TOP-MANAGEMENT
ORGANIZATION AND CONTROL

TOP-MANAGEMENT
ORGANIZATION AND CONTROL

A RESEARCH STUDY
OF THE MANAGEMENT POLICIES AND PRACTICES
OF THIRTY-ONE LEADING INDUSTRIAL CORPORATIONS

By
PAUL E. HOLDEN
Professor of Industrial Management

LOUNSBURY S. FISH
Research Associate

AND

HUBERT L. SMITH
Research Associate

PUBLISHED FOR THE STANFORD UNIVERSITY
GRADUATE SCHOOL OF BUSINESS BY ARRANGEMENT
WITH STANFORD UNIVERSITY PRESS

NEW YORK   TORONTO   LONDON
McGRAW-HILL BOOK COMPANY, INC.
1951

TOP-MANAGEMENT ORGANIZATION AND CONTROL

First Edition, February 1941
Enlarged Edition, August 1948
Fourteenth Printing, July 1952

FOREWORD

By Ralph K. Davies

*Consulting Professor, Graduate School of Business, Stanford
University, and Vice-President and Director,
Standard Oil Company of California*

American industry is today, in many ways, facing the most
critical period in all of its history. The competitive system of free
enterprise is under severe attack. Abroad it has already suffered
defeat in many lands, submerged by the force of totalitarian principles of economics. At home its right to survive is challenged by
rapidly changing conditions and new economic and political forces.
What the future holds none can foretell, but certain it is that the
character of American industrial life for generations will be determined in large measure by its ability to withstand the pressures
of today.

In the industrial field, large-scale organization especially is
now put to the test. How well prepared it is to meet the great
strain of the times remains to be seen. Whether the successes of
the past have undermined its vigor and efficiency and left it unfit
for the contest, or whether it is possessed of sufficient compe-
tence to meet the challenge of the times with further successes,
must be made clear in the relatively near future. While confident
as to the outcome, farsighted leadership in industry today does
not minimize the seriousness of the difficulties ahead.

This survey of corporate organization and practice prepared
by the Graduate School of Business of Stanford University represents a most timely contribution. The material here presented,
making available to industry the best thought and experience of a
representative group of the large corporations throughout the
United States, is a decidedly significant work. It will answer an
obvious need for enlightened and dependable information as a
basis for objective planning of management, free from personal
influences and traditional habits of thought.

To those who are actively concerned with the problem of the
organization of management, this book will be of inestimable
value. Beyond this let us hope it may prove generally stimulating

to creative thought and excite a deeper and more critical interest in this vitally important subject. For thus will it best serve the larger purpose of advancing the cause of American enterprise through pointing the way to betterment in method and increased efficiency. The law of the survival of the fittest is, in the end, inescapable.

For this most constructive contribution to the welfare of American industry, Stanford University, and in particular the able administration of its Graduate School of Business, is entitled to great credit.

PREFACE

By J. Hugh Jackson

Dean, Graduate School of Business
Stanford University

At no time in the history or development of American business has the responsibility of top management been greater than it is today. It is this central management of a business that determines the common ends toward which effort shall be directed and which maintains co-ordination between specialized functions or departments. Therefore, it is essential to have definite knowledge of the organization and functioning of these top levels of management, and to know how policies are formed, how authority is delegated, how control is effected, how departmental or divisional points of view are harmonized, how results are measured, how extravagant practices are corrected, and how waste is eliminated. To learn from the actual practices of leading American corporations the solutions to these and other problems has been the primary purpose of this research study.

Chief executives themselves are generally aware of the many problems of co-ordination and control which constantly beset them. However, experience has shown that many times expansions in management organizations are the result of immediate necessity, and accordingly the organization planning goes no further than to solve the problem currently in hand. The allocation of important functions on such a basis can only result, sooner or later, in a management organization which, although it may be moderately successful in attaining results, will speedily become so cumbersome and lethargic as to lose much of its effectiveness.

It was with this situation somewhat definitely in mind that one of the leading executives of the Pacific Coast suggested, in the spring of 1939, that the Stanford Graduate School of Business undertake a study of this type. After several months of study and discussion, during which time leading executives joined with members of the Business School faculty about the conference table, a broad program was formulated and the project undertaken. The study, accordingly, is not an academic thesis, but is rather an attempt to find a practical answer to some of the many problems constantly facing top management. The project was financed by approximately a dozen important companies, the majority of which are located here on the West Coast.

The approach taken by the School has been that no single company possesses all the best ideas on management policies and practices, and that every company could benefit from the experiences of others. It was accordingly proposed to ascertain, as far as possible, the general pattern of present-day management; then to make the fruits of such research, in the form of plans and principles, available to business executives as a guide in planning for future expansion or in gradually revamping their present organizations along more effective lines.

The program was accordingly projected on this basis; it was estimated to require approximately a year for its consummation. A data sheet, designed to give comprehensiveness and comparability, was prepared. Because of the intimate nature and the significance of the material desired, it became quickly obvious that the information could be obtained only by personal discussion with the top-management groups of the participating companies. The field work for the collection of the needed factual data required over seven months, with an additional six months to analyze and co-ordinate the vast amount of material obtained, and to write up the findings. Because the problems of the chief executives are essentially similar in all companies, whereas the work of the lower levels of management would vary greatly in different companies, the scope of the study was confined to the problems and practices of *top management*, a field which hitherto had been little explored in the manner of this undertaking.

After the broad program was formulated, the next step was to select the companies to be invited to co-operate in the study. Companies representing diversified industrial enterprises, with a reputation for progressive and enlightened management, were chosen. Also the present study has been confined to industrial companies, while banks, merchandising organizations, public utilities, and railroads have been omitted. Every effort, moreover, has been made to preserve the anonymity of the participating companies, as well as the details of their organization and practices.

On this basis, a group of thirty-one nationally known, well-recognized industrial companies were chosen. They have total assets, as shown by their published balance sheets, ranging from a little less than $100,000,000 to approximately $900,000,000. The thirty-one companies have aggregate total assets of approximately eight billion dollars, or an average of about $260,000,000 per company. They employ normally about 850,000 workers, the number ranging from 5,000 to 70,000, and averaging about 27,000 employees per company. For the entire group there is an investment of approximately $10,000 of assets for each employee. A broad classification of these participating companies by type of industry gives the following results: Building Materials, 4; Chemicals, 5; Food Products, 2; Machinery and Equipment, 9; Nonferrous Metals, 2; Petroleum Products, 4; Rubber, 2; and Steel and Steel Fabricating, 3. It would be difficult to find a group of better-managed, more efficient businesses than these thirty-one companies; in fact, it includes many of the "blue chip" companies of America.

In this volume no attempt has been made to present an exhaustive treatise on the whole field of management—as already stated, the study has been confined to the more important problems of organization and control facing the *top management*. Neither has there been any attempt to pass judgment upon or to criticize any company's plan of management. Moreover, we have definitely refrained from recommending any one plan of management organization as best or "ideal" for all companies.

Rather, the aim has been to record what seemed to be the most effective and generally applicable plans and devices found among the thirty-one participating companies for meeting their more common management problems, and to present them in a way that each company can check its own practices by them, and can take advantage, according to its own needs and inclinations, of such suggestions for the further strengthening of its own management plan. It should be realized, at the same time, that in a study of this type little or no recognition could be given to the all-important factor of personality; obviously many of the best organization and control practices found in effect in these companies were primarily the reflection of some dynamic personality or of outstanding leadership.

Finally, I come to the most pleasant part of my task, that of expressing in behalf of the Graduate School of Business our sincere appreciation to the more than forty companies which made this research study possible, either by contributing funds or by giving of their experience in the handling of major management problems. The extent of the interest and co-operation of the thirty-one participating companies exceeded all expectations. Moreover, it was most significant that the companies which have devoted the most time and effort in the perfection of their management practices not only contributed the most helpful information, but were also the most interested in learning, through the medium of this report on the activities of other companies, how they might further improve and strengthen their own management organization and plan of control. To the top executives of the various participating companies, to the members of their staffs, and to all who have given of their time or otherwise aided in bringing the study to a successful conclusion the School is truly grateful.

This volume is offered by the Graduate School of Business to those who are responsible for or interested in the best top-management organization and control in the business enterprises of the United States, with the realization that it is perhaps only a beginning in this type of management literature, but with the sincere hope and definite belief that it will suggest to many major executives a sound and practical solution for some of their more difficult problems. To the extent that this is accomplished, the School has further fulfilled its basic purpose and objective.

STANFORD UNIVERSITY
STANFORD, CALIFORNIA

TABLE OF CONTENTS

LIST OF ILLUSTRATIONS

xvii

PART A

SUMMARY AND CONCLUSIONS

FARSIGHTED PLANNING AND CLARIFICATION
OF OBJECTIVES

A SOUND PLAN OF ORGANIZATION

FULLY QUALIFIED PERSONNEL IN
ALL KEY POSITIONS

EFFECTIVE MEANS OF CONTROL

PART A
SUMMARY AND CONCLUSIONS

This report is submitted in the interest of top management. It is concerned with the fundamental problems of this particular realm of management and the means by which these common problems are being met in a selected group of thirty-one large industrial enterprises.

Top management, as used in this study, includes three groups of executives. These are (*a*) the board of directors, (*b*) general management, consisting of those executives who are concerned with the business as a whole, and (*c*) divisional management, comprising those executives who are directly responsible for the major departments, divisions, or subsidiaries of the company. Upon the vision, farsightedness, and resourcefulness of this small top group largely depends the success of an enterprise.

The primary responsibilities of top management are to provide:

Farsighted planning and clarification of objectives, visualizing the needs of the business and determining its most advantageous future course.

A sound plan of organization, enabling all of its parts, individually and collectively, to function most effectively in reaching the common objectives.

Fully qualified personnel in all key positions, insuring each individual's proper contribution to the whole program.

Effective means of control, permitting top executives to delegate wide responsibility and authority, thereby freeing themselves of administrative detail in order to concentrate on broad planning and direction.

Out of this research study have come certain definite impressions as to how top management is taking steps to fulfill most effectively its basic functions. This introductory part of the report epitomizes the foremost thought and practice found among the participating companies, for meeting the major needs and problems in this field.

3

FARSIGHTED PLANNING AND CLARIFICATION OF OBJECTIVES

There is nothing about an organization more important than its future. Owners, management, employees, and society in general are, or should be, more concerned about where a company is going than where it has been. In any institution, the responsibility for visualizing, initiating, and achieving future objectives rests with its top management. The more specifically the future course of a company is conceived and defined, the more likely is its realization. One of the greatest needs observed during the course of this study is for more adequate planning and clarification of future objectives, both near-term and long-range.

Near-Term Objectives: About half of the companies visited preplan in detail some or all of their operations for periods up to a year in advance. A few companies have fully integrated systems whereby every department and agency establishes definite objectives covering not only income and expense items, but all improvements, betterments, and contemplated changes of every nature.

Near-term decisions, however, need to be co-ordinated and directed toward long-range objectives in regard to such matters as:

Major changes in markets
Important changes in the line of products
Major changes in or expansion of facilities
Financial requirements, capital expenditures, reserves, etc.
Major personnel changes
Basic changes in the organization structure

Long-Range Objectives: Two of the companies which have outstanding plans of management establish their objectives five years ahead. Such long-term objectives are necessarily tentative, subject to modification as time and circumstances require, but they are invaluable as guideposts to assure the proper orientation, consistency, and reasonableness of the definite near-term planning.

As a rule the projected future plans are based upon estimates of expected sales volume, tempered by general economic forecasts. Able economists and well-qualified statistical agencies develop and correlate this information.

Several companies have been able to stabilize operations and employment to a substantial degree through the planning process.

In general, the successful experience which so many companies have had and the value they derive from long-range planning suggest a wider adoption of the practice by companies not now following this plan.

The lack of adequate planning frequently results from the fact that top executives are too preoccupied with matters of a current nature to concentrate upon the future needs of the business. In addition they often fail to stimulate and utilize the best thought and assistance of their organizations in formulating sound plans, policies, and objectives.

Before top management can find enough time for the planning of objectives and be assured that those objectives will be met, it must:

Devise a sound plan of organization
Have fully qualified personnel in all key positions
Institute effective means and methods of control

A SOUND PLAN OF ORGANIZATION

Top executives, no matter how competent, cannot function to full effectiveness without a sound plan of organization. A well-conceived, long-range organization program permits changes to be made in the right direction as opportunities arise. In the absence of such a plan, changes must be made on the basis of expediency, organization errors are often perpetuated, and fundamental improvements are seldom realized.

Every phase of a company's organization plan should be questioned and tested from a wholly objective viewpoint, without being influenced by present pattern or personnel, precedent or tradition. From such an analysis a plan of organization can be developed which will best meet the current and future requirements of the business.

A good organization chart for the company as a whole, with auxiliary charts for each major division, is an essential first step in the analysis, clarification, and understanding of any organization plan. The process of charting the organization is one good test of its soundness, as any organization relationship which cannot be readily charted is likely to be illogical and therefore confusing to those working under it.

Organization planning in many companies ends with the preparation of a set of organization charts. These give a good general idea of the primary divisions of the company but do not stipulate how each unit of the organization should function.

Organization charts should therefore be supplemented by written specifications defining the essential requirements of each level of management, each department, each committee, and each key job or group of similar jobs. Only by a thorough understanding of their respective parts in the whole management picture are individual executives and agencies able to devote their full energies to effective discharge of their proper functions, avoiding duplication of effort, friction, and working at cross purposes which result from lack of organization clarification. Such written specifications should cover functions, jurisdiction, responsibilities, relationships, limits of authority, objectives, and the means for measuring performance.

These same specifications also serve as the basis for training, merit rating, salary evaluation, and selective placement with respect to staff and key personnel.

Top-Management Organization: In any company, clarification of the top structure is the first requisite, since any confusion or vagueness at the top is reflected downward throughout the organization. This top structure consists of three distinct levels which differ as to function, viewpoint, and composition. These are the board of directors, general management, and divisional management. A clear conception of the proper province of each of these levels is essential in clarifying the plan of top management.

As to the board of directors, observation points to the advantage of clearly defined functions and workable size, with membership properly representative and confined to those able to visualize the needs and to make a major contribution toward the success of the business as a whole. Theirs is a trusteeship function.

The general management function in several of the best-managed larger companies is handled by a group of general executives who devote full time to planning and directing the course of the business as a whole. In smaller concerns, this function may appropriately be the province of the president and a part-time council of divisional executives.

With divisional management, the trend is toward logical, separable divisions or departments, each of which is headed by a well-qualified top executive reporting directly to general management. These executives are delegated wide responsibility and authority and are held fully accountable for results.

Operating Organization: Primary division of the operating organization may be on a functional, regional, or product basis.

The regional and product-division plans provide effective means of decentralizing the management function where it is practicable to establish separate units, each carrying proprietary responsibility for both manufacturing and sales. Each unit is, in effect, a separate business, and can be held accountable on a profit-and-loss basis.

The functional plan, on the other hand, is logical where the line of products is simple and closely related, where operations are highly centralized, or where no practicable basis exists for division along product or regional lines.

Staff Organization: In many companies, top management is burdened with problems which an adequate staff organization could appropriately handle.

Creation of certain basic staff departments appears to be overdue in several instances. Often, the same functions and effort are now found scattered among many departments and individuals. These companies are therefore already paying the price without securing the benefits of specialized attention.

Again, many existing staff agencies appear to be handicapped by deficiencies in the plan of organization. Frequently, several unco-ordinated agencies are involved with different aspects of the same general function. In other cases, staff agencies are made responsible to an executive position or management level which does not provide the authority and jurisdiction needed. Finally, it is not unusual for a control function to be organized on an advisory basis with consequently weak and ineffective results; or an advisory agency infringing upon the prerogatives of operating executives by endeavoring to function in a control capacity.

Effective handling of many staff functions requires the creation of both central departments and corresponding divisional agencies. In such cases the central agency should exercise close functional direction and co-ordination of its divisional counterparts.

Committee Organization: More confusion exists in regard to the proper organization and use of committees than with any other type of agency. In most companies there is a logical and definite place in the management plan for well-designed committees. Their functions, relationships, and composition should be as clearly defined as for any other unit of the organization.

The proper province of committees is not to perform work but rather to co-ordinate viewpoints and pass collective judgment upon definite facts or proposals. A capable agency is needed to develop the facts and present the proposals for committee consideration. Such an agency may consist of a full-time secretary or a staff department.

FULLY QUALIFIED PERSONNEL IN ALL KEY POSITIONS

Many companies appear to leave the provision of key personnel largely to providence. Others have fully co-ordinated programs under central staff direction by which top management may be assured that every responsible position is capably filled.

In these latter companies definite provision is made for inducting promising talent into the organization.

There is a carefully planned system of training and development. Executives and supervisors are expected to train their subordinates to meet most effectively the requirements of their respective positions.

Provision is made for annual merit rating. All salaried employees including key personnel are carefully appraised by competent judges. This appraisal covers capability in meeting the requirements of the job; qualification for higher jobs; most advantageous present and future assignments to assure best ultimate development; and the extent to which promotion and increased salary recognition has been earned.

A competent and impartial agency certifies as to the adequacy of candidates' qualifications for appointment to all responsible positions, as these become vacant.

Finally, firm but equitable action is taken to replace those found to be filling key positions inadequately.

EFFECTIVE MEANS OF CONTROL

A well-designed plan of control covering each major administrative activity permits top management to delegate responsibility and authority, freeing itself of unnecessary detail, yet retaining the means for assuring that results will be satisfactory.

Each plan of control embraces the following elements: an *objective* establishing what it is desired to accomplish; *procedure* specifying how, when, and by whom the plan is to be executed; *criteria* as to what constitutes good performance; and *appraisal* as to how well it was done.

It is properly the function of a capable staff agency, sometimes in conjunction with a well-designed committee, to formulate a comprehensive plan of control over each activity; to guide, coordinate, and administer its use; and to make sure that the desired objectives are realized.

Control over Policies: To be fully effective, policies must be clearly stated in writing, properly distributed to those affected, and periodically checked as to compliance. This is best accomplished through means of a well-designed policy manual, compiled and maintained by a high-caliber staff agency.

Control over Organization: Best practice provides for comprehensive, long-range organization planning, rationalization of the structure as a whole, proper design and clarification of each part, competent review of proposed changes, and the periodic check of actual organization practice. This is the logical province of a competent staff department specializing in organization problems, working through the medium of a well-designed organization manual.

Control over Key Personnel: Assurance of qualified personnel in all responsible positions requires a well-planned and ably administered program for the company as a whole. Formulation and active functional direction of such a program are logical functions of the personnel director working in conjunction with a personnel committee.

Control over Wages and Salaries: The best plans provide for (*a*) sound job evaluation and classification, (*b*) appropriate rates or ranges for each classification or bracket established in proper relation to outside wage and salary levels, (*c*) competent review of proposed changes, (*d*) suitable policies to guide administration, and (*e*) adequate checks on performance. This is properly the work of well-qualified staff specialists, often attached to organization or industrial engineering departments and working in conjunction with a wage and salary committee.

Control over Costs: The most effective control is achieved through current comparison of actual against standard costs based on optimum efficiency in handling all operations and activities. This is often supplemented by a sound plan of budgetary control. Properly qualified and co-ordinated central and divisional staff agencies make the basic analyses and determine the standards, while the comptroller's organization presents the current comparisons.

Control over Methods and Manpower: As a basis for eliminating nonessential functions and manpower, some companies make, periodically, a complete analysis of each department's activities, determining what every employee does as to function, method, and time. Examination of this data provides the basis for determining (*a*) essential departmental activities, (*b*) the best methods for performing these activities, (*c*) the number and type of people required, (*d*) the proper pattern of organization, (*e*) relative job values, and (*f*) standard costs. The same type of analysis applied to the successive steps of individual procedures provides the basis for clarification and standardization of practices. Such surveys are usually made by a well-qualified central staff agency specializing in organization and cost-control problems, or by divisional agencies under its functional direction.

Control over Capital Expenditures: Many well-managed companies use an annual capital budget as a basis for approval of a sound over-all program, which takes into proper account the financial situation, the economic outlook, and the relative needs of the business as a whole. Before final release, each individual project is subject to further careful review. After the completion of each project, a check is made to assure that anticipated advantages are actually realized. A high-caliber analytical agency working in conjunction with a well-selected appropriations committee is an essential feature.

Control over Service Department Effort: It is often necessary to establish a method for controlling demands placed upon service departments by other units of the organization. Budgetary control is used by approximately one-half the companies to regulate such staff effort. In others, control is obtained through limiting the amount of service that department heads may request, or through authorizing the service department management to question the necessity for work requested when it is thought to be of doubtful value.

Control over Line of Products: Constant vigilance is necessary to keep a company's line of products abreast of market demands and yet free from overdiversification and unprofitable items. Adequate control usually requires a competent staff agency devoting full time to analyzing market needs and to simplifying and rationalizing the line to meet those needs most effectively. Such agencies work closely with the heads of research, manufacturing, and sales, either individually or together as a committee.

Control over Research and Development: Proper control over research expenditures is a perplexing problem in many companies. Some make little effort at control, relying on the quality and judgment of the research personnel to produce satisfactory results. Other concerns effect more positive control through a well-prepared annual budget and comprehensive analysis of each project. Such analyses take into account the objectives to be accomplished in terms of savings, sales or profit potentialities, probable effect upon demand for other products, etc.

Control over Foreign Operations: The methods used by many companies in the control of foreign operations are practically the same as they employ in the domestic field. The maintenance of a separate domestic corporation within which to centralize the management of all foreign operations helps in preserving independence and freedom from too much influence from the domestic departments. The high caliber of the personnel and the greater degree of responsibility and authority accorded them are characteristic of foreign operations.

Control over External Relations: More and more consideration is being given to public reaction with regard to many company activities. In the field of public relations there is need of centralized control and responsibility. Among the companies studied, about half now have public-relations departments.

Over-All Control: One-half of the participating companies make use of some form of budgetary control as a means of preplanning and gauging over-all results. The most effective plans have the following characteristics: (*a*) they embrace all requirements and objectives for the year ahead, not only as to financial aspects but all consequential changes, developments, and improvements; (*b*) each supervisor prepares and takes responsibility for his own well-considered commitment predicated on sound standards; (*c*) a properly qualified staff agency is provided to co-ordinate and administer the plan; (*d*) flexibility to changes in the rate of operation is secured through use of a sliding scale of expectancy; (*e*) finally, such plans receive the wholehearted and active support of top management.

Another very effective system of over-all control holds separable units of the company responsible on a monthly profit-and-loss basis. This method is most practicable as applied to product divisions, regional divisions, subsidiary companies, and similar units having the aspects of a separate business.

———

However, regardless of formal systems of control, there is no substitute for firsthand observation of conditions and for personal contact with people on the job. Relieved of unnecessary administrative detail through the measures advocated herein, top executives should have more time for such contacts, which afford opportunity to refresh their knowledge and viewpoint, to observe the needs and adequacy of management, and to stimulate the morale and effectiveness of the organization. Several of the outstanding executives interviewed follow the practice of visiting systematically all major operations and field offices. In many companies, stress is similarly laid upon maintaining a wide acquaintanceship among and exchange of viewpoints with the executives of other well-managed companies.

———

The foregoing conclusions are further developed in the three parts which follow. Part B, "Organization Practices," deals primarily with the organization structure, while Part C, "Control Practices," covers a wide range of perplexing control problems and the best methods found for meeting them. These particular problems appear to be of greatest general interest and concern among the participating companies. Part D, "Board of Directors," presents a more extended discussion of certain important characteristics of this first level of top management.

PART B

ORGANIZATION PRACTICES

TOP-MANAGEMENT ORGANIZATION

OPERATING ORGANIZATION

STAFF ORGANIZATION

COMMITTEE ORGANIZATION

Section 1

TOP-MANAGEMENT ORGANIZATION

The importance of a sound and clean-cut plan of top-management organization in facilitating and contributing to the effectiveness of corporate administration cannot be overemphasized. In a few of the companies studied this field has obviously been given the attention and study it deserves. In many others it is evident that further clarification and development are needed.

THE THREE BASIC ZONES OR LEVELS OF TOP MANAGEMENT

In order to clarify this stratum of organization, it should be recognized that there are three distinct and separable zones or levels of top management. They differ as to function, and as to the viewpoint, requisite background, and experience of the responsible personnel. These three zones may be characterized as follows:

Zone 1. The Trusteeship Function is to represent, safeguard, and further the stockholders' interests, determine the basic policies and the general course of the business, appraise the adequacy of over-all results, and in general protect and make the most effective use of the company's assets. This field is the exclusive province of the board of directors.

Zone 2. The General-Management or Administrative Function includes the active planning, direction, co-ordination, and control of the business as a whole, within the scope of basic policies established and authority delegated by the board. In other words, this function involves the determination of objectives, of operating policies, and of results. This broad co-ordinative function is variously handled (*a*) by the chief executive, (*b*) by the chief executive and a part-time council of divisional executives, (*c*) by a full-time group of general executives, or (*d*) by a managing board of directors.

Zone 3. The Divisional- or Departmental-Management Function includes the management of the major divisions or departments of the company by executives fully responsible and accountable to general management for the successful conduct of their respective operations. This zone embraces the topmost level of executives concerned primarily with a particular division of the company rather than with the enterprise as a whole.

In many companies these three fundamental and separable levels of top management appear to be indistinct and confused. In some instances two or even three of these fields are administered by the same identical group of executives, as in the case of some managing boards. This frequently results in the assumption by a single agency of an excessive burden in trying to cover these three distinct functions. It is also difficult for executives steeped in the pressing problems and demands of divisional management to divorce themselves from their divisional interests and assume the broader viewpoint needed in the determination of policies, objectives, and long-range plans for the best interests of the company as a whole.

It is believed that a clear conception of the proper functions, responsibilities, and relationships of these three levels of management affords an effective basis (*a*) for testing the adequacy of any company's plan of top organization, (*b*) for making sure that each field is entrusted to a "team" whose composition and qualifications are best adapted to do that particular job, and (*c*) for passing the burden of management detail down to those in the best position to assume it.

ZONE 1.   TRUSTEESHIP FUNCTION
(BOARD OF DIRECTORS)

In this country the stockholders seldom bother, even once a year, to attend personally to the affairs of the corporations they own. As owners these stockholders have definite interests to be considered and protected. The business of a corporation must be conducted in such a way as to preserve its assets. Good judgment must be exercised in setting long-range policies, in selecting the officers, in checking results of operations, and in guiding generally the affairs of the business.

Obviously several thousand stockholders cannot personally manage the business. Therefore, they select a small group upon whom they rely to look after their interests in the enterprise. This group is the board of directors.

The point of view of the board of directors must by the nature of this relationship be identical with that of the stockholders. At all meetings of the board this viewpoint should outweigh any other consideration. In fact, the fundamental concept of the first zone or level of management is management for the benefit of those who own the business.

This point of view is not always easily maintained. Many directors are also full-time executives whose interests as members of management may momentarily be at variance with those of the stockholders.

FUNCTIONS OF THE BOARD OF DIRECTORS

It may be argued that all transactions of the business are or should be for the interest of the stockholders. At what point, therefore, should the trusteeship of the stockholders' interests, as such, cease and other more direct forms of management begin? In other words, how far should the board of directors enter into the management of the business in order properly to discharge the trusteeship function?

In substantially all the companies reviewed, the board of directors establishes broad basic policies, handles major financial matters, selects the officers and sets their salaries, and takes care of other matters of a similar character. In addition, it receives reports from the management on the company's operation since the last meeting, and passes judgment as to whether, in view of circumstances, the results are satisfactory.

These duties are of such a nature that they can be handled satisfactorily at periodic meetings. Broad policies are not subject to current fluctuation, but stand for relatively long periods. Results of operations are usually shown by monthly statistical and financial reports. Consequently, boards of directors meet at infrequent intervals. Of the thirty-one companies studied, twenty-one have monthly meetings, six meet quarterly, and only four meet oftener than monthly. Some twenty-six of the companies rely upon an executive committee of the board to handle matters requiring board action which cannot await a regular meeting.

In most companies there seems to be an unwritten but well-understood allocation of certain management decisions between the board and general management. But in addition there is a large middle ground within which the chief executive uses his discretion as to whether or not a program shall be decided by general management or presented to the board. In many such instances the action taken by general management is subsequently submitted to the board for ratification.

Any sound plan of management might well begin with the determination and definition of the functions, responsibilities, and limits of authority to be reserved for the board, and those to be delegated to general management. It is only by a clear delineation of functions that each group will know exactly what part it is to play in the management of the company as a whole. In some concerns this separation of functions has been made, and the field and duties of the board have been included as the first section of the organization manual (see example, page 218). In such companies top management has been made easier, simply because specific duties have been established, and each level can concern itself with its own particular assignment.

COMPOSITION OF THE BOARD OF DIRECTORS

Having clarified and defined just what functions the board is to assume in the management of the business, any company is in a logical position to consider what make-up of its board would best accomplish these ends, considering representation and size, as well as personal qualifications, background, and experience of its members.

At least two types of representation seem desirable on the board: one from management, the other from outside of the company. The first group brings to the board a thorough knowledge functions, because they are always available for consultation, and personal sponsorship of proposals arising within the organization. This management group should embrace a well-rounded experience and knowledge of the business as a whole and of its major functions. Such representation might, in a typical case, include the president and three or four ranking vice-presidents or other officers having a broad experience in such fundamental fields as finance or accounting, manufacturing, and marketing, respectively. It would obviously not be necessary to include all functional heads on the board in order to assure adequate representation of their of operations, the point of view of current management, and in many companies they appear frequently before the board to present proposals or explain results.

The outside representatives should have a background of wide experience in corporate affairs. Their judgment should temper proposals of the general management in the light of broad knowledge of practices followed elsewhere; but particularly it should provide an impartial, detached, analytical viewpoint which the representatives of management are apt to lose because they are too close to current operations. In addition, it is this group which must mainly be depended upon for an adequate appraisal of results, since the officer-members are in the position of passing judgment upon their own accomplishments when sitting as members of the board.

Personal qualifications desired in outside directors by executives of many of the companies studied include the following:

1. A personal financial interest in the enterprise.
2. A limited number of other directorships.
3. A familiarity with the company and its industry.
4. An independent viewpoint.
5. A willingness to criticize.
6. Sufficient interest to insure regular attendance at meetings and thoughtful consideration of company problems.
7. A broad business and executive experience.
8. No adverse interest.

Many companies experience difficulty in finding outside directors who have the requisite time, background, and experience to make a real contribution to the successful direction of the enterprise, and who, at the same time, are willing to serve on the board, in view of the usually nominal compensation and personal liability attached.

In this connection, there is an increasing interest in the idea of relying upon what may be called professional directors for some of the outside representation on the board. Such a director may be described as one who has no present full-time or active executive position in any enterprise; whose previous experience, whether broad or specialized, equips him to contribute constructive ideas and counsel on corporate policy and problems; who confines his services to a few noncompeting companies; who devotes a proportionate share of his time between board meetings to the affairs of these companies; who receives a substantial annual compensation from each company served; and who does not represent the government, the public, the management, or any financial institution, but rather the shareholders, small as well as large.

In a majority of the participating companies the board appears to be reasonably representative of both management and outside elements. In four of the concerns, however, board membership is confined exclusively to full-time executives, while some other companies have only one or two executives on the board.

As to the size of the board, it appears advantageous to keep it to a minimum consistent with providing needed representation. The board is essentially a committee, and as such its effectiveness is increased if it is kept to a workable size.

MEETINGS AND REPORTS OF THE BOARD OF DIRECTORS

As stated previously, there is a preponderance of experience to indicate that the trusteeship function can be satisfactorily discharged through board meetings held not oftener than once a month or even quarterly, with reliance upon an executive committee to act for it in the interim, if necessary.

In order to be fully effective at these meetings, however, most enlightened practice among the participating companies suggests the desirability of providing board members, in advance of meeting dates, with adequate agenda or synopses of matters to be brought up for discussion, together with comprehensive, well-designed reports of over-all progress and results of operations compared with preplanned objectives.

For a more detailed description of board practices and procedure, as observed among the participating companies, see Part D.

ZONE 2. GENERAL-MANAGEMENT OR ADMINISTRATIVE FUNCTION

The general-management function may be characterized as the active planning, direction, co-ordination, and control of the business as a whole, within the scope of basic policies established and authority delegated by the board. While both the board of directors and general management are concerned with the interests of the company as a whole, the former performs a judicial and intermittent function, that is, the appraisal and approval of major proposals and results, whereas the latter exercises an active and continuous function, involving the initiation, formulation, co-ordination, and development of those proposals and results.

Among the functions which appear to fall logically within this conception of general management are the following:

1. Maintenance of a sound and effective plan of company organization, with functions, responsibilities, and limits of authority clearly defined and properly allocated.
2. Maintenance of fully qualified personnel in all management positions.
3. Farsighted planning and clarification of general objectives.
4. Maintenance of effective systems of control over such general activities as capital expenditures, operating expenditures and results, manpower, wages, salaries, product line, and prices.
5. Review and approval of major appropriations, budgets, appointments, and salary changes as provided under these systems of control, within the limits delegated to it by the board and above the limits delegated by it to divisional executives.
6. Determination of general operating policies.
7. Recommendation to the board on matters requiring its action.
8. General co-ordination of major operating plans.
9. Appraisal of divisional or departmental performance and results.

Among the thirty-one companies studied, four plans for organizing the general-management function are found: (1) In some companies the chief executive handles this field, calling informally upon his fellow officers and divisional executives for advice and counsel as he may feel the need. (2) In other cases, the chief executive and a council of divisional or departmental executives perform the same function. (3) Other companies have set up a group of general executives to concentrate full time upon the problems of general management. (4) And, finally, in a few companies, a managing board of directors handles this field, as well as performing its natural trusteeship function. These four plans for organizing general management, as they were observed in the different companies, may be characterized and appraised as follows:

GENERAL MANAGEMENT THROUGH CHIEF EXECUTIVE

One-third of the companies rely upon the chief executive, usually the president, to carry the major burden of general management, consulting informally with divisional executives as he deems necessary. Occasionally this amounts to a "one-man show." More frequently there is such close consultation between the chief executive and his fellow officers in regard to all major moves as to approximate council action. Unless the latter condition prevails this arrangement is subject to the following analysis:

Advantage

Tendency to expedite executive action.

Disadvantages

Possibility that action may be taken without adequate consideration of all important aspects.

Lack of well-rounded experience, viewpoint, and knowledge of all
major operations, which are available only through group consideration, and which are valuable aids to and checks upon
the chief executive's judgment.

Tendency to overload the chief executive with matters that could
be handled satisfactorily by others.

Inability of the chief executive, through lack of time and energy,
to accomplish satisfactorily all the important functions and
objectives of general management.

Failure to develop fellow officers to major stature through sharing
the responsibility of general management with them.

Consequent maximum disruption of the enterprise when the chief
executive finally retires or leaves the business.

GENERAL MANAGEMENT THROUGH CHIEF EXECUTIVE AND COUNCIL OF DIVISIONAL EXECUTIVES

Another third of the participating companies look to the chief executive and a part-time but formally constituted and representative council of divisional executives, called together from their divisional duties as necessary, to handle the broad administrative functions of general management. Characteristics of this plan may be summarized as follows:

1. The president (sometimes together with a chairman, vice-chairman, or executive vice-president) is the only executive devoting full time to general management.

2. In a few companies, he makes some of the decisions and exercises some of the functions of general management himself, taking up other matters with the council. In other companies,

nearly all the decisions appear to be reached through the council, in order to assure that all aspects of each matter are given adequate consideration.

3. In all cases, the council, variously termed executive council, president's cabinet, officers' board, operating committee or management advisory committee, is a formally constituted agency, with members appointed by the chief executive, holding regular meetings weekly or oftener as required to transact business. Authority of the group is that delegated by the chief executive, who may ordinarily overrule any decision of the cabinet.

4. Council membership ranges from five to seventeen with an average of eight. Besides the chief executive, it usually includes the principal divisional executives whose interests or advice are most often of general concern.

Divisional members of these part-time councils devote their major time and attention to divisional interests, getting together as necessary to advise with the president in regard to general problems. The relative merits of this plan of general management appear to be as follows:

Advantage

Regular participation of representative divisional executives in council deliberations should assure adequate consideration of divisional interests and points of view. In addition, such participation should result in better understanding of and compliance with council action.

Disadvantages

In the largest companies the problem of general management becomes so complex that it is questionable whether or not the part-time attention of a representative group of divisional executives is sufficient to find and chart the most profitable course for the business to follow, involving as it does the forecasting of general conditions, formulation of operating policies and objectives, coordination of plans, review and approval of major proposals, and appraisal of results.

It is difficult for divisional executives, absorbed in their day-to-day divisional problems and responsibililties, to cast this all aside and take a sufficiently broad company-wide viewpoint to be fully effective in the field of general management during the few hours a week in which they may serve on the council.

Insufficient attention is often devoted to broad planning for and direction of the business as a whole, because these can, without immediately apparent results, be deferred in favor of seemingly more pressing divisional matters.

There is a natural tendency for divisional executives to bring into the council divisional problems which properly need never concern it.

GENERAL MANAGEMENT THROUGH A COUNCIL OF GENERAL EXECUTIVES

In one-fourth of the companies studied, particularly those which have devoted the most attention to organization planning, the boards of directors have delegated the field of general management to a full-time group or council of general executives. This group determines operating policies and objectives and concentrates upon the broad direction, co-ordination, and control of the business as a whole. In order that they may devote their full time and energies to this important purpose, council members are usually relieved of direct responsibility for individual divisions or departments through effective delegation to divisional executives.

This arrangement for handling the general-management function, which appears to be particularly effective and toward which there is a discernible trend among the larger concerns, has the following typical characteristics:

1. In all those companies having such a plan, the board confines its sphere to proper trusteeship functions, the intermittent character of which necessitates meeting not oftener than once a month.

2. The executive council usually consists of the three to nine (average six) top active officers of the company, ordinarily the president and ranking vice-presidents, so chosen as to embrace a wide range of experience, background, and knowledge of the company's principal operations, such as manufacturing, marketing, and finance. As a rule, it is largely the same group that represents management on the board.

3. This group meets daily to weekly as required to transact its business, but the members devote their full time to the broad interests of the company as a whole.

4. While the members are not, as a rule, in charge of any specific phase of the company's operations, this responsibility be-

ing effectively delegated to divisional executives, they are usually looked to by the other members of the council and by divisional executives for consultation, co-ordination, and advice within the field of their special experience and background. Thus, particularly in companies which are set up on a product-division basis, council members with a broad manufacturing, marketing, or financial background are able to provide the necessary functional co-ordination between divisions.

5. This is ordinarily done on an advisory basis, however, divisional executives being accountable to the council, not to its individual members. In almost no case would a divisional executive expect to receive a "yes" or "no" decision from an individual council member; such decisions emanate only from the council as a whole. In this connection, it is noteworthy that in companies working under this plan even the president usually takes action through the council rather than as an individual.

6. In the words of one company, the council consists of a president and several "assistant presidents," each of whom has the same company-wide interest and viewpoint as the chief executive, thus multiplying the seasoned consideration of corporate problems.

7. Divisional executives consult members of the council to secure the benefit of their advice on major problems, to enlist their support on specific proposals in advance of council action, and to keep them informed as to what is going on. These contacts are voluntary, not mandatory, and though usually made with a designated council member, divisional executives are free to consult with any of the members at will.

8. Every effort is made to hold divisional executives fully responsible and accountable for successful conduct of their respective operations. They are expected to make their own decisions in regard to strictly divisional matters and to burden council members only with matters whose character or magnitude, as delimited by the council, make them of general concern. Even these matters are presented as well-considered and substantiated proposals for the council's final action.

9. Divisional executives appear frequently before the council, either at their own instigation to present some matter for decision, or upon request to explain or defend proposals or results.

This plan of general management appears to have the following advantages and disadvantages over other plans observed:

Advantages

Each of the three zones of top management is occupied by a separate agency, designed and constituted to do the most effective job in that particular field. This is broadly true even though usually all members of the general-management group and some members of the divisional-management group may also function as directors at periodic board meetings.

With a small group of top executives concentrating full time on the problems of general management and divorced from the problems and administrative routine of divisional management, the broad planning, direction, and co-ordination so vital to the success of the business as a whole are facilitated and assured.

The small executive group is able to take action easily, effectively, and informally, calling in divisional executives for specialized counsel and advice as necessary.

The time and energy of the top and, presumably, highest-paid officers and executives are devoted to the broad problems of the company as a whole, instead of being dissipated in handling responsibilities which divisional executives with their specialized experience may appropriately assume.

Throwing the full responsibility of divisional management and administration upon divisional executives serves to develop these men to their full potentialities.

Disadvantages

Smaller companies may not feel able to afford a separate group of major executives concentrating on the broad, general aspects of the business as a whole, preferring to call in divisional executives to consult with the chief executive on general problems as necessary.

In such smaller organizations, too, the problems of general direction and co-ordination are less complex and may not require the full time of a general executive group to do them justice.

GENERAL MANAGEMENT THROUGH THE BOARD OF DIRECTORS

Two of the thirty-one companies studied rely upon a managing board of full-time executives to handle the entire burden of general management as well as their natural trusteeship function. In comparison with other plans observed, this arrangement is subject to the following appraisal:

Advantages

Most of the principal functions and activities are directly represented in management deliberations through membership of the responsible executives on the board of directors.

General management is kept thoroughly familiar with all major aspects of the business.

Co-ordination of interdivisional interests and development of a company-wide viewpoint are facilitated.

Disadvantages

Such a large group (the full board of directors) is unwieldly in taking management action.

It is necessary to involve the whole board for frequent and extended periods in deliberation over problems that affect and are of prime interest to only a few members.

With the divisional management so heavily represented there is a natural tendency to burden the general group with the consideration of purely divisional problems which properly need never concern it.

ZONE 3. DIVISIONAL- OR DEPARTMENTAL-MANAGEMENT FUNCTION

Divisional management provides the active direction and management of the respective parts or divisions of the company within the scope of operating policies and authority delegated by general management. These parts may be operating departments, such as manufacturing and marketing, or staff departments, product divisions, regional divisions, or subsidiary companies.

Divisional executives are therefore defined as the topmost executives directly in charge of one or more of these divisions or departments, whether they be called vice-presidents, directors, general managers, managers, or presidents (as in the case of some subsidiaries). They are all directly accountable to the chief executive or to general management for the successful conduct of their respective parts of the business.

Divisional executives are distinguished from general executives in that they are immediately concerned with divisional or departmental rather than company-wide interests. A thorough knowledge of divisional operations and problems is therefore of greater moment than a wide knowledge, experience, and viewpoint of the company as a whole which are so important in the zone of general management.

The following considerations are of primary importance in the successful functioning of divisional management:

Logical Divisions.—Whatever the nature of the division assigned to each divisional executive, whether a functional division, like manufacturing or marketing, a staff department, a product division, or a subsidiary company, sound organization requires that it be a logical, separable, clean-cut part of the whole. This facilitates the clear conception and definition of functions, objectives, and relationships, and, through the fact that records of performance naturally follow the same channels, makes it possible to measure divisional results effectively.

In some companies, certain divisional executives appear to have an unrelated hodgepodge of activities under their direction. In other companies, the primary divisions are confined to single major functions, product divisions, departments, or logical groups of closely related activities. This appears to facilitate their effective management by permitting concentration and specialization of executive attention.

Number of Divisions.—The number of divisions reporting directly to general management varies widely. In one well-organized company practically all activities head up to four divisional vice-presidents in charge of manufacturing, marketing, financial, and purchasing activities, respectively. The other extreme is reached in the case of a company set up on a product-division basis, where there are ten product-division managers and fourteen staff and service department heads, all reporting to the president. It appears that under this latter arrangement, unless some special provision is made to the contrary, the demands upon the president's time for maintaining necessary contacts with such a large number of divisional executives might prove burdensome. There is a prevalent conviction that the number of subordinates reporting to a single executive should be definitely limited in order that each may get the attention he needs without overburdening his principal.

Responsibility, Authority, and Accountability.—General management, whether it consists of the president or a full-time group of general executives, should keep itself free of divisional detail, concentrating its full time and energy upon the larger problems of over-all direction and control. Divisional executives should be expected to handle their strictly divisional problems without burdening their principals, assuming as nearly full proprietary responsibility and accountability for the successful conduct of divisional operations as is consistent with the need for over-all co-ordination and control. The most effective steps found among the participating companies for insuring and furthering this objective are:

Clear-cut delineation of the functions, responsibilities, and relationships of each divisional executive through job specifications in the organization manual.

Delegation to divisional executives of adequate authority, commensurate with these responsibilities, within limits specifically defined.

The establishment of definite objectives and suitable measures of what constitutes the divisional job well done. This may take the form of budgetary planning, standards of performance, or other devices of control.

Effective current comparison and appraisal of actual results against the preplanned objectives, and the taking of necessary action to stimulate improvement where it is needed.

A conscious effort on the part of general executives to render advice and counsel as requested, but to give no decisions, as individuals, within the field delegated to divisional executives. The latter are expected to make up their own minds, take appropriate action, and stand accountable for results.

Insistence that matters presented for the action of general management be submitted in the form of well-substantiated proposals or recommendations.

Effective use of staff agencies to analyze and digest proposals as a preliminary to general management's consideration.

OPERATING ORGANIZATION

The operating organization embraces those divisions or departments concerned with such primary functions as production and marketing. These units are usually the largest. Normally, they have the most people and spend the most money. How they are organized has an important bearing upon the ease and effectiveness of management's direction and control.

The present form of operating organization in many companies is a result of tradition, merger, or unplanned growth. Many concerns have found or are beginning to find that as their businesses expand in extent and diversity, the same plan of management that sufficed in earlier days is no longer adequate. It is increasingly difficult to find and develop men who have sufficient firsthand experience and knowledge of all the operations under their jurisdiction to prescribe intelligently for all conditions, or even to pass judgment upon results. With so many irons in the fire it becomes more and more difficult to "keep on top of the job."

There is, therefore, a definite urge and trend toward decentralization of management, breaking the big fields down into smaller, logically separable units headed up by well-qualified executives who are delegated wide responsibility and authority and held definitely accountable for results. Limiting factors are, of course, the caliber of available personnel and the adequacy of the means of control. The general objective is to assign to each individual down the executive scale the maximum responsibility which he has the capacity to assume, so that a $20,000 executive is not spending most of his time at $3,000 work. Thus top management is relieved of administrative detail, while action is facilitated and maneuverability is increased.

THE THREE BASIC TYPES OF OPERATING ORGANIZATION

There are three fundamental "chassis" upon which to mount the operating organization:

Functional—as when one divisional executive is in direct charge of all manufacturing, another in charge of all marketing, and so forth.

Product Division—as when each of the separable product lines is set up as a more or less independent business under a divisional executive who may be responsible for his own manufacturing, marketing, and other functions.

Regional—as where a divisional executive is in direct charge of all phases of the business within a well-defined geographical district or region.

FUNCTIONAL PLAN

This is the traditional plan of organization and is the type most commonly found in industry. It merely carries the principle of division of labor into the realm of management. That it is the natural and customary form of organization is doubtless due to the fact that human capacities, abilities, interests, and desires seem to follow functional lines. It is unusual for an individual to have the same genuineness of interest and aptitude for sales that he has, say, for production. For this same reason, men are usually trained and developed along functional lines, and the normal course of progression and advancement follows such channels.

Under the functional plan of organization the problem of functional co-ordination is simplified. With all of the factories, for example, responsible to a single executive supported by an adequate staff, the problem of standardizing and co-ordinating policies, operations, facilities, methods, costs, and procedure is relatively simple from an organizational standpoint. This plan does, however, throw the entire burden of co-ordinating the various functions into a profitable and successful whole upon general management, because it is very difficult to measure directly and to hold each functional division accountable for its individuals contribution to company earnings.

Undoubtedly the functional plan of organization is the most logical where a single product or a small number of related products are made, where operations are highly centralized, or where there is no practicable physical basis for establishing responsibility along product or regional lines. On the other hand, as operations increase in size, and, as the line of products becomes more and more extensive and diversified, it becomes increasingly difficult to effect adequate direction and control through a single executive channel over a primary function such as manufacturing or sales.

PRODUCT-DIVISION PLAN

Under this plan of organization, divisional executives are responsible for all functions, except general staff and service activities, involved in the manufacture and sale of a single product or related group of products. Sometimes the product divisions are integral parts of the company, and sometimes they are subsidiary companies.

The principal advantage of this plan of organization, where it is practicable, is that it often provides a very effective basis for the decentralization of management. Each product division, carrying primary responsibility for its own product determination, prices, manufacturing, and marketing, has all the aspects of a separate smaller business. Consequently, it can be held fully accountable on a profit-and-loss basis, which is the ultimate measure of successful operation. General management is able to delegate a wide measure of latitude and authority to such units, implanting a stimulating sense of proprietary responsibility in the divisional executives. Therefore, general management can confidently rely upon an effective profit-and-loss control to insure satisfactory results, knowing that if each of the component "businesses" is profitable, the enterprise as a whole is bound to be successful.

This plan of organization can be most effectively used in the case of large companies with a diverse line of products which it is feasible to make in separate factories and market through separate selling organizations. Examples of this type are found in the major automobile companies, the larger chemical concerns, and in general manufacturing enterprises making a number of more or less unrelated products, each involving its own technical, manufacturing, and sales problems. Where, however, the various products are derived from a common source, as in the case of the oil and steel companies, it is relatively difficult to use this type of organization because it is impracticable to divide responsibility for the manufacture of different products in a single plant.

One large company with many divergent lines of products, having had difficulty in directing and controlling its expanding operations on a functional basis, has within recent years broken these operations down into some twenty product divisions. Each division is responsible for its own product engineering, manufacturing, and sales direction, although making use of a common selling organization in order to eliminate duplication of field coverage.

Another company, although its factories make several lines of products, has organized sales on a product-division basis. Each division has primary responsibility for its own product determination, quality, costs, delivery, prices, and sales operations, while relying upon a common manufacturing department to operate the factories. This arrangement calls for a high degree of co-operation between product-division executives and plant management in order to avoid confusion of responsibility and interests.

While facilitating control and affording an effective basis for decentralization of management, the product-division plan of organization presents a special problem of co-ordination. With wide latitude delegated to product-division executives in the running of their own businesses, it is still necessary to provide adequate co-ordination between divisions with respect to policies, practices, methods, and costs, within the common fields of manufacturing, marketing, etc. This purpose is generally accomplished by setting up central staff agencies to exercise overriding *functional* direction, supervision, and control within each of these fields and to assure realization of the company's over-all objectives. These staff agencies generally follow the plan of organization described on page 41. In some cases they head up to designated members of the general-management group.

Generally speaking, an operating organization divided along product lines is likely to develop more all-round men. The assumption of a high degree of proprietary responsibility and authority, as well as the driving necessity of operating as profitably as possible, affords experience in all phases of business. In functional organization, on the other hand, there is a natural tendency for divisional executives to become specialists in experience and interests, rather than all-round businessmen. Then, too, a functional executive, when advanced to the level of general management, frequently is reluctant, consciously or unconsciously, to relinquish direction over the department he formerly managed. This trait of human nature is so strong that one of the participating companies adopted the expedient of creating several subsidiary companies with a full complement of officers in an effort to concentrate the full attention of general executives upon broad company affairs.

REGIONAL PLAN

This plan of organization is one in which a divisional executive has charge of all company activities within a given geographic area. Its most logical application is in the management of remote operations which are more or less self-contained, with both manufacture and distribution serving the same territory. Under these conditions the regional division becomes virtually a separate business and can be held fully accountable for profitable operation just as in the case of a product division.

Like the product setup, therefore, this plan of organization affords an effective basis for decentralization of management. High-caliber divisional executives, located on the job and invested with wide responsibility and authority but guided by sound general policies, may appropriately be expected to take prompt and effective action based upon firsthand knowledge of local needs and conditions, without referring any but major matters to the home office. The retarding effects of absentee management and remote control are thus largely avoided. At the same time regional executives are developed into all-round businessmen.

Regional divisions may be integral parts of the company or subsidiary corporations, depending upon tax or legal considerations or previous status as separate concerns. The plan of management and control appears to be about the same under the two systems, both reflecting the same high degree of autonomy and full accountability for results on a profit-and-loss basis, and both having local staff and service agencies looking to the central staff offices for functional guidance and co-ordination. This study reveals a tendency, however, in the case of domestic subsidiaries of this type, to abandon the corporate form in favor of operation as divisions of the parent company.

While finding it impracticable to go the whole way toward regional management, several companies set up on a functional basis were found to be making effective use of the regional principle for decentralizing functional responsibility. One company with some fifty factories and sales coverage throughout the United States has established three regional offices headed by vice-presidents in charge of all local activities and supported by a very complete staff organization. The regional vice-presidents receive functional direction from the home-office executives in charge of manufacturing and sales. Likewise, regional staff assistants are functionally co-ordinated by the corresponding general staff offices. Under this arrangement most of the local problems are handled on the job by high-class supervisors and staff specialists thoroughly familiar with local needs and conditions, leaving only the broader aspects of direction, co-ordination, and control for the home-office organization. Incidentally, the number of individuals the head-office executives need to contact is greatly reduced.

It is not uncommon to find the Pacific Coast operations of a company set up on a regional basis, even though some other plan or organization obtains elsewhere in the company. The remoteness of this area from Eastern headquarters suggests the reason for this plan.

In many large companies all three of the foregoing plans of divisional organization may have application. If a trend toward any one type may be regarded as discernible, based upon the thirty-one companies studied, it is perhaps in the direction of the product-division plan.

Section 3

STAFF ORGANIZATION

The two preceding sections have dealt respectively with the directive and operative branches of management. The various staff departments make up the facilitative or third essential branch. The organization of this group of departments, even though in the aggregate they involve less personnel than the operating group, is of increasing importance in industry. As a rule, organization of the primary functions, such as manufacturing and marketing, is reasonably definite and well understood. With the staff departments, however, this is not the case, and analysis of the organization plans of most of the companies surveyed testifies to the need of better understanding and further clarification in order to make this important part of the management machinery fully effective.

As the managerial process grows in complexity, the time, ability, and comprehension of single executives become increasingly inadequate and must be supplemented by staff agencies able to furnish specialized assistance and advice. An adequate staff organization, designed to take full advantage of specialized knowledge, concentrated attention, unified effort, and definite accountability for results within its appropriate fields, can go a long way toward relieving the burden and increasing the effectiveness of management. Such an organization may be relied upon (*a*) to determine needs and formulate appropriate plans, objectives, and controls; (*b*) to review, co-ordinate, digest, and pass expert opinion upon proposals; and (*c*) to keep executives informed of significant developments; and thus make it possible for management to concentrate its attention upon matters requiring its consideration.

Staff departments do not create new functions but concentrate specialized attention upon certain phases of the management problem as these reach extensive proportions. Before emerging as the specific activities of full-fledged staff agencies, the same functions are found scattered among various individuals in different departments. As the business grows in size and complexity, it becomes

36

increasingly necessary and profitable to set up a well-qualified agency to concentrate upon achievement of desired objectives within each logical field, rather than to rely upon the casual interest and variable understanding of individuals and agencies to whom it is often of secondary concern. In many cases a company does not realize that it is overdue for specialization in some such field, and that it is already paying the price of a fully effective staff agency without securing the benefits of specialized attention.

One of the important considerations in the organization of general staff agencies is the determination of the management level and executive position to which each should logically report. Too often this allocation is based upon mere expediency—the fact that a certain executive may know something about the subject, or may be carrying a somewhat lighter load than his associates. This often results in burdening major divisional executives with a miscellaneous group of unrelated activities and interests. It also tends to impair the effectiveness of staff effort through lack of interest, restriction of action, and difficulty in obtaining necessary support of top management.

Observation within the companies surveyed suggests the following principles as a sound guide to such assignment:

1. If the effort of a staff agency is to be expended primarily in behalf of one branch or division of the company, it would seem logical that it be made responsible to the divisional executive concerned. For example, an agency organized for inspection and control of quality would normally be found on the staff of the divisional executive of manufacturing.

2. If, on the other hand, the agency is intended to serve two or more divisions impartially, it should report to general management either directly or in combination with other closely related general staff functions.

In order to be fully effective, central staff agencies concerned with such general functions as personnel, organization, cost control, and public relations must be free of department obligation, influence, or bias, and able to take a broad objective viewpoint based solely upon the best interests of the company as a whole. Within their respective fields, these agencies must be in a position to investigate and call attention to unsatisfactory conditions in any division or department of the company, and to initiate steps toward their correction. This is rendered difficult if the agency reports to one of the divisions concerned, because the interests of the staff executive may often conflict with those of his superior. Furthermore, other divisions affected can hardly be expected to receive favorably recommendations coming from the same level of management, particularly where these may be construed as reflecting upon the adequacy of divisional administration. For example, a personnel department attached, say, to manufacturing would probably be handicapped in prescribing for the needs of personnel in the sales departments.

Such agencies, handling important specialized functions of general, rather than divisional, concern, therefore, can properly accomplish their purposes only as the agents of general management. Only under such auspices are they in a position to secure the effective support and co-operation of the various divisional executives with whose activities they must properly be concerned.

3. Sometimes, in order to minimize the number of agencies reporting directly to general management, it is desirable to group certain of the smaller, closely related staff functions under a single staff executive reporting to general management. As an example, the comptroller may appropriately head up tax, insurance, real estate, and auditing activities, as well as accounting. Likewise, functional responsibility for organization and cost control may be vested in a single executive. Such an executive should have the time, understanding, and interest properly to guide and secure the necessary support for each of the staff activities entrusted to him. In addition, by the nature of his position and jurisdiction, he should be free to maintain an impartial company-wide viewpoint, without any interests which might conflict with those of his various staff functions.

TYPES OF STAFF ORGANIZATION

Another major consideration in the setup of a staff agency is the determination of its proper status in the organization—its functions, objectives, limits of authority, and relationships with other departments and agencies. In this regard there appear to be four more or less well-defined bases from which to choose, either individually or in appropriate combination:

Control basis	Co-ordinative basis
Service basis	Advisory basis

It is most important that each staff agency be established on a basis suited to its major purposes. A control function set up on an advisory basis is likely to be weak and ineffective, while an agency which should be advisory may easily overstep its proper province if it attempts to operate as a control organization.

These four general types of staff effort may be characterized as follows:

CONTROL AGENCIES

One common type of staff agency is that set up to "take over management's worries" within a certain field. Such agencies are expected to conceive needs, crystallize objectives, formulate and develop required plans, methods, and means of control, follow results, and take all appropriate measures necessary to insure that the ends desired by management are actually achieved. Agencies of this type include the following:

Organization	Personnel Administration
Cost Control	Accounting
Industrial Engineering	Auditing
Standard Practice	Credit
Budgetary Control	

In addition, companies organized on a product-division basis frequently have staff agencies of this type to provide necessary functional co-ordination and control over those aspects of manufacturing, marketing, and engineering common to all divisions. In many cases, such staff departments are concerned with functions which are inherent responsibilities of the line organization and from which the latter cannot appropriately be relieved. However, if these functions are left entirely to the casual interest, variable understanding, and unco-ordinated effort of the many line executives who are often heavily burdened with other matters, results are usually far from satisfactory. It is therefore customary to set up a properly qualified staff agency to exercise an overriding functional responsibility and accountability for seeing that the desired objectives are achieved. Needless to say, this dual responsibility calls for a clear-cut definition and understanding of the respective functions, authorities, and relationships involved, as well as the exercise of proper tact and understanding in their performance.

The following considerations are of primary importance in organizing such control functions:

1. If it is to be fully effective, the control agency must be directly responsible to a level of management having jurisdiction over its entire field of activity.

2. The control agency should be held definitely accountable for seeing that desired objectives are realized and should take whatever steps are necessary and appropriate to this end. Too often such agencies are established merely on an advisory basis. This seriously impairs their value and effectiveness from a control standpoint.

3. The staff agency must usually accomplish these ends with little or no direct authority and without conflicting with the natural line responsibilities involved. Its means are therefore normally limited to:

a) Crystallizing plans and objectives for management's ratification.

b) Formulating and developing adequate means and systems of control for insuring realization of these objectives.

c) Securing necessary acceptance, co-operation, and support through discussion, education, and recommendation.

d) Following and gauging the adequacy of performance within its given field, working with the executives concerned toward the elimination of unsatisfactory conditions, and keeping general management informed of over-all progress and results.

e) Passing upon proposals and developments within the given field as a basis for final approval.

f) In general, advising and assisting all executives and departments concerned in reaching the desired objectives.

It is usually impracticable in a large organization to attempt to exercise such control functions in their entirety from a central office. Besides overloading the central agency with matters which can be better handled on the ground, this arrangement gives the appearance of relieving rather than guiding and assisting the line executives in the exercise of their proper responsibilities within such fields, and often causes unnecessary friction and resentment.

In order to obtain the advantages of decentralization without impairing over-all control, therefore, many concerns have established counterparts of the central control agencies on the staffs of divisional and regional executives. This is particularly true in the case of accounting and personnel functions. Usually such agencies are directly responsible to the line executives whom they serve, and functionally responsible to the central staff office. Experience among the participating companies indicates that this arrangement can be made very practicable and effective, despite the dual-responsibility feature, provided the following principles are observed:

1. Just as it is the primary function of the central control agency to assist general management in achievement of certain objectives for the company as a whole, so it is properly the province of these local affiliates to assist their departmental principals in realizing these same ends. By being members of the local organization the local staff representatives are often in a position to obtain better co-operation and results than a central agency could obtain.

2. In order to assure the necessary over-all co-ordination and control, however, it is most important that the local staff offices have the same viewpoint and understanding of the general program, objectives, policies, and procedure that the central staff agency has.

3. To this end, the central staff executive should have a determining voice in the selection of his functional representatives, at the same time making sure that his nominees are acceptable to the local management. Wherever practicable, such selections can well be made from within the department concerned in order that the individuals chosen may already have the confidence and support of the local organization.

4. These local staff executives should, wherever practicable, have the benefit of training through the central staff office in order that they may have a thorough understanding of general objectives and policies. Where this cannot be anticipated and arranged as a logical step in their long-time training and development programs, it may be necessary to bring such men to the central office for a few weeks of intensive training before they assume their departmental responsibilities.

5. The central staff executive should maintain close contact with his local affiliates through field visits, home office conferences, and direct correspondence. In order to avoid conflict with obligations to the line organization, it is important that this interchange be confined to equipping the local staff agencies to serve their local principals most effectively in accomplishing the common objectives, rather than to giving them definite instructions.

6. Any matters likely to conflict with local instructions or interests should be taken up through the local or departmental executives. Any general policies or mandatory plans of control should likewise be handed down through line rather than staff channels.

One of the participating companies, with world-wide operations, has a most impressive plan of staff organization along these lines. The central staff executives responsible for accounting, personnel, engineering, research, and purchasing functions, all set up on a control basis, have a determining voice in the selection of their functional representatives. They usually appoint someone who has had several years of training in the central staff office and who is therefore able to bring to the local organization a broad knowledge of the company-wide program in that field. The central office keeps these men informed of all developments of interest and expects them to "sell" their local principals on any needed changes. In the event that they are unable to get done the things that need to be done, these local staff agencies have the right of appeal to their central staff offices.

SERVICE AGENCIES

The chief objective in establishing a staff service department is usually to relieve each of the operating departments of the necessity of performing some function common to all, and, through assignment to a single well-qualified agency, to secure the advantages of specialized attention, better service, closer co-ordination and control, and usually lower costs. The extent and cost of such effort, scattered through many departments and consequently hidden from view, are frequently very great. It is only when they are brought out into the open and assigned to a single agency that their magnitude is appreciated and control measures can be undertaken. Then, too, a central agency can often justify a higher caliber and wider diversity of specialized talent than would be feasible for any single department. Such activities as the following are frequently consolidated and set up on a service basis:

Research and Development	Tax
Engineering and Construction	Real Estate
Purchasing	Insurance
Statistical	Motor Vehicle Selection, Op-
Traffic	eration, and Maintenance

Where it is practicable to centralize such functions in the home office, no difficult organizational problems are presented. In the case of the larger companies, however, such centralization may result in lack of full understanding and appreciation of the needs, problems, and viewpoints of the departments and regional organizations served, or, again, remote handling may occasion undue delay. To meet this condition central staff departments frequently establish local service units or departmental liaison men who take care of routine local requirements and look to the central office to handle or assist with major or special problems.

Where the staff function is not logically separable from line activities and responsibilities, however, and it is therefore impracticable for the staff organization to take it over in its entirety, local needs and requirements may best be met by setting up staff agencies under divisional and regional managements. Under these circumstances, the central staff office may assume the province of a control agency, carrying responsibility for the functional supervision and co-ordination of these local affiliates, and taking appropriate steps to insure the adequacy, uniformity, and economy of service rendered. A typical example of this type is the plant engineering function usually embracing plant maintenance and power plant operation. Because of the intimate relationship of these functions to other manufacturing activities, it is not practicable to take them out from under plant management. Considerable advantage may accrue, however, from having the chief engineer of the company standardize methods and practices, eliminate duplicated effort, and exercise a major voice in the selection and training of the various plant engineers.

CO-ORDINATIVE AGENCIES

Sometimes a staff agency is set up to co-ordinate and handle functions in which two or more departments have a joint interest. Examples of this type include:

> Order and Distribution Department
> Production Planning Department
> Merchandise Department

In such cases, no one of the primary departments concerned is normally in a position to appreciate fully the needs, requirements, and consequences of contemplated plans, schedules, and changes, with respect to the others. A separate agency, designed to embrace a comprehensive knowledge and understanding of the various interests concerned, is therefore set up to work closely with the different departments, developing, co-ordinating, and securing agreement upon plans that take into proper account the different needs and requirements.

In some cases such agencies are vested with authority to make final decisions in regard to products, production schedules, and similar matters. Others develop the facts and submit their recommendations to general management for decision. From an organizational standpoint they logically follow the same principles outlined for service agencies.

ADVISORY AGENCIES

The primary purpose of many staff agencies is to render specialized advice and counsel to management upon request. Such agencies normally have no directional, administrative, or control functions, but give authoritative opinions when asked, and often bring to management's attention developments of interest within their respective fields. Among the functions which are largely advisory in character and fall within this group are:

> Legal
> Economic
> Public Relations
> Labor Relations Aspect of
> > Personnel Administration

The effective organization of such agencies, as a rule, presents no unusual problems. They normally report to the president or general management, or to the divisional executive most closely concerned, but are usually available for consultation by any interested executive or department.

The same general principles outlined above with respect to general or central staff agencies may, with equal propriety, be used as a guide in the organization of departmental staff activities. The problems and relationships are essentially the same, the only difference being in the scope of operation.

EXTENT OF STAFF ORGANIZATION

The necessary information regarding the extent of staff organization is available for twenty-six of the participating companies.

These data reveal that the number of general staff departments in a single company runs from eight to twenty-five. All told, more than fifty different staff agencies were found. The extent to which these companies have specialized agencies to handle the more common staff functions is indicated as follows:

Accounting 26
Purchasing 26
Traffic 26
Product or Process Research 24
General Engineering 24
Credit 23
Tax 23
Personnel Relations 22
Legal 21

Patent 20
Insurance 18
Budgetary Control 16
Cost Control or Industrial Engineering.......... 13
Order and Distribution........................ 13
Public Relations 13

Market Research 9
Real Estate 9
Economics or Statistics....................... 8

Organization 4
Merchandise 4

OBSERVED NEEDS AND TRENDS IN STAFF ORGANIZATION

No attempt will be made to discuss the complete roster of staff functions and agencies, because in many cases their scope and practices are well known and differ mainly as to detail. Certain staff activities, however, are of particular interest from an organizational standpoint, either because of new developments or trends, or because particular needs or weaknesses were observed in the course of the survey. These are discussed below.

PERSONNEL AND INDUSTRIAL RELATIONS DEPARTMENTS

While the personnel and industrial relations function has central staff representation in most of the companies studied, in only a very few cases did this activity appear to be operating under a plan of organization conducive to the full accomplishment of its logical purposes.

Most of the personnel agencies appear to be primarily concerned with labor relations and the problems involved in handling rank-and-file personnel. In this field, for the most part, they seem to be quite effective. As a rule, however, they apparently play little part in the constructive development of staff, supervisory, and executive personnel. This is one of the major problems on which management must necessarily look to active staff assistance if the important objectives outlined in Part C, Section 5, are to be fully realized.

Then, too, instead of having a single, strong staff agency taking full functional responsibility for all appropriate aspects of personnel administration and industrial relations throughout the company, many concerns have several agencies handling different parts of this general field with little or no effective co-ordination between them. Sometimes the split is made on a functional basis, as when there are separate agencies to handle personnel relations, labor relations, and so on; in other cases, individual departments, such as manufacturing and sales, have independent personnel agencies. Under this plan it is difficult or impossible to achieve the uniformity of thought, purpose, and practice which is so important in this field.

Another handicap to the full value and effectiveness of such agencies is the fact that, in order not to conflict with the natural responsibilities of the line organization in regard to personnel matters, the personnel or industrial relations department is set up on an advisory rather than a control basis. Under this arrangement it is not in a position to assume the active, functional direction and supervision of the entire program, "getting done the things that need to be done" in this field. On the contrary, it must sit back and wait to be asked for advice, often aware of unsatisfactory conditions which it is powerless to correct except by the dubious expedient of complaining to the chief executive. Other companies have demonstrated the practicability of organizing this important function on a control basis, as defined above, and are apparently able to secure the advantages of this type of setup without relieving or conflicting with the natural responsibilities of the operating organization.

In this same connection, central personnel agencies set up on an advisory basis generally lack the power of selection, training, and, sometimes, even freedom of contact and correspondence with the various divisional or department staff agencies handling the same function. Without such authority the director of personnel is often obliged to work through departmental representatives whose qualifications, background, and viewpoint may be wholly inadequate. This seriously impairs efforts to achieve the desired over-all objectives.

Another common weakness in organizing a personnel department is to make it responsible to a divisional executive and then expect it to function effectively for the company as a whole. Because the major portion of rank-and-file personnel is found in the factories, some companies place the personnel and industrial relations department under manufacturing, possibly overlooking the major need for similar staff supervision with regard to sales, office, and supervisory personnel, or at least making it difficult for the personnel agency to function effectively over this broader field.

Again, in two or three companies the personnel department reports to the legal department, presumably to take advantage of specialized knowledge of labor laws and bargaining procedure. Regardless of personal qualifications, this organizational relationship might easily make it difficult to secure the confidence of the company's workmen, because emphasis is placed upon legal rights rather than upon equitable human relationships. It may be significant in this connection that, in the two participating companies which have experienced major labor difficulties in recent years, the labor relations department works under the legal department.

Observation among the companies surveyed indicates that the following features are usually desirable in the organization of the personnel staff:

1. There should be a single, high-caliber, central staff agency, under a director of personnel responsible to the president or to general management for functional direction, co-ordination, and control over all personnel and industrial relations matters.

2. In the case of a large company, such an agency might appropriately have subdivisions as follows:

a) **Research and Analytical Section,** keeping informed on the best thought on personnel matters and benefit plans throughout the country, analyzing labor laws and requirements, following the company's own practice, initiating and formulating needed changes in plans and policies, and maintaining the personnel policy manual designed to insure uniform and appropriate procedure in all departments.

b) **Employee Benefits Section,** concerned with the proper application of the various employee benefit plans to specific cases, making necessary analyses, and recommending appropriate action to the employee benefits committee in each instance.

c) **Training and Development Section,** formulating, guiding, and co-ordinating the company program for assuring properly qualified personnel in all positions from top to bottom. As explained in Part C, Section 5, this would involve such activities as scouting specialized talent, developing and assisting in the administration of the rating program, co-ordinating all training and development activities, and analyzing candidates' qualifications for appointment to key positions for the personnel committee.

d) **Employment Section,** functionally supervising all employment offices; co-ordinating personnel and manpower requirements between different departments, making sure that surplus in one division is absorbed as far as practicable before new men are hired; helping develop more suitable placements for personnel in other departments; checking the possibility of advancing qualified employees already on the payroll to fill vacancies before hiring outsiders; making certain that new men hired are up to standard; and, in event of major layoff, that the least-valuable employees in the entire organization are released.

e) **Labor Relations Section,** to advise operating executives in regard to the maintenance of satisfactory labor relations, collective bargaining, avoidance of labor trouble, and the handling of difficulties when they arise.

f) **Medical Section,** to be responsible for all medical service and staff.

g) **Safety Section,** functionally supervising and co-ordinating the company's safety program.

3. The director of personnel should have the power of selection and training of, as well as functional supervision over, all

departmental and divisional personnel men—making sure, however, that his selections are acceptable to the operating executives concerned and taking care to avoid all conflict with proper divisional interests.

ORGANIZATION DEPARTMENTS

Increasing realization of the importance of organization analysis, planning, and clarification is evidenced by the fact that at least four of the participating companies have, within recent years, set up well-qualified central staff agencies for this purpose. In each case the agency assists the top executives in developing and maintaining plans of organization which will best facilitate management and control of the enterprise.

These agencies are usually headed up by a manager or director responsible to the president and supported by from one to a dozen specialists having wide experience and familiarity with the different major functions or fields of operation, such as production, marketing, technical, and office. Owing, no doubt, to their comparatively recent origin, none of the agencies observed has as yet fully achieved its logical ultimate province and place in the organization. Their functions are found to vary considerably, and in no one case do they embrace the full field of usefulness for such a department. Among them, however, practically all the activities appropriate to such an agency are represented.

The primary responsibility of an organization department is, logically, to determine needs, formulate plans, and secure necessary acceptance, co-operation, and support, to the end: first, that the company may have the best possible plan of organization to meet its requirements; second, that the appropriate functions, objectives, relationships, and limits of authority may be properly clarified and defined for each level of management, each department, each committee, and each key job; and, third, that the size of the company's organization (manpower) may be kept at a minimum necessary to handle the essential work. This normally involves such specific activities as the following:

1. Developing an ultimate or ideal plan of organization to work toward as appropriate opportunities are presented.
2. Developing and maintaining an organization manual clarifying and defining the approved plan of organization by means of organization charts, job specifications, and similar devices.

3. Initiating or reviewing proposed changes in the plan of organization, making sure that they are desirable and as far as practicable consistent with the ultimate plan, and recommending appropriate action.
4. Making a periodic review of organization practice to see that it conforms to the plan, or that the plan is amended as necessary to meet changed requirements.
5. Making necessary organization surveys to determine essential work, manpower, and organization requirements.
6. Developing and administering a plan of control over payroll and manpower, such as a payroll budget.

Such an agency should also have an important voice in designing the general plan of control over such activities as capital expenditures, operating expenditures, wages and salaries, appointments to key positions, and changes in the line of products. These control schemes are an inseparable part of organization planning, involving the allocation of functions, assignment of responsibilities, and delegation of authority.

The process of analyzing and clarifying job functions and setting up job specifications affords the best possible basis for determining relative job values. Therefore, as confirmed by the practice of two of the companies, the organization department is in a logical position to serve as the analytical or fact-finding agency in connection with the company's wage- and salary-control program, involving such phases as:

1. Appraising relative job values.
2. Determining prevailing wage and salary levels on the outside.
3. Recommending appropriate wage rates and salary ranges for all jobs as necessary to maintain a rational and equitable wage and salary structure.
4. Reviewing all proposed wage changes from the standpoint of justification, effect on other related rates, and similar factors.
5. Analyzing all proposed salary changes from the standpoint of conformance with the approved salary structure, and other considerations.

Two companies have found it advantageous to look to their organization agencies to exercise functional control over not only payroll costs, but over all elements of cost.

In companies which lack an organization department, such

functions are often assigned to the industrial relations or industrial engineering departments.

In order that it may be in a position to discharge all of these responsibilities effectively and assure the proper co-ordination of similar effort throughout the company, the organization agency should be set up on a control basis, with closely related departmental affiliates, following the general pattern outlined on page 41.

The need and appropriate functions of a staff agency specializing in organization and related management problems are discussed more at length in Part C, Section 4, "Control over Organization."

COST-CONTROL DEPARTMENTS

While all the participating companies stress the importance of cost reduction and control, very few have organized this function on a basis which facilitates and assures most effective over-all results in this field. Many companies have cost-control agencies doing an impressive job in specialized fields, such as an industrial-engineering division working on direct factory expense, an analytical agency concerned with the reduction of certain phases of selling expense, and perhaps a group of specialists working toward standardization and increased efficiency of clerical operations. Very often, however, there is little, if any, co-ordination among these agencies as to method, viewpoint, or results, and frequently their activities embrace only a portion of the entire field of operating costs.

About half of the companies have budgetary-control plans, often administered by a budget division responsible to the comptroller. The effectiveness of such a plan, however, is largely dependent upon the caliber of the basic estimates of optimum performance upon which the budgets are based. Quite often, the central budget division lacks the knowledge, jurisdiction, or any effective basis for co-ordinating and satisfying itself as to the soundness of detailed budget estimates, and must be content with mere statistical analyses and comparisons.

These conditions suggest the desirability of unifying and co-ordinating all staff effort devoted to cost reduction and control under the functional direction and supervision of a single, well-qualified staff department, upon whom top management may confidently rely to make sure:

1. That suitable yardsticks, measures, and objectives are established for all elements of cost in all departments. These standards should represent not merely best past performance, but the best performance of which the organization and facilities are capable.
2. That all supervisors and executives are currently informed through simple, well-designed, and co-ordinated reports, as to how their actual costs compare with the standards or budgets.
3. That action, commensurate with the need, is taken to correct the conditions which stand in the way of optimum performance.

This general plan of control is approached or realized in several of the participating companies. In some cases a budget- or cost-control division of the comptroller's organization is responsible for general administration and co-ordination of the program. This arrangement has the advantage of providing ready access, familiarity, and control of cost and performance records. On the other hand, the accounting personnel may lack the requisite knowledge and understanding of operations and industrial engineering practice, unless special provision is made for this type of representation. In other companies, a strong industrial engineering department may perform some or all of these functions on a company-wide basis.

Two of the companies surveyed have found it advantageous to combine responsibility for organization and cost-control activities. The logic of this arrangement proceeds from the following considerations:

1. Control over the form and the size of organization are almost inseparable. Thus the organization department is logically concerned with effecting control over what is one of the largest items of cost—the payroll.

2. Individuals in organization work necessarily have the analytical ability and firsthand familiarity with functions and operations throughout the company which are almost indispensable requirements in the development and administration of an effective over-all plan of cost control. In many cases they would qualify as industrial engineers. While in other cases they may not be authorities in such specialized fields as time and motion study, scrap control, and mechanization of operations, they should be in a position to recognize the problems and requirements and be able to secure the necessary specialized advice.

3. In order, therefore, that top management may be able to look to a single well-qualified agency to take responsibility for co-ordinating the entire program, it selects the organization department which has a natural concern with respect to the larger part of the field—manpower and payroll. In this case it becomes an organization and cost-control department. This agency, of course, looks to the comptroller's organization to furnish the reports and figures required in the control plan.

Whether or not the cost-control function is assigned to the organization agency, it would logically follow the same plan of organization as a typical staff control department. This general plan, providing for maximum practicable decentralization of control through departmental affiliates, closely co-ordinated by a strong central agency, is described on page 41.

DISTRIBUTION-SERVICE DEPARTMENTS

There appears to be a growing tendency to consolidate and co-ordinate within a strong staff department the various functions and operations lying between manufacturing and selling that have to do with keeping the sales department properly supplied with merchandise. This field might be characterized as the "service of supply" to the selling organization. This development, grouping activities otherwise scattered among several departments, is of particular interest because it tends to rationalize a field of administration which often lacks clarity in organization.

Among the activities that can be appropriately assigned to such an agency are the following:

Order and Distribution—receiving orders from the sales organization, consolidating the orders, allocating them to the manufacturing plants, and following them through to shipment.

Stock and Inventory Control—anticipating sales requirements, seeing that they are properly supplied, keeping field inventories at a minimum and the turnover at a maximum, initiating action as warranted to discontinue slow-moving items, arranging for the disposition of obsolete stocks, and so forth.

Warehousing—operation of regional warehouses to supply the sales organization.

Traffic—the usual functions of a traffic department.

This arrangement recognizes the natural, close relationship between these four functions and, at the same time, leaves the two major operating departments free to concentrate upon their primary functions—production and selling. One large and well-organized company has recently created just such a department under a general manager, with subordinate managers responsible for each of the four functional fields indicated. A number of the other companies have combined some but not all of these functions.

MERCHANDISE DEPARTMENTS

Several companies have likewise seen fit to establish a department to handle the many analytical and co-ordinative functions concerned with product and price determination. It occupies the twilight zone that lies between sales, manufacturing, product engineering, and research in regard to these fields. While no two merchandise departments have exactly the same functions, there is a tendency to assign them a wide variety of analytical problems. The following list of functions is characteristic:

To serve as a clearinghouse for all product suggestions from customers, inventors, the field force, or the engineering and research departments.

To study product lines with a view to the creation of needed new items, simplification and elimination of obsolete, duplicate, or unnecessary products, and the redesign of others to cover the field more effectively.

To study packaging from the standpoint of standardization, simplification, appearance, and protection.

To make market surveys and analyses to find new uses for products, and to study and make recommendations in regard to customer service and policies.

To work up all price and discount schedules in accordance with general price policies.

To issue all catalogues and price lists and check advertising material from a technical standpoint.

To investigate and test competitive products.

To co-ordinate production schedules, inventories, and other factors in regard to changes in the line of products.

In other companies many of these functions are handled by a group of analysts and specialists serving as a products committee which takes final action in most cases.

ECONOMIC PLANNING AGENCIES

The growing recognition of the importance of sound economic analysis and forecasting as a guide to top management in planning the conduct of the business is attested by the fact that about one-third of the companies have economic research and statistical agencies, often heading up to an economist responsible to the president or general management. Many top executives have been brought to a realization of the major effect which general economic conditions and the business cycles have upon their own operations, and the importance of shaping their forward plans in regard to sales, production, labor, inventories, capital expenditures, and general financial policies in accordance therewith. While it is by no means infallible, many concerns have found that the use of such research can materially reduce the chances of being caught unprepared or overextended, and several companies appear to have been remarkably successful in anticipating major changes in the trend and promptly trimming sail accordingly.

The functions of such economic and statistical agencies normally include:

Analysis and forecasting of general economic conditions and their probable effect upon company sales, prices, employment, inventories, raw materials, and so forth.

Preparation of reports and charts showing trends and forecasts in these different fields for the guidance of executives.

Preparation of master forecasts of sales and production for a year or more ahead.

Industry analyses and statistics, sometimes including participation in efforts toward standardization and simplification of products throughout the industry.

In some cases such agencies make fundamental analyses as to the propriety of entering a new field of business or some other major venture. They may also be involved in studies looking toward stabilization of the company's operations and employment, with respect to seasonal and even cyclical fluctuations. The value of such effort, assuming it is adequate, lies in the extent to which it is used as a guide to operation. In several companies, projected operating plans and capital expenditures are carefully considered each month or quarter, in the light of the general business forecast, and in accordance therewith are modified as necessary.

PUBLIC RELATIONS AGENCIES

One of the most recent activities to be accorded departmental status is public relations. Approximately half of the participating companies have such staff agencies, usually under a director responsible to general management. Other concerns are considering the establishment of such an agency. There is, however, a wide variation of opinion as to the proper functions and scope of such a department. In this connection the following conception, obtained from the head of public relations for one of the larger companies, will be of interest in clarifying this field:

Public relations in its fundamental sense has to do with the creation and shaping of policies which, if sincerely practiced and effectively made known to the public, will be reflected in public good will. Publicity is merely the technique by which these policies and actions are effectively presented to the public. Public relations calls for a point of view, it asks questions: What is going on inside as well as outside this business that may affect the public's viewpoint towards us? What are the policies that govern the conduct of this business; are the individual and collective contacts of the corporation with the public, including the employees, such that the impression created will be favorable and preferential toward the enterprise and everything connected with it? Does the determination to do what will create that impression permeate the whole organization?

Public relations is a part of management. The public relations aspect should always be considered when decisions are made. The public interest and attitudes should be taken into account when establishing policies and operating practices.

The duties of the public relations men are varied. Many of them are difficult to distinguish from sales promotion. Some of the things handled are:

Speeches: Edit from a public relations view; what to say—what not to say and reach the people intended.

Reception: Make contacts pleasant, for callers, for salesmen calling to sell goods, for customers visiting plants or offices.

Meetings: Get proper executive representation at meetings; at conventions, etc. Persuade top executives to attend and suggest attitude to take.

Stockholders: Prepare good informative letter to the stockholders for president's signature to be included with the dividend checks; issue other letters to stockholders occasionally to notify them of new developments.

Complaints: See that complaints are handled tactfully.

Advertising (Contributions) : Handle such cases as that of a preacher who wants $150 for an advertisement in a church publication.

Government Relations: Keep within the scheme of things and still on a sound business basis.

Newspapers: Contact newspapers and publishers in advance of meetings where the president will be. Arrange for them to meet and talk with the president and other top executives before the meetings. Top executives should not talk about war, politics, government, etc., and should avoid political or other partisan activities. A fundamental rule is never to ask a paper to print or not to print.

Publicity: Help prepare and/or censor all institutional releases, annual statements, etc.

PRODUCT-DIVISION CO-ORDINATING AGENCIES

Where a company is organized on a product-division basis, there is usually need of some special means for co-ordinating the aspects of manufacturing, marketing, and engineering and other functions that are common to all divisions. This is usually done by setting up for each of these functional fields, as necessary, a central staff agency responsible to general management for standardizing and co-ordinating operating policies, methods, practices, facilities, costs, and similar items. These agencies generally follow the plan of organization described on page 41.

The functions assigned to one such department, co-ordinating certain manufacturing activities of nearly twenty product divisions, are as follows:

Production control

Allocates production between divisions where several are involved.

Programs flow of raw materials and semifinished products between divisions.

Referees questions of defective work between divisions and plants.

Passes on whether to manufacture or purchase related or auxiliary equipment involved in a given project.

Exercises functional supervision over the system of planning and scheduling in all plants.

Advises general management relative to the status of production.

Quality control

Establishes and standardizes sound inspection practices.

Analyzes defective work arising at the various plants in consultation with local managements.

Watches inspection expense.

Facilities and methods

Studies best practice throughout own and similar industries.

Assists divisions in preparation of annual and special-equipment budgets, studying needs and advising them as to best selection based on maintenance, cost, performance, etc.

Reviews all capital budgets; follows up all budget appropriations and expenditures.

Works with purchasing department in contacting suppliers for bids and proposals.

Conducts manufacturing laboratory to try out all new tools and devices offered by suppliers and establishes proper feeds and speeds, thus making it unnecessary for each division to try out the same equipment.

Prepares bulletins covering new and better shop and production methods for distribution to all divisions.

Cost and methods control

Deals with the whole problem of efficiency and cost reduction at all plants.

Co-ordinates methods of analysis and control and aids in establishing standards covering such things as tools, materials, and performance.

Studies best practices of machining, welding, toolmaking, grinding, and other shop operations.

Construction control

Acts as liaison between divisions and outside architects, engineers, and contractors for reconstruction, additions, or new structures.

Checks appropriations and estimates for new construction.

Works with local, state, and city authorities as to codes, permits, floor loads, and the like.

Section 4

COMMITTEE ORGANIZATION

Of the various mechanisms of management, none is more controversial than committees. Some companies are intolerant on the subject; others overdo the idea. Committees are charged with wasting time, slowing down action, stifling individual initiative, producing compromises rather than clean-cut decisions, and lessening the sense of individual responsibility.

The committee plan obviously is not without its limitations, but when properly used, organized, and administered, committees provide a most effective device for co-ordinating activities and points of view. Informal meetings of executives are essentially no different from formal meetings of the same group sitting as a committee, except that there may be less regularity and orderliness in the former. A president conferring with individual top executives separately may conserve the time of the latter, but incurs an extravagant waste of his own time.

Despite their alleged shortcomings, committees are an important device of administration. They are appropriate at every level of the management scale. The board of directors is a committee, and most boards have several subcommittees. At the general-management level, the executive council or cabinet is in effective use, as brought out in a preceding section of this report. At the operating level of management, committees are of equivalent value and from one to ten such committees were found in most of the participating companies.

Where experience with committees has been unsatisfactory, the trouble usually lies either in improper use or in faulty organization and administration of the committees. The following considerations, suggested by observation in the participating companies, appear to be of primary importance in making committees effective.

Province of Committees.—From the standpoint of organization the regular company committees provide general management with additional advisory, co-ordinative, and control agencies. In this regard they supplement the staff departments, management having at its disposal the use of either type of agency. There is no overlap in purpose or functions, however, between the staff departments and the committees. The staff organizations are composed of experts, specializing by function, as indicated in the previous sections. They are called upon when specialized work or expert advice is required within their respective fields.

Committees should be created only when it is desired to obtain the *co-ordinated best judgment of a particular group*. Committees are no substitute for high-quality executive talent; they are not effective in offsetting defects in the organization structure; neither do they adequately correct weaknesses in the plan of management. The true function of committees is to deliberate upon previously developed facts, to exchange viewpoints, and through collective judgment to recommend action or endorse conclusions. Committees are not expected to be fact-gathering agencies; neither should they be assigned work to do. It is a waste of the time of all the members to endeavor to develop facts from which to find solutions through group discussion.

Before any committee is established, careful consideration should be given to its necessity. Very often an existing staff agency can more effectively handle the subject, and unless there is some particular reason for wanting group judgment it should be assigned to the staff agency. But if there are repetitive situations upon which the opinion of a selected group would be valuable, then a committee becomes useful. The purposes for which committees are most effective are:

1. To co-ordinate activities and points of view of the members. For example, it is often desirable to have some agency wherein the various departments can outline operating schedules, inform each other of intended developments or projects, and otherwise keep each other up to date. This gives each department represented a chance to explain its needs and co-ordinate its activities with those of the other departments.

2. To provide general management with well-considered recommendations on matters of company-wide concern as a basis for final action. Thus if general management desires the consensus of judgment of the department managers, there is an agency through which to obtain that co-ordinated opinion without soliciting each one separately.

3. To provide the rounded judgment of a well-qualified group in lieu of that of one individual, agency, or department. On such matters as salaries, appropriations, employee benefits or promotions, committees are an essential part of the control machinery in many of the companies visited. The various department managers refer their proposals to the committees established in these fields for their unprejudiced analysis and appraisal. Within specified limits, approval by the department manager and endorsement by the committee constitute final authorization. In case of disagreement, or beyond the limits specified, the proposal is referred to higher authority for final decision. This arrangement relieves the top management of routine approvals. In addition it removes the pressure and the onus which usually attach to any one individual who has final approval on matters which affect the destinies of individual employees, such as salaries, ratings, and appointments. A more sound and impartial consideration is also assured.

A committee may serve any one or all three of these needs, depending upon its purpose. As a by-product, committees give the people who serve upon them the wider knowledge and experience which come from considering problems on a company-wide basis. They therefore have a worth-while training value. Some companies find that particular aptitudes and abilities of the members are disclosed through committee work.

Need for an Auxiliary Working Agency.—One of the common misuses of committees is to assign problems to them for solution. A solution requires development of facts and an interpretation of those facts into conclusions. This involves work. The usual committee has no one to do such work. Consequently, the chairman or secretary generally undertakes the job, as and when other duties permit, and eventually presents the matter in proper form for committee consideration. To obviate this difficulty, some of the companies studied implement their committees with a full- or part-time secretary to keep minutes, gather and analyze data, follow up action, and relieve the chairman and members of detail. Where the volume of work warrants, the secretary may have several full-time assistants.

Another device is to designate an appropriate staff department as the working agency to develop and present conclusions and recommendations together with a brief summary of facts for committee action. In such cases it is not unusual for the committee chairman to be head of the staff group performing the analytical work. Very often the proposals, as well as the facts and supporting data, are prepared in the departments concerned and passed directly to the committee, or are sent to the committee by the general management.

These devices are used to expedite action and conserve the time of the committee members. Their use assures that the committees will receive for attention only well-analyzed proposals in proper form for consideration. This is important, since many companies want only the very best judgment on their committees—usually the highest divisional executives, whose time is valuable.

Well-Defined Functions, Responsibilities, Authority. — Since committees are a definite part of the organization, their exact status and relationship with the other parts of the company should be clearly established. In this regard they warrant exactly the same treatment as any department or position. The functions, objectives, relationships, and limits of authority of each committee must be stated in order that its purpose and proper use will be understood alike by the committee members and the rest of the organization. This clarification is particularly important in the case of committees because of the occasional tendency to unload problems upon them which are foreign to their real purpose. When this is permitted, the committee starts to grow; members are added to encompass the new subjects. As this process continues there eventually comes a point at which the committee must be abandoned or reorganized and restored to its original status and duties. Therefore it is well to emphasize that committees, like staff departments, are established to deal with particular specialized subjects, and care should be taken to keep their efforts confined to the proper field.

Membership Chosen to Assure Objectives.—Since group judgment of the members is the most important committee contribution, its membership largely determines its worth. The members of a committee should be selected for their functional or departmental point of view, as well as for the dependence placed upon the personal judgment of the individuals. Thus on some committees it is essential to have certain departments represented. Such is the case in a products committee where the points of view of the sales, research, and manufacturing departments are required. On other committees, particularly those having control functions, the analytical ability, background, and unbiased viewpoint of the members may be more important than departmental affiliation.

The number of members should be kept to a minimum consistent with necessary representation. In the case of the products committee mentioned above, three members in addition to a working secretary are sufficient. But if the purpose of the committee were to co-ordinate the activities of all the company departments, there should probably be a representative from each major operating and staff department.

In the interests of expediting action many companies use only top divisional or departmental executives on their committees. The members are then qualified to speak for the departments they represent; their judgment is also presumably the best in the company within their respective fields. Where care is exercised to make sure that all proposals are analyzed and worked out in advance, membership on such committees does not unduly burden the time of the members.

Appointment of members to such committees is made by the president or executive council. Needless to say, the members should be selected with care and with due consideration to the particular purpose the committee is to serve.

Procedure Designed to Obtain Prompt, Effective Action.—Administration of committees has an important bearing upon their success and effectiveness. When the committee is large, such as some of the co-ordinating committees, it is important to keep meetings orderly and businesslike. The chairman is usually selected not merely on the basis of his position, but particularly on his ability to keep discussion relevant, to bring out the best thoughts of the members, and to summarize opinion.

To the extent practicable, agenda are prepared and made available to members well in advance of the meetings. Where any controversial, technical, or complex proposal is to be presented, a summary is included with the agenda. The members are thus given an opportunity to analyze the proposal, and to obtain the views of their staff aides before attending the meeting. By this means it is possible to obtain the well-considered judgment of the members, rather than a hurried concurrence or a postponement of action. In the case of the control type of committee, such as those handling salaries and appropriations, a summary of every case to be considered at the meeting is supplied each member in advance. The committee meetings then require only sufficient time to discuss such features as the members wish to raise; they are already familiar with the matters presented and have had time adequately to judge their faults and merits.

In routine cases or in those where the facts clearly indicate only one possible course of action, the proposal may be circulated to the desks of the members for signature without the formality of a committee meeting. The more controversial cases are presented in regular meetings so that all members have the benefit of the discussion and exchange of views.

One of the companies requires members to sign the final draft of any proposal and to assume full individual responsibility for the decision taken by the committee. Other companies record the vote in the minutes of the committee meeting, thus tending to increase the sense of responsibility of the members. Copies of the minutes in brief form are supplied to the president or members of the executive council in some companies in order to keep them advised of committee action.

GENERALLY APPLICABLE COMMITTEES

Data were obtained on more than seventy-five committees within the divisional zone of top management. There are at least a half-dozen which might well be considered by any large concern for inclusion in its plan of organization. In the particular fields they cover, these committees offer the best means for obtaining the type of co-ordination and control required.

CO-ORDINATING COMMITTEE

Every company has the problem of co-ordinating the activities of its various operating and staff departments. Lacking such co-ordination, there is confusion of effort because the departments act individually without proper understanding of the plans, problems, and needs of other departments. For example, new facilities may be constructed by one department, when another has suitable facilities idle; plans for producing a new product may be perfected, while features covering its distribution and sale are neglected.

Before taking final action on some contemplated move or policy, it is often important for the top executives to find out from the department managers what the probable effect of such action would be upon the departments. A co-ordinating committee is an effective device for accomplishing these purposes. In general, the functions of such a committee are:

1. To develop opinion and viewpoint of the key executives in regard to contemplated moves and policies as a guide to top management in taking action. This includes such matters as changes in the wage and salary structure, changes in personnel policies and benefit plans, and feasibility of proposed systems of control.
2. To discuss and co-ordinate management plans, policies, aims, and objectives, so that all departments and key executives have a clear and uniform plan of action. Subjects to be discussed include such matters as establishment of production schedules, major developments in the various departments, contemplated changes in the line of products, activities of competitors, budget results, and methods of increasing net profits.
3. To consider the need for changes in policy, systems of control, and other matters of a general nature, making appropriate recommendations to general management as necessary.
4. To provide each of the members with an understanding of the operations and problems involved in the other departments, thus broadening viewpoints and the opportunity for co-operation.

The membership consists of the key executives who are heads of major operating and staff departments. All principal departments are represented, since the committee serves in a company-wide capacity. Because of its importance and scope, a full-time or part-time secretary is provided. Regular meetings are scheduled and the members reserve a definite time when all are available. In case there is insufficient business, meetings are canceled and the secretary notifies the members. One of the participating companies insists that every member be present at the first meeting each month, which is attended by the president and other top executives, and at which production schedules and plans for the month are outlined and discussed. Less stress is placed upon attendance at other meetings. Authority of the co-ordinating committee is usually limited to recommendations.

WAGE AND SALARY COMMITTEE

One of the most frequent causes for concern among the participating companies was found to be salary administration. In a majority of the companies each individual case is considered on its own merits, and control is achieved through personal approval by some executive in high position. It is not unusual to find that the president must finally approve every single increase in salary. In doing so he depends largely upon recommendations of others, for seldom does he know the person, the position, or the circumstances which might justify an increase. In ten of the companies, committees have been established to administer salaries. Most of these committees are composed of top divisional executives, and in two cases the president and ranking vice-presidents are the members.

Committee or no committee, this system places a burden of detail upon the top executives. Their authority cannot be safely delegated, however, until there are some limits to control its use. It is therefore necessary to establish salary group limits within which all the jobs in the company are appropriately classified and placed. When such a rational salary schedule is once set up and approved by the top executives, it is a simple matter to delegate authority for salary administration within the limits provided. Many companies have a similar schedule covering wages, although union contracts in many cases govern rates.

Once the limits have been established as a guide, a wage and salary committee becomes an excellent control agency through which to provide uniform and equitable wage and salary administration. The functions of such a committee consist of:

1. Review of the basic wage and salary scales and recommendation of changes therein.
2. Classification of new jobs, fitting them into the existing wage or salary structure.
3. Review of all requests for changes in individual classifications.
4. Review of wage and salary rates in each department to insure conformity with basic company schedules.
5. Approval of changes in individual salaries within specified limits (usually up to $5,000 or $6,000 a year).

Best practice observed among the participating companies leads to the conclusion that membership on the committee should be held to a minimum. The director of organization, because of his familiarity with jobs and their value, his company-wide viewpoint, and his impartial attitude, makes an excellent chairman. The director of personnel, because of his knowledge of the people, his access to rating reports, and his equal impartiality and company-wide viewpoint, makes a good second member. The third and last member should be the department or divisional executive whose requests are being considered.

A competent analytical agency is very necessary to review and analyze every request, develop all the facts, and present conclusions and recommendations on each case to the committee for its action. In a majority of the cases this consists of making certain that the proposal is within the proper limits. In special circumstances, however, it may be necessary to analyze the work done on the job, in order properly to appraise the proposal in light of the true facts. In two of the companies with organization departments, this analytical work is performed in that department. In other companies the personnel department has analysts for this purpose.

Authority of the committee regarding salary increases may be final up to the specified limit provided the three committee members agree. In case of disagreement, the case is referred to higher authority for decision. In one of the participating companies agreement of the chairman of the salary committee and the manager of the department concerned constitutes final action up to $5,000; recommendations are also made on salaries up to $15,000 a year. Any changes in the basic wage structure or salary schedule are recommended to general management, the committee having no final authority in matters of this importance.

Meetings are held upon call of the chairman, as business requires. Records are maintained of the net results of the increases granted.

APPROPRIATIONS COMMITTEE

Another field in which a committee is effective is in control over capital and other large expenditures. Some companies deal with each such expenditure as and when the need arises. Control is embodied in a series of approvals, and usually top management must finally authorize any project involving as little as $500 or $1,000. In order to shift this burden downward in the organization some other method of control must be substituted in order that authority may be safely delegated. Establishment of an appropriations committee is not in itself the answer, although such a committee becomes an excellent agency through which to control such expenditures after an appropriate plan and limits have been authorized.

In many of the companies visited an annual capital budget is used to limit the total amount to be expended by the company for capital betterments during the year. This budget also provides for allotment of the total sum among the various departments. An appropriation request must be submitted before proceeding on any individual project, regardless of the fact that it was included in the budget. A thorough analysis is made to be sure that each and every project is necessary and in order. The appropriations committee is charged with control over this field and its duties include:

1. Assembling the annual capital budget from departmental estimates, classifying the projects in order of urgency and merit, and presenting the material to higher authority for approval in principle.
2. Reviewing individual requests for appropriations received from departments, determining whether they are included in the annual budget, and passing upon their soundness. This involves a thorough analysis of each project with regard to such considerations as necessity, cheaper alternatives, justification for each part, cost, effect on operations, pay-out, and improvement in quality.
3. Approving those appropriation requests which are sound, are included in the budget, and are within the limit assigned to the committee (say $1,000 to $25,000).
4. Recommending to higher authority those projects above $25,000 which are found to be sound and those under $25,000 which are required but which were not included in the budget.

Membership, as with any committee, should include only those who definitely add to the group judgment. In this case it could appropriately include the chief engineer, because of his ability in judging the soundness of construction plans, costs, and alternatives; the comptroller, for his financial and economic viewpoint, particularly as to availability of funds and correct time for undertaking the project; the director of organization and cost control, for the benefit of his viewpoint on cost reduction, effects upon the organization and manpower considerations; and the divisional executive concerned, who attends to present his case and see that all factors are given consideration. Others may be requested to attend when necessary, such as the research manager to advise on new developments.

The most important feature of this particular procedure, however, is the analytical agency which reviews all the proposals and by whose analyses the committee must be very largely guided. A very capable individual—one of the stature of a departmental manager—is required to head the analytical work. Upon the projects presented the company will spend very large sums, and it is therefore essential to have in this position a person able to present consistently high-quality, accurate analyses. This person might also be the chairman of the committee, he and his staff constituting an independent, full-time agency concerned with appropriation analyses. In some companies a section of the engineering department makes the analyses. Others object to this on the ground that the engineering department also works out the designs, methods, and savings, and is therefore not in a position to criticize and reject its own work. For that reason they prefer an independent agency embodying adequate engineering talent.

PRODUCTS COMMITTEE

Five of the companies were found to have products committees. In practically every company it is necessary to co-ordinate the viewpoints of the sales, manufacturing, and research departments in regard to changes in the line of products. In addition, some system is needed to relieve top management of the necessity for passing upon every change, however minor, in the company's products. Finally, some capable agency is needed to take over responsibility for analyzing the needs and simplifying the line of products to the end that the company may be in the strongest position from a competitive and profit-making standpoint. A logical solution to these needs is a products committee, the functions of which are:

1. To stand responsible for review and analysis of the product line, and for initiation of action designed to eliminate unprofitable products or sizes, illogical items, and obsolete items.
2. To review and pass upon research and development programs

aimed at maintaining a line of products best suited to the market.

3. To review proposals to add, change, or drop products from the line, or to change brands, packages, or labels, taking into consideration effect on volume, displacement of other products, cost of manufacturing, new equipment necessary, market trends, profit possibilities, and competitive products.

4. To investigate and pass upon requests for test or development of products requiring work in excess of a fixed sum, e.g., $1,000.

Three members are required on this committee. They are the divisional executives in charge of research, manufacturing, and sales. It is usual for the research director to be chairman of the committee. As in the case of the appropriations committee, an excellent analytical agency is essential for successful results. This agency prepares the analyses in suitable form for consideration by the committee, devoting full time to analysis of the product line and problems concerned therewith. Approval by the three committee members assures that the interests of their respective departments have been satisfactorily provided for. Authority of the committee is final when the three members are in full agreement, except as limited by the procedure covering capital expenditures, and where major changes affecting company policy are involved.

PERSONNEL COMMITTEE

In many companies selection and appointment of personnel to key positions is left to the next two higher levels of authority; for example, the superintendent and the plant manager pass upon appointments to foremanships. This method of control may be reasonably effective if means are available for ascertaining the best-qualified candidates, the most outstanding of whom is appointed. It usually limits consideration to employees within the division where the vacancy exists, to the exclusion of perhaps better-qualified prospects in other divisions of the company. An even more serious possibility is that the decision may be influenced by prejudice, personal acquaintanceship or preference, promotion of the next in line regardless of caliber, and similar factors.

In seeking a better check and control to insure selection of the best-qualified person for each key spot, several of the companies have set up a disinterested agency to pass upon and certify as to the adequacy of candidates' qualifications before final selection and appointment. A personnel committee can serve as a very effective agency to this end, functioning as follows:

1. Receiving from the executive concerned his preliminary nominations of individuals he considers qualified for the vacancy.
2. Reviewing the qualifications and experience of these nominees to determine whether they meet the requirements of the job.
3. Suggesting consideration of other better-qualified candidates.
4. Furnishing the executive concerned with a list of candidates, all of whom it is willing to certify as qualified to fill the job, from which to make his final selection.
5. Serving as the agency for conducting the merit rating of the more important managerial and executive positions in the company.

The membership of the committee would logically include the director of personnel as chairman, because of his knowledge of the personnel, access to and analysis of rating reports, and company-wide viewpoint. The director of organization is a desirable second member because of his knowledge of job requirements and of the background and experience required to fill them properly. The divisional executive concerned with the appointment is an essential third member. The staff of the director of personnel serves as the analytical agency.

Authority of the committee is limited to passing upon qualifications of candidates. It makes no selections of personnel, but its action eliminates from further consideration those who are not well qualified. This affords a sound basis for delegating to divisional managers authority for making appointments up to a specified salary level. Above this level confirmation of general management is required. Details covering the control methods involved in rating and appointing personnel to key positions are discussed in a later section (see pages 117–26).

PENSION AND BENEFITS COMMITTEE

Nine of the participating companies have committees for administering their pension and benefits plans. The usual functions assigned to such a committee are the following:

1. To investigate and review all pension cases, all extensions of benefits, all severance allowances, and all other discretionary applications of personnel policies.
2. To take final action upon all cases falling within established policies.
3. To recommend to general management action to be taken on questionable cases, for which there is no precedent.

As chairman of the committee, the manager of the pension and benefits section of the personnel department is a good choice. His staff logically serves as the working agency for the committee, investigating cases, gathering facts, preparing analyses, and presenting recommendations. The director of personnel, because of his company-wide viewpoint and knowledge of company policy, makes a good second member. The divisional or departmental executive whose employee is concerned becomes the third member.

The working agency develops information and maintains lists of employees eligible for retirement or other benefits and presents the cases to the committee at the appropriate time. Divisional executives present their special cases. The committee's action is final on cases covered by established policies.

By this method top management is relieved of the detail of passing upon each case within this field, and considers only those cases for which there is no precedent. Even on the latter a thorough analysis and a well-considered recommendation accompany the proposal. Future cases of a similar nature are then handled by the committee in accordance with the precedent established by general management in the cases it decides.

OTHER REGULAR COMMITTEES

In addition to those of the type described above, a variety of other committees are in use in the thirty-one companies visited. For example, nine companies have committees whose primary assignment, in one way or another, has to do with analyzing future business conditions and translating these into terms of company expectancy. Stabilization of company operations is a major objective in several instances; others give particular attention to the field of procurement and inventory practice, being charged with appraising the outlook for raw material prices and recommending a program for forward buying.

Other groups of committees have to do with financial considerations and include insurance committees, dues and donations committees, and investment committees. Patent, public relations, real estate, advertising, printing, and forms are among numerous other interdepartmental committees found in use by one or more of the participating companies.

One other important group of committees embraces the functional or departmental committees, in contrast to those covering interdepartmental subjects. Such committees are particularly found in the fields of manufacturing, engineering, sales, and office administration. Within their respective departmental fields, the functions of these committees follow closely those of the company-wide co-ordinating committee. Membership is comprised of departmental executives and important staff assistants. Committee action is final in certain respects and advisory in other matters. Principles covering committee organization apply equally to these departmental committees, the only difference being that they exist within one single department and are concerned only with its problems.

SPECIAL COMMITTEES

Occasionally new situations arise upon which the judgment of a special group would be of value. Accordingly a special committee may be appointed to take care of that need. As in the case of the regular committees, the true function of such special committees is to pass judgment upon the matters presented to it in proper form for consideration. They are not the proper agency to work out details or gather facts. Such development work should be assigned to the most logical staff agency and presented to the committee only when there is a concrete proposal for its consideration. If no staff agency can properly undertake the special work, some individual and the necessary assistants may be divorced from other regular duties to spend full time on the problem, and thus constitute a temporary staff unit.

As soon as any special committees have served their purpose, they should be promptly dissolved by the same agency which created them.

PART C

CONTROL PRACTICES

THE BASIC PROCESS OF CONTROL

CONTROL OVER POLICIES

CONTROL OVER RATE OF OPERATION

CONTROL OVER ORGANIZATION

CONTROL OVER QUALITY OF KEY PERSONNEL

CONTROL OVER WAGES

CONTROL OVER SALARIES

CONTROL OVER COSTS

CONTROL OVER METHODS AND MANPOWER

CONTROL OVER CAPITAL EXPENDITURES

CONTROL OVER SERVICE DEPARTMENT EFFORT

CONTROL OVER LINE OF PRODUCTS

CONTROL OVER RESEARCH AND DEVELOPMENT

CONTROL OVER EXTERNAL RELATIONS

CONTROL OVER FOREIGN OPERATIONS

CONTROL OVER DEMANDS UPON EXECUTIVE TIME

CONTROL OF OVER-ALL PERFORMANCE

THE BASIC PROCESS OF CONTROL

One of the most challenging problems of management is to give authority to those capable of exercising it and yet retain control in the hands of those ultimately responsible. If management is to function effectively, devoting its major attention to planning, directing, and co-ordinating activities, it must be freed at every level of the unnecessary burden of detail.

This burden is generally associated with approvals; it is lightened to the degree that authority for final approval is delegated to others. Usually it is not from choice that executives become buried in detail; they are more often the victims of an inadequate system of control. They cannot safely delegate the authority reposed in them because there is no adequate means of control which permits this to be done.

The obvious remedy for this situation is the installation of procedures and limits designed to control the use of delegated authority. A logical place to start is with any feature which is particularly bothersome and takes considerable time. It may be approving salary increases, authorizing capital expenditures, or any one of the recurring items which require executive attention. Many such problems are company-wide in scope, and a good control procedure would lighten the burden on not only one, but many executives.

Control is a basic process and whatever the type or whatever the subject it embraces the following elements:

1. **Objective**—what is desired

2. **Procedure**
   a) Plan—how and when it is to be done
   b) Organization—who is responsible
   c) Standards—what constitutes good performance

3. **Appraisal**—how well it was done

Conceiving the control required is the first requisite to its attainment. This involves the determination of the objective, i.e., the final results wanted, and then the careful development of a procedure which will bring about those results.

Such a procedure may require changes in the plan of organization, additions of staff groups or committees to serve as control agencies, and numerous other adjustments. This development work is not a one-man affair. The best talent and thinking on the subject available in the organization should be enlisted to help design the procedure. A careful firsthand inspection and analysis by competent people is usually an essential preliminary step to determining what the procedure should be. After the planning is done and the design is complete, each of the parts must be assigned to individuals for accomplishment. Concurrent with development of procedure is the establishment of standards of performance, which indicate for each separate part of the procedure what constitutes good performance and how it is to be measured. The procedure and the results expected must be made known to all those who are affected. Authority is then safely delegated downward in the organization, in accordance with the limits specified and subject to the control procedure.

The final aspect of control is checking to make certain that the procedure is working as intended and bringing about the results desired. The necessity for current approval is limited to those exceptional cases which are not covered by the procedure. Executive attention needs to be devoted only to those matters where performance fails to meet expectancy. Supervision becomes more effective through following results and instituting action toward correction and betterment where needed. As the control procedure becomes well established, those who are responsible may check their own performance and report causes for unsatisfactory conditions, together with the steps planned or already taken to correct them.

One by one this treatment can be extended to the recurring items requiring executive authorization. The sections which follow immediately are devoted to methods in use for controlling individually a number of the more important and difficult problems facing top management. Each time a well-planned control procedure is substituted for personal approvals, additional time is made available to the top executives for the far more important over-all planning and control of the enterprise, which is aimed at securing maximum effectiveness of the company as a whole, rather than control of any individual problem.

Section 2

CONTROL OVER POLICIES

There is a good deal of loose talk about policies. The word is variously used to mean departmental procedure, usual custom, basic course of action, or management decision. As used in this chapter it means the guiding principles established by the company to govern actions, usually under repetitive conditions. For example, a decision by top management to reward an employee for some special act does not constitute a policy; but an announcement that each such case under similar circumstances is to receive such an award may be called a policy.

From the standpoint of management, policies constitute one of the primary instruments of co-ordination and control. They provide consistency of action, without which current operation is not effective and desired ultimate objectives are not likely to be reached.

The distinguishing features of policies seem to be that they constitute the basis for governing future actions; accordingly they must be made known to those who are responsible for handling such actions. Under this interpretation, policies become the laws of conduct for the business, and as such they are a device for permitting authority to be delegated within the organization. Their primary purpose is to sanction in advance the action to be taken in repetitive situations. This makes it unnecessary to refer each case as it occurs to higher authority for decision; it can be handled at the point of occurrence without delay.

Under these circumstances it is important that policies be carefully and adequately expressed so that those in the organization will understand under what conditions and to what extent the rules are to apply. Further, since the policies are to cover actions in the future, and since man's memory is not infallible, it seems most important that the policies should not only be clearly expressed, but that they be in writing in order that:

1. All members of the organization will have the same interpretation of them.

2. They can be reviewed from time to time and changed to meet current conditions.
3. They can be checked for compliance and proper understanding within the organization.
4. They will not become obscure through the passage of time.

DETERMINATION

Policies are of varying degrees of significance in the conduct of any enterprise. They may be classed as basic, general, and departmental. As such their determination rests at different levels in the management organization.

Basic policies are those which establish the long-range objectives and chart the destinies of the company. An existing, impending, or future set of conditions may require the establishment of a company position. The need of such a company position results from firsthand contact with a new situation and may arise in some division or department of the company. Initiation of the basic, long-range policies may, therefore, emerge at almost any management zone in the organization. The formulation of basic policies usually reposes with the chief executive, or with a group of executives charged with general management of the enterprise. Most companies have an executive council comprised of its key men. It is this group which translates the needs into terms of recommended company position. The final authorization or adoption of basic policies rests with the board of directors. In fact, this is one of the fundamental functions of that agency of top management. Examples of basic policies found during the course of the study are:

Compensation for all employees shall be at or above prevailing rates.
Additional manufacturing capacity shall be provided on a decentralized basis.
All distribution of products shall be through exclusive agents.
Each year's depreciation shall be reinvested in plant facilities.

General policies are ones which may be regarded as of short-range or everyday operating significance, but which affect some or all divisions of the company. Authorization of such policies usually lies in the general-management group, and may also be formulated there. As with basic policies, the initiation may arise at almost any managerial level. General policies are always in conformity with basic policies. Examples of such policies are:

Whenever the annual volume of a product falls below an economic manufacturing-lot size, the product shall be considered for elimination.

Until further notice the company will meet all competitive prices.

All supervisors shall be furnished a monthly statement of all costs for which they are responsible.

No department will hire new employees until its present force is working forty hours per week.

In practically every company, the head of a department adopts policies for the guidance and conduct of his own immediate field of operation. Such departmental policies must not conflict with either basic or general policies, or with the activities of other departments. Interpretation of policies into terms of departmental operation is the prerogative of each department head. With practically every company the establishing of supplementary departmental rules and regulations growing out of policy interpretation is regarded as a responsibility of department management. The following are typical departmental policies.

All reports required for the monthly closing shall be dispatched to the head accounting office by the fifth of the following month.

Any purchasing commitment covering requirements beyond ninety days' consumption shall be approved by the general purchasing agent.

Extension of credit in excess of $50.00 shall be granted on the basis of a satisfactory credit report.

All customer complaints shall be referred to the office of the general sales manager.

PROMULGATION

Once a policy has been established, the next step is to convey its meaning to those who are to be guided by it. Among the thirty-one companies studied only a few follow the practice of compiling or assembling statements of company policy into a policy manual. A few other companies issue policy declarations in bulletin, general instruction, or executive memorandum form. Some of these preserve a set of such releases in binders, which serve as a book of rules or "bible." In some companies written policy declarations are supplemented by statements of objectives and collateral information helpful by way of interpretation. Other companies notify executives concerned by means of a letter from the president. A few simply pass policy statements down the executive scale by word of mouth, a method conducive to misunderstanding and variable interpretation.

For most companies it is usual to find that department heads issue written policies and policy interpretations for guidance of personnel in their own departments. Similarly it is a rather general practice for personnel policies to be set forth in printed booklets which are given wide distribution both within and without the company. To a lesser degree it is found that purchasing policies are printed and made available to vendors as well as buyers.

Some companies maintain a manual of company policies. One of these states that "a policy is not a policy unless it is in writing." It answers the argument that some policies cannot be put in writing with the statement that "perhaps the reason behind the policy cannot be written, but the policy itself must be clearly stated for the guidance of all."

The preparation and maintenance of the company policy manual cannot be entrusted to some clerk. It demands the attention of a high-caliber person to do the job properly. But this effort is well repaid as top management is relieved of the burden of decision caused by poor understanding and lack of policy guidance within the organization.

COMPLIANCE

Control over policies, as of every other phase of business, is not complete until some check is instituted by which to measure performance in the light of expectancy. This in turn presumes that the expectancy has been made known to those who are to be checked. In order to preclude all possibility of misunderstanding and to make any such control effective, the expectancy must be reduced to writing. Once the policies have been clearly stated in writing, they can be checked to see that the organization complies with them.

None of the companies studied seems to have hit upon any inclusive scheme by which policy interpretation or compliance can be checked. Where monetary matters are involved, the auditing staff is the natural and commonly used agency. Some companies go further than this and look to their auditors to check against policy violation in many other directions, such as prices, credits, discounts, and purchases.

All policies are not as easily checked as, for example, whether or not purchases involving a certain sum are being made on a basis of bids. However, in the field of employee relations, examination by higher executives of grievance files would afford a check on compliance with certain personnel policies. A similar analysis of customer complaints would provide a check in another field. Perusal of rejected credit applications would serve to check the application of credit policies.

Section 3

CONTROL OVER RATE OF OPERATION

Determination of the future operating program and co-ordination of all departmental efforts in keeping therewith is one of the important problems of management. Basic policies often have a determining effect upon this activity. Some companies operate their factories at economic capacity and expect the sales department to dispose of the output. The exact opposite is found in other companies where production is required to accommodate itself to the primary interests of distribution. Stabilized employment with its essential of leveled plant operation is the controlling policy in other concerns. Again, rigid limits on investment in raw and finished inventories may have a determining effect.

Another factor having an important bearing upon the rate of operation is the nature of the product line—whether perishable, subject to style obsolesence, standard or custom-built, durable or nondurable, simplified or diversified. Other important variables are the nature of the market, method of distribution, and degree to which production is decentralized.

In no company studied does the sole responsibility for projecting the rate of operation into the future reside in any single agency. Generally the final approval rests either with the president, the group of top executives representing general management, or the board of directors. The formulation of the plan and often the responsibility for its administration after it has been authorized, are delegated to staff agencies specializing in this field. Committees representative of the different staff and operating departments affected are frequently used to review and co-ordinate the various aspects of the plan before its presentation for final approval. Although intimately concerned with the problems and interests of production, sales, and other branches, such staff agencies and committees usually have an independent status from an organization standpoint. Thus, they are in a position to function in the best interests of the company as a whole rather than those of any single department. Staff and committee members are usually

84

recruited from the different departments served, which tends to assure a proper understanding of departmental problems.

As a rule the projected operating rate is largely founded upon estimates of expected sales volume tempered by general economic forecasts. Many of the co-operating companies have able economists and well-qualified statistical agencies which play an important role in developing and correlating this information. In a number of cases the value and accuracy of their studies and forecasts were found to be most impressive.

Long-range expectations are generally translated into an operating program for a period of one year ahead, although one company gives some definition to a five-year plan. On the whole, the twelve-month programs have a high degree of definiteness and detail. All are subject to modification on a monthly or quarterly basis in the light of changing conditions.

In general, the successful experience which many of the companies have had and the value they derive from long-range planning suggest the desirability of a wider adoption of the practice by those companies not now following this plan.

TYPICAL PLANS

The extent to which control has been brought to bear upon this important aspect of management is best indicated by a few of the plans in use, which are presented in skeletonized form. One company, whose product lines are numerous and whose markets are varied, has adopted the following procedure:

The determination of its future operating rate is the product of three factors: a policy of reasonably stabilized production and employment, a five-year forecast of general conditions, and a comprehensive system of budgetary control. From the standpoint of establishing the level of operations, the company's five-year outlook serves to locate the guideposts for only the most general direction which advanced planning should follow. Detailed considerations are confined to the ensuing year. Four months before a new fiscal year, the company's economist prepares a master forecast of sales and inventory program. A committee, composed of the economist, together with the heads of the finance, accounting, and production-planning departments, reviews the master forecast in the light of anticipated business conditions, calling in various department heads for counsel and advice. Production, sales, prices, inventory, and other component elements of the forecast are examined. Out of this joint deliberation, recommendations covering the broad outlines of the coming year's operating program are submitted to the top-executive group. Upon approval by general management, the program is then passed to the production-planning department which schedules production by individual items for each month to all plants. Comprehensive monthly reports of actual versus planned performance are made by product and by divisions as a final phase of control.

Another company, whose products are standardized, and fall into the durable-goods classification, and are produced for stock, programs its rate of operations as follows:

Projected schedules are tentative for one year ahead, fairly definite for a month ahead, and definite for the ensuing week.

The foundation for preplanning is the analysis made by its statistical department, which follows closely all available information on economic conditions having a direct bearing on the company's operations. At a specified time each year this department receives estimates from all regional sales offices for the next year's sales expectancies. These estimates are tempered by the statistical department's appraisal of general economic conditions, together with statistics of the entire industry, inventory and price trends of the company's basic raw materials, market conditions, and similar factors.

Based on this analysis, a forecast is made of sales, production, and stock requirements by months for a year ahead. The department then submits to the president a master operating schedule showing units of each major class of products to be produced by each plant for the next month. With the president's approval, this schedule is turned over to another department whose function is to see that plants produce and the sales territories are supplied with the products necessary to meet sales requirements. Incidentally, this latter control department reports directly to the president, thus giving the department a status independent of both sales and production. Based on a constant analysis of current inventories and sales trends by sizes, types, and geographical areas, this department breaks down the approved monthly schedule into production items and places specific orders on the plants. Coincident with the definite weekly orders, the department also gives each plant a tentative forecast for a month ahead.

A third company projects its operating program one year ahead but places firm orders on its plants only four months in advance. The production problems of this company are complicated by an extensive line of products made up of many thousands of component parts. Its procedure is as follows:

Advanced planning is the function of a staff department reporting to the sales vice-president. From a division of the comptroller's office this department receives economic forecasts in terms pertinent to company operations. This information, coupled with estimates submitted by branches over the country, provides the basis for establishing a twelve-month sales estimate broken down into product lines. The head of the department submits and explains this estimate to a committee consisting of the vice-presidents of manufacturing, purchasing, and sales, the treasurer, and the comptroller. This agency determines the final sales estimate.

From the gross figures are deducted plant and warehouse stocks in order to derive the projected manufacturing schedule. This schedule provides the manufacturing department with an over-all picture for the ensuing year but is not an authorization to produce. Firm production orders are issued four months in advance and allocated to specific plants with stipulations covering product items and delivery dates. The follow-up of production, both as to time and items, is a function of the same staff department.

A somewhat different procedure is followed by another company whose products are manifold, about half being made to special order, and all of the durable-goods classification:

The organization plan of this company is of the product-division type. Much latitude is permitted division managers with respect to advance planning of operations which are programmed definitely by months for three months ahead. Ultimate check is provided through budgetary and profit-and-loss control.

Because of the high degree of decentralization in programming future operations, it is necessary to provide divisional managers with more significant economic forecasts and better forecasting methods than they could develop individually. A central economic staff directly responsible to the president has accordingly perfected a technique for measuring the probable business trend in terms of the company's own line of products. Despite the statistical technology involved, the system has been simplified, set up in book form, and made available to division managers for their guidance in forecasting. The economic staff prepares its own over-all company estimates, using the same forecasting method. From divisional and departmental heads advance estimates are gathered quarterly covering three periods of six months each—a total of eighteen months. The composite forecast is then sent to all managers to give a uniform basis for guiding and adjusting their own thinking.

INVENTORY ASPECTS

For the purposes of this discussion inventories will be separated into two classes: (1) raw materials and purchased items, and (2) finished goods and fabricated parts. Control of the first group is tied in with procurement policies, while control of the second group is an integral part of advance-planning operations.

A large group of the participating companies have simplified the control of raw material and other purchased inventories by a policy of buying as needed. Another group of the companies engages in forward or market buying of basic raw materials. Inventory control in these instances is a function of general management. Maximum and minimum limits are frequently established, within which the purchasing staff has freedom of action. More often, however, the control is centered in a committee of major executives, which acts upon such economic and technical information as may be provided by staff departments. In an occasional instance extraordinary advanced commitments are submitted to the board of directors for approval.

Finished-goods inventories are planned and controlled in most of the companies as a specific phase of determining future rate of operation. This is a particularly important feature of advance planning with those companies whose products are reasonably standardized and whose sales are seasonal. The kind and amount of finished inventory are scheduled quite as definitely as the rate of production. Hence, whatever procedure is instituted to establish and control rate of operations will include finished-goods inventories as well. One company uses the simple expedient of limited storage space as a control of inventories for both raw materials and finished products. While this plan seems to work satisfactorily in this instance, there is little to commend it from a scientific standpoint.

STABILIZATION ASPECTS

A conscious effort is being made by many of the participating companies to stabilize production and employment over periods of both seasonal and cyclical fluctuations. Maintenance of a qualified and contented personnel, better operating performance, lower costs, and recognition of social responsibility are the main objectives. A reduction in the payments under the unemployment-insurance tax is usually a distinctly secondary reason.

Production to stock is the customary method of cushioning the seasonal ups and downs of sales. Shut-down vacation plans, varying working hours, a sliding scale of discounts on advance orders, and paying salesmen a bonus for off-season sales are a few of the other expedients used.

Softening the effects of cyclical fluctuations is a much more challenging problem. Production for stock is effective on a short-range basis, but impracticable for the long sweeps of the business cycle. However, among the participating companies, many of which are in industries subject to the most violent of swings, positive steps have been taken to stabilize operations, with particular emphasis on job security. Pre-eminent among such efforts is the policy of guaranteed employment. Fortunate indeed is the company whose line of products, method of distribution, financial situation, and methods of control permit such a policy.

Long-range forecasting receives most frequent mention as an aid toward stabilization. Several companies assay the value of forecasting in the following terms:

It enables projected operations to be translated into terms of needed manpower.

It avoids building up an abnormal plant and working force which cannot be sustained.

It prevents expansion to accommodate boom peaks; an adherence to a normal program of expansion is followed even at the loss of some business. It guides the management in its policy of keeping production facilities just short of sales requirements and of buying to cover excess requirements.

Other stabilization practices used to greater or lesser extent among the participating companies include the following:

Establishing a stabilization fund during good times to be used for semi-relief purposes during dull times, e.g., giving four days' pay for three days' work.

Withholding introduction of new products so as to build up sales when business conditions sag.

Deferring or spreading certain major capital and maintenance projects which can be used for fill-in work during slack times.

Varying the proportion of construction and maintenance work handled by outside contract, to offset variations in the labor demand.

Setting aside funds during active periods to cover the cost of constructing projected, but not immediately needed, facilities during dull periods.

Recording worker versatility to permit job switching and interdepartmental transfers.

Guaranteeing employment on a variable basis in accordance with the length of service.

CONTROL OVER ORGANIZATION

A sound and clean-cut plan of organization is essential to facilitate the effective management of any enterprise. Only when they understand thoroughly their respective parts in the whole picture of management are individual executives and agencies able to devote their full energies to the effective discharge of their proper functions, avoiding the overlap and duplication of effort and the confusion, friction, and working at cross purposes which invariably result from lack of a clean-cut plan.

In only a few of the companies visited did it appear that organization design and clarification had received the attention it is believed to warrant. As a result, in many cases, obviously capable executives were observed to be more or less overburdened with detail and, therefore, handicapped in discharging their responsibilities.

Maintenance of a logical and effective plan of organization is not a matter of chance, of "letting nature take its course." It requires continuous study, development, adjustment to changing conditions, and review of actual practice to see that the plan is properly understood and working effectively. Control over this important activity is usually effected through:

Organization Planning	Initiation and Approval of
Organization Charts	Organization Changes
Job Specifications	Periodic Review of Organi-
Control Specifications	zation Practice
Organization Manual	Organization Training
	Staff Agency Required

ORGANIZATION PLANNING

In most companies, major consideration is devoted to planning and designing the line of products which will best fit the market. Relatively little attention, however, seems to have been devoted to planning and designing the organization structure to facilitate

91

the management and control of the business. In this field, as in any other, a sound plan is the better part of achievement.

While some companies recognize the need for a general over-hauling and clarification of their organization plans, very little is done about it, first, probably because they lack a well-qualified staff agency to do the work, and, second, because any needed major changes might impinge upon some of the major executives or their ideas. In this connection, several of the participating companies have in mind the development of an ultimate or "ideal" plan of organization—not as it is, but as it should be—to serve as a guide to the gradual strengthening and clarification of the structure, *as it becomes opportune to make changes*, through re-tirements and other eventualities. Thus, when changes *are* made, they will be made in the right direction and in the course of time a clean-cut, rational plan of organization can be achieved without any major disruption of personnel.

Comprehensive organization planning entails the following procedure:

1. Keeping familiar with the best thought and practice along in-dustrial organization lines throughout the country—through review of the literature on the subject, and exchange of ideas with other leading concerns.

2. Questioning and testing the soundness and adequacy of every phase of the organization plan from a wholly objective view-point, without being influenced by present pattern or personnel, precedent or tradition. This involves the careful analysis of present organization charts, functions, responsibilities, and relationships.

3. Blocking out, in chart form, an "ideal" or ultimate plan which will most effectively meet the basic requirements of the busi-ness. This entails clarification of the various zones or levels of management and the agencies which are to handle them, making sure that the primary divisions of the company (whether functional, product, regional, or staff departments) are logical, distinct, and designed to facilitate effective man-agement.

4. "Designing" and writing the specifications for each level of management and each key job, or group of similar jobs; de-fining and clarifying functions, responsibilities, objectives,

limits of authority, and relationships with other parts of the organization. (See "Job Specifications," page 94.)

5. Comparing the ideal or ultimate plan thus designed with the *present* plan, and noting and classifying the changes needed to achieve the ideal pattern, as to (*a*) those which can appropriately be undertaken at once, and (*b*) those which should await a more opportune occasion, such as the retirement of incumbent personnel.

It is believed that this process of analysis and clarification applied to any organization plan cannot fail to develop many opportunities for further strengthening and improving the existing structure, thus increasing the effectiveness of management.

ORGANIZATION CHARTS

Comparatively few of the companies surveyed have comprehensive company organization charts, graphically portraying their plans of organization. Even some of the largest companies, with world-wide operations and many subsidiaries, have no organization charts to facilitate proper understanding and study of their organization arrangements. This condition is apparently due to lack of appreciation of the need and value of such charts, reluctance to indicate relative ranking of executive positions which might give rise to dissention, or lack of staff assistants experienced in making simple, effective charts.

The companies which do have comprehensive organization charts appear to have the soundest organization plans. Furthermore, in the course of preparing charts for the companies that did not have them, many obvious organization weaknesses were brought to light which would not be readily apparent except through the charting process. It is therefore felt that a good organization chart for the company as a whole, with a break-down chart for each major division, is an essential first step in the analysis, clarification, and understanding of any organization plan. Sample charts showing typical company organization plans are shown following page 73.

In some companies organization charts are held very closely, only a few top executives being permitted to see them. In other companies all staff and supervisory employees are given copies of the general organization charts and a comprehensive explanation of the whole plan of organization. These latter concerns consider that a proper understanding of the general organization structure and the relationship of their own particular units to the whole is an essential part of the training of these employees. Certainly a clear understanding of the general organization plan on the part of key personnel is eminently desirable, and this would be difficult to accomplish without the rather general use of suitable charts.

Incidentally, the process of charting an organization plan is one good test of its soundness, because any organization relationship that cannot be readily charted is very apt to be illogical and confusing to those working under it.

JOB SPECIFICATIONS

After the organization structure is planned, the next logical step is to clarify and define the essential specifications and requirements of each level of management, each department, each committee, and each key job or group of similar jobs. This establishes the conditions which, if fulfilled, will result in the contribution by each job or agency of its proper maximum to the success of the enterprise.

Such clarification of job specifications and requirements serves the following important purposes:

1. It gives each job holder a clear conception of his proper part and relationship in the organization as a whole. This definition of just what is expected of him makes it possible for him to concentrate his full energies and attention toward accomplishment of these specific objectives.

2. It affords an invaluable basis for "breaking in" new appointees and training them to meet the requirements of the job.

3. It provides a sound and logical basis for the periodic appraisal and rating of individual performance and capabilities, in terms of the requirements of the job.

4. It serves as an ideal basis for job evaluation so essential in an effective plan of salary control.

In defining each job and writing its specifications to fulfill these purposes, it is desirable to cover the following ground:

Basic functions.

Scope, indicating the general extent of jurisdiction.

General objectives or responsibilities in terms of conditions which will be met when the job is well done. These general objectives are sometimes supplemented by specific annual objectives arrived at in consultation between the job holder and his superior.

Means of control—how realization of these objectives is to be measured.

Relationships with other units of the organization.

Limits of authority.

A typical specification developed along this line to cover a district sales manager's position is shown in Figure 6. To those who have no such system of job clarification, such an analysis might appear rather formidable. It must be remembered, though, that time spent in crystallizing the plan of operation for each key job will be amply repaid through facilitating, and making easier and more effective, the handling of the many matters and problems with which that job is concerned.

The first step in developing such job specifications is, normally, to determine the present practice as to functions, objectives, relationships, and limits of authority for each agency, key job, or group of similar jobs. From this information the rationalized plan or specifications can be worked out to permit the job to function most advantageously in its relation to the whole organization. It normally falls to a staff agency, specializing on organization problems and working in close collaboration with the executives concerned, to develop the required information and evolve the job specifications.

CONTROL SPECIFICATIONS

In the process of developing job specifications the need becomes apparent for designing and clarifying the general plan of control over activities with which each such position is concerned, such as expenditures, appointments, and salaries. This need may be advantageously met through development of "control specifications," prescribing the general plan for controlling each such activity on a company-wide basis. Such specifications should indicate the respective functions, responsibilities, and relationships of the different agencies having a part in the control of a given activity. They should establish, by levels of management, the source and limits of authority and the method to be followed in appraising results.

With such control specifications or "enabling acts" approved for activities requiring company-wide control, it becomes an easy matter to pick out the provisions relating to any one key job and

DISTRICT SALES MANAGER
(Western District)

BASIC FUNCTION

Responsible to the general sales manager for distributing and marketing all company products in the Western District (California, Oregon, Washington, Idaho, Nevada, and Arizona).

SCOPE (figures indicate approximate magnitude)

Business

Potential business ......$10,000,000/yr.	Potential accounts 12,500
Business enjoyed .... 3,000,000/yr.	Accounts served 3,600

Operating Expenditures: $ 560,000/yr.

Organization: Total personnel, 150

District sales manager 1
Key assistants 2
Branch managers 15
Salesmen 77
Warehousemen 30
Clerks 25

Facilities:

District office 1
Branch offices 15
Branch warehouses 15
Motor vehicles 126

GENERAL OBJECTIVES AND RESPONSIBILITIES

Control through

1. To *sell* the largest possible volume which can be profitably marketed at the prices prescribed by the home office. Quotas, based on analysis of available business and accounts, to be developed and agreed upon with the general sales manager and incorporated in the annual budget.

    Comparison of sales performance against budget.

2. To maintain a high standard of *service*, with the customers thoroughly satisfied, the company well and favorably known, and no complaints.

    Analysis of sales performance and complaints.

3. To maintain all *costs* and manpower at a minimum as represented by standard costs and reflected in the annual budget.

    Comparison of actual against standard costs and budget.

4. To develop and maintain a fully effective *organization* with fully qualified personnel, thoroughly trained in the requirements of their respective jobs (as specified in the organization manual), and enthusiastically co-operating in their fulfillment.

    Analysis of sales performance, rating results, number and caliber of men developed for promotion, turnover, morale, and organization practice.

5. To be active in the promotion of *improvements* in products, methods, and facilities—abreast of the best-known practice.

    Number and caliber of improvements suggested or developed.

RELATIONSHIPS WITH OTHER UNITS OF ORGANIZATION

1. Directly responsible to general sales manager for performance of the above.
2. As member of general sales manager's council, responsible for participation in the discussion, co-ordination, and solution of problems common to all districts.
3. Functionally responsible to sales comptroller for supervision of local clerical activities and for conformance with prescribed accounting practices.
4. Functionally responsible to sales organization and cost-control manager for co-operating in the clarification and co-ordination of organization plans, and for the development and compliance with suitable manpower and cost standards.
5. Functionally responsible to sales personnel manager for co-operating in the general personnel development program.
6. Functionally responsible to general credit manager for conformance with established credit and collection policies.
7. Functionally responsible to sales operating manager for safe and efficient operation and upkeep of warehouses, motor vehicles, and other facilities.

FIGURE 6.—Typical

LIMITS OF AUTHORITY

1. On expenditures

All expenditures to be covered by annual or supplementary budget allowances approved by general management. Within this general authorization, further restrictions are imposed as follows:

New facilities: May approve up to $25; above this, submit to general sales manager (Attn. sales operating manager).

Maintenance: May approve up to $100; above this, submit to general sales manager (Attn. sales operating manager).

General sales expense: Limited only by approved budget, except specific items as follows:

Policy adjustments (returns and allowances): May approve items up to $100; above this limit, submit to general sales manager.

Disposition of obsolete and excess stock: May approve disposition entailing losses up to $100 per lot; above this limit submit to general sales manager.

Donations and subscriptions: May approve up to $10; above this submit to general sales manager.

Purchase contracts, leases, etc.: No authority.

2. On personnel

Additions to force: To be anticipated in and limited by budget. Before hiring, clearance to be obtained through sales personnel manager (*a*) that there are no suitable surplus personnel available in the company, (*b*) that there are no suitable employees elsewhere who should be considered for promotion to this job, and (*c*) that prospects for Class F jobs (salesmen, etc.) or higher are properly qualified.

Promotions and appointments: Full authority to fill jobs below Class F. Class E and F appointments must be approved by the sales personnel committee which will satisfy itself as to adequacy of the nominee's qualifications and give proper consideration to any markedly better-qualified candidates from elsewhere in the department. Appointments above Class E must be submitted through the general sales manager for approval.

Dismissals for cause: No limitations.

Layoff and demotion on account of lack of work: Full authority to lay off personnel below Class F, with under 10 years' service and merit rating below "average." Above this limit, clearance must be obtained from the sales personnel committee to the end that the least-deserving employees in the organization may be released.

3. On compensation

Wages: Full authority to apply established daily or hourly wage rates for prescribed work. All changes in wage scales must be submitted through general sales manager for approval.

Salaries: Full authority to change salaries for positions below Class F within prescribed policies and bracket limits. All salary changes affecting positions in Class F or higher, and all changes in job classification to be submitted through the general sales manager for approval.

4. On sales prices and contracts

No authority to determine prices—responsible for maintaining prices established by home office. Has full authority to execute sales contracts in accordance with approved form, terms, and prices.

5. On operating methods and policies

All changes in branch or district boundaries, plan of organization, or general channels and methods of distribution must be submitted to the general sales manager.

The district manager is expected, however, to initiate recommendations looking to change of plans or policies wherever, in his considered opinion, this would be to the company's interest.

Note: Classes D, E, F, etc., refer to particular brackets of the company's salary scale. Class D, for example, includes positions with salary evaluation between $250 and $300 per month; Class F, $200 to $225 per month.

Approved (date)

General Sales Manager
Director of Organization

Job Specification

write them into the job specification for that position. For this reason, the control specifications should be developed as soon as familiarity with the general plan and requirements of organization permit. A typical control specification prescribing the plan of control over capital expenditures is shown on page 173.

The staff agency primarily concerned should ordinarily take responsibility for designing the general plan of control over any such activity. Thus, the director of personnel would ordinarily formulate the plans of control over the various important phases of personnel administration. Organization aspects—including the designation of appropriate control agencies, allocation of functions, and delegation of authority—should logically be passed upon by the agency responsible for the organization program as to soundness and consistency with the general company plan of organization. Finally, any company-wide plan of control should normally have the approval of general management, or even of the board of directors, if of sufficient interest or importance.

ORGANIZATION MANUAL

To systematize and facilitate control and administration over the organization aspects of management, and to insure that all concerned have a clear conception of their proper parts in the over-all picture, several of the companies have developed a comprehensive organization manual. A complete manual, of which only pertinent portions need be issued to any one executive, logically includes the following:

1. The ideal or ultimate plan of company organization—including organization structure and specifications for major jobs and levels of management, and projecting desirable changes to be made as opportunity permits. This material would normally have very limited distribution.

2. A comprehensive set of organization charts for the company as a whole, with a break-down chart for each major division—representing the current, approved organization plan.

3. Approved job specifications prescribing the functions, responsibilities, objectives, limits of authority, and relationships of each organization unit, including

Board of Directors	Committees
General Management	Field Executives
Divisional Management	Key Jobs

4. Approved **control specifications** prescribing the general plan of control over important problems common to all departments, such as

Plan of Organization	Wages and Salaries
Capital Expenditures	Promotion and Transfer
Operating Expenditures	Hiring and Dismissal
Manpower and Payroll	Line of Products

Preparation and maintenance of the organization manual is a natural function of a staff organization department working in close collaboration with the executives concerned. It is probably unnecessary to emphasize the importance of clear thinking and expression and the avoidance of all unnecessary detail in the preparation of such a manual. It is generally conceded that the plan of organization, establishing as it does the pattern of management, warrants the attention of men of the highest caliber. In some companies even the president or chairman devotes an appreciable share of his time to this important work. In short, it is a job for management, not a clerical assignment.

The same process of organization and function clarification applies with equal propriety all down the line to the bottommost job. In most cases this can appropriately be handled as a matter of divisional or departmental development, following the general pattern established for the management organization.

From the foregoing, it is self-evident that a well-designed organization manual is a very effective aid in (*a*) achieving and maintaining a sound plan of organization, (*b*) insuring that all concerned have a proper understanding of the general plan and their proper parts and relationships thereto, (*c*) facilitating the study of organization problems, (*d*) systematizing the initiation, approval, and issue of necessary organization changes, and (*e*) serving as an effective guide in connection with the training, rating, and compensation of key personnel.

Two of the participating companies have done a splendid job of organization clarification through what they term the "consultative plan of management." Under this plan executives meet frequently with their subordinates and staff assistants to consider and discuss the problems of management, such as organization structure; proper allocation of functions, responsibilities and authority; long-term objectives; measures of accomplishment; and procedure. Out of these discussions evolve the best possible plans for the solution of these management problems. The plans thus derived constitute the organization manual. This process of "self-determination" has been found to be very stimulating and effective in clarifying viewpoint and understanding, and in contributing to the training and development of the key personnel who participate. It is believed, however, that such a program is a logical supplement to, rather than a substitute for, an able staff agency concentrating on organization matters. Such an agency, responsible for developing the general pattern of organization and for guiding, co-ordinating, and assisting the efforts of divisional executives within this field, should contribute materially to the speed and effectiveness of the program for clarifying organization.

INITIATION AND APPROVAL OF ORGANIZATION CHANGES

The initiation and formulation of changes in the plan of organization may arise from within the department or division concerned or may result from organization planning, surveys, and similar directed studies. In any event, it is desirable that all important proposed changes be carefully reviewed as to basic soundness, harmonious relationship with the existing company plan, and conformance with the ultimate plan of organization. This analytical function is normally assigned to the organization department in companies that have such an agency.

Practice in regard to approval and authorization of organization changes may be summarized as follows:

1. The general plan of organization for the board of directors is usually prescribed in the by-laws. Within the latitude thus provided, the board normally establishes its internal organization and prescribes which functions, responsibilities, and limits of authority it wishes to reserve to itself and which to delegate to general management. As a rule, it also approves the general plan of organization for handling the general-management function and passes upon major changes in the plan of divisional organization, such as the creation of a new major division, or a change from a functional to a product-division basis.

2. Subject to the board's interest or approval, general management normally works out the plan for handling its functions, as delegated by the board. General management also prescribes the basic plan of divisional organization and the functions, responsi-

bilities, and limits of authority of divisional executives. In some companies, it also concerns itself with major changes within a division, such as increasing the number of major sales districts.

3. Within the broad pattern of company organization and specific limitations imposed by general management, divisional executives are normally free to make any adjustments considered necessary in their organization plans. As a rule they personally approve any important changes within their respective divisions. Proposed changes which affect the interests of other divisions or the general company plan are referred to general management for approval.

In this connection, one or two of the participating companies have not only a central organization department, but also have affiliated divisional staff agencies available to advise and assist divisional executives with their organization and control problems. This arrangement, injecting a common approach and viewpoint into the consideration of organization matters, tends to insure that changes approved within a division are consistent with the present and projected plans for the company as a whole.

In companies having organization manuals, changes in organization are ordinarily submitted for consideration and approval in the form of revised sheets for the manual. In one company, all changes in organization, position, title, or salary are referred by the divisional executive concerned, through a staff agency specializing in the analysis of organization and salary problems, to the salary committee (consisting of the president and two general vice-presidents) for approval. The staff agency then handles the drafting and distribution of all announcements, notifications, and necessary changes in the organization manual, thus assuring proper uniformity and effectiveness.

PERIODIC REVIEW OF ORGANIZATION PRACTICE

Even with a sound basic plan of organization, there is definite need for a periodic review to see that practice and understanding are in accordance with the plan as intended and to note the need for adjustments in the plan to meet the changing requirements of the business. At best, it is a difficult problem to make certain that all executives throughout the organization have the proper understanding and viewpoint in regard to the general plan of organization and management, and their logical parts in it. Thus even with the best of intentions, there is apt to be a divergence of practice which militates against the effective and harmonious working of the plan as a whole.

Perhaps the most effective way to determine how well the plan of organization is functioning is to review the demands upon executive time and attention in each key office, taking into account personal contacts, telephone calls, reports, and correspondence, and considering the adequacy of presentation and action taken in each case. Such analyses should disclose any weaknesses of organization plan or practice and suggest means of protecting and relieving the executives concerned of all matters which do not justify their attention. This process is described more at length on page 199.

Another approach in checking organization effectiveness is through analysis of actual control procedure covering such matters as operating expenditures, capital expenditures, manpower, appointments, and salaries. Finally, an excellent check on organization practice can be made in conjunction with the comprehensive analysis of all operations and activities undertaken as a basis for determining cost and manpower standards.

Such methods should effectively bring to light for correction and improvement needs and weaknesses in organization plan and practice. They should thus serve as a basis for making sure, first, that the plan as set up in the organization manual is adequate and fitted to current requirements, and, second, that through proper understanding and use, full advantage is being taken of the plan to facilitate the management of the business.

ORGANIZATION TRAINING

Top management, advised and assisted by organization specialists, and consulting with the executives concerned, may devise, prescribe, and maintain a sound plan of organization along the lines outlined in the foregoing paragraphs. However, full organization effectiveness requires the intimate understanding, close cooperation, and intelligent application which can come only through systematic training of the entire executive and supervisory personnel in organization principles and practice.

One or two companies have made notable progress in this direction by enlisting the active interest and participation of executive, supervisory, and supporting personnel in the consideration and formulation of organization and control plans. This is done through periodic conferences which are a part of the training and development program conducted by these companies.

STAFF AGENCY REQUIRED

The foregoing discussion establishes the fact that control over organization is one of the most vital problems of management. Moreover, the problem is continuous and not intermittent. As with any other problem of management, its control must be a specific responsibility of some agency. In a large enterprise the problem assumes such proportions, if handled adequately, that it is a full-time assignment, not of an individual, but of a staff department comprised of qualified personnel under able direction. The very nature of the problem and its manifold aspects suggest that the responsible agency report to the president or the general-management group. Several of the companies studied have set up staff agencies of this kind.

For further details as to the logical plan of organization and functions of such an agency, see "Staff Organization," page 49.

CONTROL OVER QUALITY OF KEY PERSONNEL

Just as it is important to design the plan of organization to facilitate and meet the needs of management, so it is essential to develop personnel who can come as close as practicable to meeting the requirements of the positions which constitute that organization, and so to assure its full effectiveness.

It is recognized that the personal element necessarily plays a large part in selecting men for key positions, and the ideal specifications as to individual qualifications, background, and experience are more often only approached than completely met. However, experience clearly shows that a great deal can be done toward developing men who can adequately meet essential job requirements through having a clear idea of what those requirements are and then using this as a guide in the various phases of personnel administration. While most of the participating companies seem to recognize the importance of this problem, only a few of them appear to have programs that are fully co-ordinated and effective. Others rely largely upon the initiative and judgment of individual executives, often with far from impressive results.

The most effective plans observed in this study have many or all of the following features in common:

Careful selection of candidates for training

Comprehensive training to meet job requirements

Gradual, systematic development through selected positions of responsibility

Thorough, periodic rating of individual performance and capabilities in terms of job requirements

Effective control over appointment to responsible positions

Disposition of those proving inadequate in key positions

Definite assignment of responsibility for developing, guiding, and co-ordinating the entire program

Practices among the participating companies in regard to each of these important aspects of control over quality of key personnel are outlined in the following paragraphs.

SELECTION

The first step in developing an adequate supply of well-qualified talent for ultimate placement in responsible positions is that of selection. A few companies still rely largely upon rank-and-file personnel, hired at random, who have gradually, over the years, achieved some measure of distinction over their fellows, for successive advancement to all positions of responsibility. Nearly all the concerns studied emphasize the importance of developing and selecting rank-and-file employees, wherever possible, to fill the more desirable positions for which they can adequately qualify, thus providing needed incentive and outlet for the best men in this bracket. They do not, however, confine their selection to this group.

About half the companies make a practice of taking a substantial number of selected college graduates into the organization each year for training and ultimate development as salesmen, staff men, supervisors, and executives, according to their talents. Administration of this activity is generally centralized in the personnel department.

In ten of the companies, representatives visit leading universities and technical schools each spring to interview, interest, and finally sign up the selected graduates, either at the schools or later at company headquarters. This function is usually performed by the director and/or assistant director of personnel, although in many cases candidates are finally interviewed and passed upon by several interested executives before they are actually hired.

Two major companies discontinued the scouting of talent, preferring to make their selections from applicants who come to them for employment. This method has been adopted, first, because it tends to assure that the recruits really desire to work for a particular company and have not just been talked into it; second, because through previous extensive recruiting these companies had found themselves unable to provide suitable opportunities for such a large number of exceptional new men each year; and, third, as a result of the depression and their wide reputation as desirable companies for which to work, they are able to secure an adequate supply of high-grade men from the many who make application. Even these companies admitted, however, that during good times they might have to resume scouting in order to secure the number and caliber of men required.

The number of exceptional prospects secured in this way by individual companies runs from half a dozen to several hundred a year. In most cases the total number is based upon definite departmental estimates of the number required to maintain an adequate supply of "come-along" material in training, and the number of suitable training jobs available. In this connection, some companies which formerly inducted up to five hundred such recruits into their organization each year, have found themselves oversaturated with talent in relation to the promotional steps available. As a result, many of these high-grade trainees have become dissatisfied with their lack of progress. These companies have accordingly reduced the annual intake of such talent until they can absorb and provide adequate opportunity for the men they now have.

One company, whose entire plan of management is outstanding, has a particularly effective program for assuring that an adequate supply of high-caliber talent is inducted into the organization each year. This company believes in hiring the best prospects obtainable and makes every effort to weed out inadequate candidates during the process of selection before they are hired, rather than wasting time and money in putting them through its comprehensive training program and then finding them deficient. In one year, for instance, the personnel manager and his assistant visited forty of the leading colleges and technical schools throughout the country, interviewed approximately twenty-five hundred prospective graduates commended to their attention, and offered application blanks to about two hundred fifty of the best prospects. These applications (with photographs) were then reviewed with the company executives concerned, who selected the one hundred fifty most promising for personal interview. These one hundred fifty from all over the United States were invited to come to the home office at company expense, where they were personally interviewed and appraised by these same executives. The best one hundred forty (the cream of the twenty-five hundred) were finally hired. As a result of this procedure the company has secured a remarkably high percentage of able men whose engagement is usually permanent.

In another company the industrial relations department, headed by a vice-president, is expected to be on the lookout for exceptional talent, either recent graduates or more experienced men, and to take them onto its own payroll if need be, until they can be placed in other departments to advantage. For example, this department recently hired and placed at $600 per month an outstanding prospect for development into a works manager's position, keeping him on its own payroll until the division management concerned was thoroughly sold on his value.

In another company the vice-president in charge of operations, impressed with the need for developing able men for key positions in the organization, personally scouts and hires for training and development up to a dozen outstanding men each year from the leading schools and from other sources. He also takes an active personal interest in the actual training program for these men.

Another company makes extensive use of mentality and aptitude tests which it has found to be quite dependable as an aid to judgment in appraising candidates. It has decentralized responsibility for recruiting and hiring prospects, relying upon home office review of application forms, photographs, and the results of these tests for necessary co-ordination and control.

While most of the companies make a practice of training and developing their own men for key positions, a few occasionally resort to hiring outsiders, who have already made their mark, to fill particular jobs for which adequate talent is lacking within the organization. As an example, several companies have hired experienced public accountants and industrial engineers who have previously worked for them on a professional basis. Others have hired automobile company executives who could bring them an authoritative knowledge of mass production and assembly-line methods. All recognize the hazard to morale in bringing outsiders in to fill responsible positions toward which insiders might reasonably aspire. One company learned from painful experience that this situation becomes acute when the ousider, failing to develop the loyalty and support of his newly acquired organization, is permitted to bring in a clique of his former associates upon whom he feels he can rely with greater confidence.

TRAINING

After insuring an adequate supply of potential talent within the organization, the next step in achieving a uniformly high caliber of key personnel is through training. The need for training applies to all positions from top to bottom. Just as the workman needs to be taught how to handle his job most efficiently, so every supervisor needs to learn how best to perform his supervisory functions. Even managers and presidents are not born as such, and can profit from studying the most effective methods of management.

Often, it is assumed that because a man has been on the job a long time there is nothing further he can learn about it. Yet there is hardly a job that cannot be made more effective through analysis of its requirements and learning how to meet them to best advantage. Many men in key positions are heard to remark, in effect, "No one has ever really shown me how to handle this job; I'm just doing what I saw my predecessor do. If he was wrong, I'm probably wrong too."

To meet the need for training, some companies have, at considerable expense, set up a company school with a wide variety of general courses available to all who were interested. In most cases, this effort is considered to have fallen short of the mark, scattering the shots too promiscuously—spending time and money to train employees in subjects for which they might have little aptitude or ultimate chance for use, and thus raising false hopes.

The general consensus among the companies which have comprehensive programs is that the most profitable and effective training is training on the job for the job, as well as the training of selected candidates for the job ahead. This type of training is specific and purposeful rather than general and abstract, and is fundamental to the interests of both the individual and the company; it shows each man how he can do his job better.

Obviously, the first requirement in any such program is a clean-cut conception and definition of the proper functions, responsibilities, relationships, and objectives of each job, as provided in a comprehensive organization manual. The training process then consists of seeing that each man understands and knows how to do his job, that is, how to discharge his proper functions and responsibilities and meet his objectives. At the same time, individual deficiencies disclosed by periodic ratings become the object of special coaching or assistance.

Such training is a primary function of management. While staff-training divisions, conference leaders, and special training courses all have their essential parts, there is no substitute for the active interest and participation of the entire management organization in assuring the full value of any training program. Just as it is the natural province of a foreman to train each man for his job, so is it the proper function of the superintendent to train his foremen, of a manager to train his superintendents, and of a general executive to develop his managers to full effectiveness.

Training practices in the companies surveyed are discussed below under the following captions:

> Student Training
> Supervisory Training
> Executive Training

Student Training

Practically all the companies that take in a substantial number of selected graduates each year have a comprehensive training program. This is designed to fit these men, together with any promising material from within the organization, as rapidly as possible for productive work as salesmen, staff men, or minor supervisors. From this general level they normally progress to positions of greater responsibility according to their talents and the opportunities available. These student-training programs are of three general types:

1. Normal progress through earned promotion from job to job
2. Accelerated progress through brief assignment to selected jobs
3. Intensive training school

One company which does a splendid job in the selection, training, and development of all its personnel, relies upon the first method, with normal, well-planned progress through successive actual jobs, to develop its exceptional recruits as well as others. Another concern states in its manual for employees: "Two fundamental principles govern this company's training activities: (*a*) the most effective training is training-on-the-job, combined with individual coaching; and (*b*) training is a continuous process, lasting throughout a man's career with the organization."

Most companies, however, attempt to take advantage of the superior qualifications of these recruits to accelerate somewhat this natural training process. In many cases this is accomplished by successive assignment to a series of minor jobs chosen to give the trainee as wide a background and experience as possible within a reasonable time, along lines which will be of greatest value in his intended field. He is left on any job only long enough to learn it, prove himself out under fire, and become familiar with the surrounding operations and activities. This usually includes a year or more through such factory jobs as helper, laboratory assistant, timekeeper, and inspector, to acquire the general knowledge of products and operations needed by men going into production, engineering, accounting, or sales work. Trainees are expected to make good on each job and are treated like any other workman. They are carefully watched and rated by the supervisory staff. In some cases, to avoid conflict with the unions or displacement of regular workers, the trainees are assigned as extra men. Compensation practice is divided between paying them the rate of the job, or paying a special training salary. One company pays them the rate of the job, representing what they actually earn, and then gives them a supplementary check to bring them up to an established training salary. In most cases trainees are expected to do outside studying and some classwork, usually at night or Saturday mornings.

One company, using this general plan, insists that all men brought into home-office staff positions or going into sales work have at least two years of such factory experience and a brief period of training through selected general-headquarters offices.

In another company training-through-actual-work is supplemented by frequent contact and discussion with major executives. The vice-president in charge of operations, who is active in recruiting the talent to be trained, meets periodically with the half-dozen or more trainees at his home. In addition, he takes one at a time on his frequent trips of inspection to the various operating properties. This affords an excellent opportunity to appraise capabilities and develop interests. All trainees likewise come into the home office every Saturday to meet with the other major executives, in turn, for discussion of the various phases of the business.

The third and most accelerated general type of student training, applied most extensively to prospective sales personnel, is through an intensive training school, in which classroom work is given major emphasis, along with some opportunity to observe and acquire a general familiarity with different pertinent operations and activities.

One of the participating companies has a very effective plan of this type, embodying the following features:

1. All trainees spend the first week going through a carefully worked out orientation course conducted by the personnel department (training division) and designed to give the students a good general picture of company organization, operations, policies, and products.

2. Those destined for sales are then put through an intensive sales training course under the direction of an assistant general sales manager. This involves study of products, prices, and selling methods, including actual and sound-movie demonstrations of good and bad practices. Considerable time is spent in factories and laboratories. After nine months of such training, the trainees are assigned to branch sales organizations where they serve a brief apprenticeship in customers' retail stores. They are then turned over to selected regular salesmen, whom they accompany for one or two months in order to observe how it is done, and are coached in making their own contacts. Every two years thereafter each salesman is brought to headquarters for a one-week "postgraduate" conference to bring his knowledge of products, manufacturing and selling methods, and general policies up to date. Major executives meet with these conference groups.

3. After the one-week orientation course common to all trainees, those going into research or engineering are assigned to different engineers to observe and help with projects selected to give them as wide an experience as possible. This is interspersed with observation of manufacturing and control operations and weekly quizzes. By the end of twelve months the trainee is expected to be fitted for work as a junior engineer.

4. The comptroller's organization likewise has a carefully designed two-year program which provides for working the trainees through various factory and headquarters offices as clerks, so as to make them familiar with the figures from source to final use. Here again, the practical work is supplemented by special study, quizzes, and group conferences.

Another company, using much the same plan, tries out prospective salesmen on minor sales work in the field for a few months to see whether or not they appear to have selling ability before bringing them to headquarters for a six-week intensive training course.

Many companies have instructor-supervisors attached to each sales district who break in new salesmen on the job, demonstrate the proper techniques with actual customers, and then coach and criticize the trainee's own efforts. This process is repeated periodically throughout the salesman's career, the instructor spending several days with each man on the job, demonstrating the proper methods, pointing out weaknesses, and assisting in their correction.

Supplementing this procedure, one company, with some three thousand salesmen operating all over the United States, insists that every branch manager spend at least one full day a week making the normal rounds with one of his salesmen (in turn). During this contact he observes the salesman's strength, corrects his faults, assists with difficult accounts, and maintains a firsthand acquaintance with the trade and its problems. This company likewise expects each regional manager to do the same for his branch managers, maintaining a log to be sure that this is actually done at the intervals scheduled.

It will be seen from the foregoing discussion that in most cases the divisional managements concerned are expected to assume a major part in the direction of training programs designed to fit men for their respective operations, usually looking to the personnel department (training division) for general assistance and co-ordination as necessary.

Supervisory Training

Many of the companies studied appear to appreciate the vital position of foremen and other immediate supervisors as management's key men in assuring high quality, low costs, and satisfactory employee relations. In general, these concerns have comprehensive supervisory training programs to develop such men to full effectiveness and to impress them with their responsibilities as members of management. Other companies were found to have done very little along this line, except for casual individual efforts or occasional meetings. In this connection it is considered significant that among the participating companies, the two or three that have experienced major labor troubles in recent years appear to lack fully effective supervisory training programs. Without adequate recognition and training, members of this important group are often found to be wanting in loyalty and in their support of the management and its policies.

While many comprehensive supervisory training programs have been described in trade and technical journals, the following plans or features observed during the survey appear to be of special interest. One large company has a very comprehensive program toward which it budgets some $70,000 per year, presumably to cover the time of men attending the training conferences. Development, direction, and administration of the program is handled by the different levels of the supervisory organization. All supervisors, including department managers and selected staff men, participate in the training. A high-caliber training director enlists the interest and support of general and operating executives and generally guides and co-ordinates the program which is specifically designed to help participants do a better job. This program embraces the following fields:

Principles of Organization: organization plan of the department concerned; the distinction between responsibilities and relationships of operating and staff departments.

Personnel Administration: existing policies and their background; advance discussion of changes in policy; analysis and handling of complaints and grievances; and similar matters.

Cost Control: proprietary viewpoint; purpose of accounts, analyses, records; budgetary control plan and procedure; types of expense and their control.

Quality Control: principles of quality control; inspection practices; salvage methods.

Planning and Scheduling: explanation of the whole system of production planning and stabilization, from the top down, presented by those responsible.

Other companies have somewhat less comprehensive programs along similar lines. Some of them appear to have made effective use of training courses and material obtained from an outside service specializing in this field.

In addition to basic student and supervisory training programs, one company has three special features of particular interest:

1. Men promoted from the ranks into their first supervisory positions are given a special two- to three-week preparatory course of special training, usually at company headquarters.

2. The personnel and industrial engineering departments are

used extensively as training grounds for men going into supervisory positions.

3. All foremen, supervisors, and selected staff men from all over the United States are brought in to headquarters every three to five years, in groups of fifteen or twenty, for a "postgraduate" training conference lasting one week. This is very carefully programmed to be of greatest value and inspiration to the men, widening their conception and knowledge of company organization, policies, and management methods and objectives, as well as bringing them up to date on product and process developments. The major executives participate actively in this program.

While all the foregoing plans naturally emphasize to foremen and other supervisors their community of responsibility and interest with and as a part of management, two supplementary devices are of especial interest:

1. Impressed with the fact that employee representatives frequently meet with major executives in their private offices and then gloat over their foremen who had never had that opportunity, the senior vice-president of one company has recently inaugurated a plan under which each major works manager is expected to invite all his supervisory people, in suitably sized groups, to lunch and to spend part of the afternoon in his office informally discussing their common problems. The vice-president himself started the ball rolling by bringing groups of foremen from a near-by plant to his New York office. The response to this plan has been most enthusiastic.

2. In another concern which has its headquarters at the main plant, the president, vice-president of manufacturing, treasurer-comptroller, and budget director meet with the foremen once a week for two to three hours to discuss such matters as current problems, present and proposed policies, and costs. The supervisory staff also has lunch every day with the top executives.

Executive Training

Some companies appear to trust to luck or sporadic individual efforts to produce adequately qualified candidates for executive positions when they are needed. Other companies, impressed with the value of having only the highest-caliber personnel in every major position, have a well co-ordinated training and development program to this end. This assures an adequate supply of candidates who have the requisite personal qualifications, training, and background to make them fully effective in the positions for which they are in line.

Executive training has two important aspects. One is to train executives to function most effectively in their present jobs. The other is to provide, through successive appointment to selected positions in different departments, the wider background and experience which may eventually qualify them for higher executive positions. Both these activities fall within the natural province of management, to direct the program and, through contact with their subordinates, to take an active part in their development. In both cases, training-on-the-job is of primary importance. Here again, clarification of job requirements is a first essential.

Many companies attempt to earmark their potential executive talent or promotable material. Executives are expected to devote special attention to the progressive development of such men within their organizations and their progress is the subject of periodic discussion with major executives.

Some of the co-operating companies insist that each executive train an adequate successor as a condition precedent to his own advancement. To this end, one company goes to the length of insisting upon double desks for all executives, with a candidate for ultimate responsibility sitting opposite, usually functioning in a "foot-loose," "assistant-to" capacity. Even the president follows this practice, with a high-caliber assistant sharing his own double desk. While admitting that the practice of maintaining these extra training positions is somewhat expensive, the company feels that the benefits far outweigh the costs. Advantage is taken of opportunities to send these trainees out to the field to investigate problems and to relieve field executives during their vacations, thus supplementing their inside training.

Two of the participating companies do a most impressive job of training executives through use of the so-called consultative plan of management. Under this plan of sharing management problems and responsibilities with subordinates, functions and objectives as well as methods and measures of accomplishment are clarified through joint discussion and agreement. This gives each man a clear conception of the requirements of his job and the best thought of his principals and associates as to how to discharge them.

Another company achieves something of the same effect through close contact between subordinate executives and their principals in connection with its five-year planning and development program (see page 207).

In still another company, the top executives meet monthly with from fifty to two hundred of the key operating and staff heads to discuss problems of major concern, review proposed changes in policy, and develop and co-ordinate the thinking of their key men.

DEVELOPMENT THROUGH RESPONSIBLE POSITIONS

As to the second aspect of executive training—progression through selected jobs to widen experience and familiarity—the following practices are most interesting:

1. A number of the companies follow the progress of their promotable material closely, and when, through periodic appraisal, they feel that a promising man has realized the full measure of training and experience from his present assignment, they try to find a suitable promotion or arrange a lateral exchange ("swap") of jobs. In either event the objective is to widen the individual's experience and provide an opportunity for his continued growth. In making appointments, such companies frequently try to make as many logical shifts of key prospects as practicable in order to multiply the number of opportunities for further development.

2. Many concerns recognize the special training value of work in certain jobs and departments which afford familiarity with a wide circle of activities, such as organization work, industrial engineering, cost control, personnel activities, and the various "assistant-to" jobs. Full advantage is taken of the opportunity to rotate promising men through these departments in connection with their long-term training. In the same way, service in a subsidiary company may afford familiarity, on a smaller, simpler scale, with most of the problems of the parent company.

3. In making any appointment, from the lowest to the highest, one large company considers not so much who can most quickly fill a particular job (usually the "next-in-line"), but who will profit the most through the experience and training which the opportunity affords, and so be of greatest ultimate value to the company. To this end, it considers all individuals throughout the department at the level next below the vacancy and selects the man who, in its judgment, would get most out of the assignment.

In the case of the more important positions, this consideration extends to qualified men throughout the company. It is assumed that within a few months an able man, with the help of his associates, can learn to handle the work. No difficulty is experienced through disappointment of the "next-in-line" or "heir apparent," as all key men know the system and are hopeful of appointment not only to the one position directly ahead but to any of the many positions on the next higher level. The result of this practice is that executives have a remarkably comprehensive knowledge of the operations and of the key personnel throughout the company.

In order to crystallize and effectuate the program of executive development through service in a logical succession of well-selected assignments, it is desirable to consider and record for each key position in the company the training jobs or fields in which the candidate should preferably have served, indicating the logical order of promotion where practicable. For instance, if the key position carries major responsibility for production, costs, and labor relations, it would be considered desirable for the candidate to have had some experience in the production, industrial engineering, and industrial relations departments. While such specification would of course not be on a hard and fast basis, being subject to the availability of openings and other considerations, it would tend to systematize the development program and so make it more effective.

RATING OF PERSONNEL IN KEY POSITIONS

One of the most important and fundamental requirements in a sound and equitable program of personnel administration is the thorough periodic rating or appraisal of individual performance and capabilities on the job. Important as this is in the case of rank-and-file personnel, it becomes doubly significant in connection with staff, supervisory, and executive positions, where errors in selection and deficiencies in performance are of maximum consequence. As applied to this group, comprehensive personnel ratings serve as an invaluable guide and basis for

Early discovery and elimination of unsuitable men.

Recognition and correction of weaknesses through helpful discussion, special training, and more suitable placement.

Discovery of talent, and with the most advantageous training, development, and placement thereof.

Bringing to attention the "forgotten man" who needs or deserves
    promotion, change of placement, or increase of pay.

Selection and appointment of best-qualified men to key positions.

Disposition of inadequately qualified men in key positions.

Equitable compensation of individuals within ranges appropriate
    to the job.

Stimulation of morale through assurance that recognition is based
    on merit only.

Stimulation of supervisor's interest in personnel administration.

Establishment of a permanent record of employees' qualifications,
    avoiding sole reliance upon personal knowledge of supervisors
    who may be shifted.

Generally assisting management in maintaining and improving the
    quality of personnel in all responsible positions.

Practically all of the co-operating companies make some attempt to size up their key personnel from time to time. Where this
function is left to individual initiative, judgment, and method,
however, results are likely to be inaccurate, inconsistent, and un-
reliable. Even with a systematic rating plan, overcomplexity, improperly qualified raters, and the tendency of preconceived judgments, prejudices, and partialities to influence appraisals may
seriously impair its value unless special precautions are taken. A
few of the companies have developed very effective rating plans,
in some cases extending to top executives. Many of the other
companies recognize the limitations of their present efforts in this
field, and look with interest to learning of other more effective
plans.

From observation among the companies studied, the following considerations, applicable to the rating of personnel at all
levels, are of primary importance.

Appraising Performance in Terms of Job Requirements

Just as the most effective training appears to be training on
the job to meet the requirements of the job, so rating to determine
how nearly these requirements and objectives are being met seems
to be the soundest basis for appraising performance. Such ratings
are practical and concrete and are in terms which management can
do something about; they are not theoretical generalities.

This process is greatly facilitated through the use of job specifications, which establish the major objectives and means of meas-

uring their realization, for each key job or group of similar jobs. Rating sheets are designed and co-ordinated for use in appraising accomplishments in terms of these objectives. For example, basic objectives common to all supervisory positions, and forming the basis of the rating sheet for such positions, might include

1. Accomplishment—getting the required work done satisfactorily as to quantity, quality, and time.
2. Costs—keeping costs at a minimum.
3. Betterment—developing improvements in methods, products, processes, facilities, or other fields.
4. Personnel—making sure that every job is filled by a well-qualified, thoroughly trained employee, fully understanding and enthusiastically discharging the proper functions and responsibilities of his job.

While deficiencies in personal qualifications such as initiative, judgment, leadership, and personality may be of interest in explaining why these major objectives have not been met and what is to be done about it, and thus may be worth noting on the rating sheet, the extent to which job objectives are being realized is the primary consideration in appraising performance.

Appraising Potentialities and Best Placement

After rating performance on the present job, any comprehensive appraisal should also take into account, as an entirely separate consideration, what line of work the employee is best fitted for and what are his ultimate prospects. This will serve as a guide toward placing and developing him to best advantage both to himself and to the company. This portion of the appraisal should logically cover such questions as the following:

1. Does employee appear to be naturally fitted for his present line of work?
2. If not, for what other job or line of work does he appear to be best fitted?
3. For what higher jobs, both in this and other departments, does the employee now appear to be a properly qualified candidate?
4. For what type and level of responsibility does the employee appear to be an ultimate prospect, e.g., foreman, superintendent, manager, specialist?
5. Through what succession of jobs should the prospect advance

in order to round out his experience and training and develop his full potentialities?

Well-Designed Rating Forms

The consensus of the best thought and practice among the participating companies as to design of rating sheets is as follows:

1. Simplicity.—They should be kept as simple as possible consistent with the essential information to be developed.

2. Concreteness.—As indicated above, they should deal in concrete terms of job requirements rather than theoretical generalities.

3. Uniformity.—They should be uniform as to general scope, viewpoint, and form for all departments of the company, thus facilitating advantageous placement, transfer, and promotion between departments.

4. Co-ordinated Series.—While preserving uniformity as to basic form and scope, rating sheets should be adapted to the particular needs and nomenclature of the different well-recognized fields in order to assist the raters in appraising performance and capabilities. Thus, there might be a series of well co-ordinated rating sheets applicable to such fields as management, supervision, selling, technical work, clerical work, and production.

5. Gradations.—The most common practice is to use five gradations in appraising each job factor or objective, representing "exceptional," "better than average," "average," "below average," and "poor" performance, respectively. This appears to be consistent with the general accuracy of the rating method, as the use of fewer gradations lacks specificity, while a greater number becomes unnecessarily elaborate.

6. Gradation Descriptions.—Many companies characterize and describe the different gradations under each qualification in order to assure accuracy and uniformity of judgment in making appraisals. A few concerns go further and scramble the order of gradation under the different qualifications so that raters will not let their over-all judgment of a man influence their appraisal of each qualification. While possibly justifiable in some circumstances with untrained raters, this practice appears unnecessarily confusing and prevents a quick appraisal of each man's strengths and weaknesses from his rating sheet.

7. Numerical Evaluation or Weighting.—After the apprais-

als have been made, many companies resolve them to a numerical basis, through assignment of points to the various qualifications and gradations, according to importance, in order to facilitate ranking and grouping.

8. Final Ranking and Grouping.—Many companies finally grade their different classes of personnel on the basis of their numerical ratings into five groups, corresponding with the gradations described above, as follows:

    Top   5 percent = Exceptional
    Next   20 percent = Better than average
    Next   50 percent = Average
    Next   20 percent = Below average
    Bottom 5 percent = Poor

While these percentages may vary somewhat in smaller groups, experience in scholastic, business, and military circles indicates that, in any large and representative group of individuals, the proportions indicated should be reasonably accurate, affording a good over-all check on the soundness of the ratings and providing a common denominator to insure a uniform basis of appraisal throughout the organization.

Consensus of Several Best Judgments

Many rating plans fall far short of meeting expectations because reliance is placed upon the judgment of one man, normally the immediate superior, in making appraisals. Under this plan, each supervisor or executive is handed a bunch of rating forms and asked to rate his subordinates. As might be expected, results are apt to be colored by the many differences in viewpoint, inadequate knowledge of rating principles, preconceived judgments, and personal likes and dislikes. To get around this, several companies secure independent appraisals from the several supervisors and executives most familiar with each man's work. These opinions are then reconciled and co-ordinated, usually by the personnel department, consulting as necessary with the individual raters, and resolved into a final rating.

One company has made very effective use of the conference method of rating to assure the uniformity and reliability of appraisals. Under this plan, carefully selected and thoroughly trained conference leaders or chairmen, usually from the personnel organization to assure impartiality and proper viewpoint, meet with the several supervisors and executives having closest familiarity with the performance of the individuals to be rated. The chairman's function is to educate the raters as to rating principles and viewpoint, to develop and co-ordinate the different opinions and judgments through questioning and discussion with the other members, to reconcile and record results, and, in general, to assure that the ratings are sound and impartial, reflecting the true facts. As all judgments are obtained from the supervisory members of the group, the staff chairman need not necessarily be familiar with the individuals rated. In order to do a good job, all raters are given advance notice of those to be rated, together with copies of the rating forms on which they may indicate their tentative opinions prior to discussion at the meeting. In order to avoid preconceived judgments, previous ratings should not be referred to until after the new ratings are completed.

In appraising the more important managerial and executive positions on this basis, it is usually desirable for the director of personnel to function as the impartial chairman, soliciting and co-ordinating the judgments of the several higher executives in best position to appraise the performance and capabilities of the individuals in question. This arrangement has precedent in two of the companies surveyed. In one, the director of personnel, in collaboration with the sales vice-president and general sales manager, recently rated all district sales managers and reviewed the ratings with the president; in the other, the vice-president in charge of personnel, in collaboration with the appropriate executives concerned, each year rates the top two hundred fifty executives of the company.

Effective Use of Ratings

Sound ratings and appraisals are of value only to the extent that they are actually used as the basis for the following aspects of personnel administration:

1. The individuals rated should be informed of their weaknesses and guided and assisted in their correction through special training and supervision.

2. Improperly placed personnel should be reassigned to better advantage.

3. Key employees who do not fully measure up to requirements after repeated efforts toward their improvement should be re-

moved from these positions in order not to jeopardize the effective functioning of the organization.

4. Candidates for promotion and appointment should be selected from among those shown to be outstanding on the basis of sound appraisals.

5. Financial recognition can be advantageously accorded on this basis.

6. Once a year the director of personnel should submit a report to general management covering progress and results under the personnel-development program. This report, based upon a comprehensive analysis of the annual ratings, should indicate, by departments and levels, the extent to which key jobs are adequately filled and properly backed up and the measures under way or recommended to strengthen weaknesses.

While personal knowledge and judgment of a man will always play an important part in the final selection, advancement, or disposition of key personnel, a good rating plan, properly administered, can be invaluable in providing the basis for a sound and equitable program designed to assure that every responsible position is filled by a fully qualified individual.

APPOINTMENT TO KEY POSITIONS

The most important requisite in assuring fully qualified personnel in every responsible position is an adequate system of control over selection and appointment to such positions. Too often other considerations than the basic qualifications essential to effective performance of the job appear to govern such appointments. In many cases outstanding salesmen are made sales managers in recognition of their individual selling records, only to find that they have few, if any, of the qualifications needed in a manager. Another common fallacy is to assume that eminence along technical and scientific lines is all that is required to manage a technical department successfully.

In many companies, appointment to key positions is left to the individual judgment and approval of the next two higher levels of authority. Where selection is made from among the best-qualified candidates within a division, as disclosed by analysis of comprehensive ratings or appraisals, this method of control may be reasonably effective, although it usually precludes consideration of better-qualified prospects from other divisions. Where such a sound factual basis is lacking, however, the decision is often adversely influenced by limitations of personal judgment, superficial impressions, personal familiarity, prejudice, or the fact that some individual, although of mediocre caliber, has some familiarity with the job through having served as assistant.

In seeking a more positive control to assure selection of the best available candidate for each opening, several companies rely upon some disinterested agency to review the qualifications of the proposed and available candidates and recommend the several who appear to be best qualified for final selection by the department head concerned.

In one large company having world-wide operations, practically all appointments from foreman on up are referred to the director of personnel, who passes upon the qualifications of proposed candidates and suggests able men who should be given consideration from other parts of the company. His suggestions serve as a basis for final approval by the divisional executive, or, in more important cases, by the president. In giving his opinions, the personnel director consults freely with departmental personnel men.

In another company the local executive and his staff confer and nominate their first, second, and third choices to fill any key vacancy, i.e., foreman or higher. These names, together with ratings and substantiating reasons, are forwarded for review and recommendation of the divisional executive and personnel director and, in more important cases, for final approval by general management.

In still another concern, all appointments to salaried jobs above a certain level are cleared through the salary committee, which passes upon the individual's qualifications, proper salary, and title, and approves the appointment and issues notification thereof. This committee consists of the president and two vice-presidents. A high-caliber staff agency makes the necessary analyses.

A Suggested Control Plan

A suggested plan of control over all appointments, incorporating the best features of several schemes observed, is as follows:
1. All vacancies to be filled by the best-qualified candidates available, taking into proper account:
    a) Job specifications and requirements, as outlined in organization manual.

b) Candidates with highest ratings available within local departmental organization who have been certified upon their rating sheets as fully qualified for such a job.

c) Candidates from other departments with sufficiently higher ratings and qualifications to be worthy of consideration.

d) In the case of jobs suitable for training purposes, such as staff and "assistant-to" jobs, candidates for whom service in such a job has been specified as the next logical step in rounding out their experience and development.

e) Properly qualified surplus personnel in the same or other departments.

2. As a basis for final approval, all proposed appointments and promotions to be passed upon by an impartial reviewing agency as to adequacy of qualifications and proper consideration of all suitable candidates. The appropriate branch of the personnel organization would function as the reviewing agency, thus assuring a broad and impartial viewpoint and familiarity with the general personnel administration and development program. In the case of higher jobs, a personnel committee such as described on page 70 would perform this function.

3. The executive concerned to submit his preliminary nominations, in order of preference, to the reviewing agency. This agency would satisfy itself that these nominees are fully qualified to meet the requirements of the job, and would suggest consideration of other better-qualified or surplus personnel, giving its reasons in each case.

4. From this list of approved candidates, the executive concerned to make his final nomination and submit his choice for formal endorsement of the reviewing agency and final approval in accordance with a schedule such as the following:

Appointment to	Review and Approval of Qualifications by	Final Approval of Appointment by
a) Positions under $200 (nonsalaried, clerical, etc.)	Local (or divisional) personnel man	Subdivisional or field executive
b) Positions between $200 and $300 (salesmen, minor supervisors, etc.)	Divisional personnel committee (or personnel man)	Subdivisional or field executive provided divisional personnel agency concurs (if no concurrence, then as in *c*)

Appointment to	Review and Approval of Qualifications by	Final Approval of Appointment by
c) Positions between $300 and $500 (key supervisors, etc.)	Divisional personnel committee (or personnel man)	Divisional executive
d) Positions between $500 and $750 (assistant subdivisional and field executives, etc.)	General personnel committee (or personnel director)	Divisional executive provided general personnel agency concurs (if no concurrence, then as in e)
e) Positions over $750 (except as in f)	General personnel committee (or personnel director)	General management
f) Officers, general and divisional executives	General personnel committee (or personnel director) on request	Board of directors

Such a plan should go far toward insuring (a) that all those properly eligible are given consideration, (b) that final selection is made only from among qualified candidates, and (c) that major executives are relieved of detail in connection with the consideration of minor appointments and yet may be reasonably assured that good choices are being made. The executive concerned would retain a major voice in the selection of the members of his staff, provided he picks properly qualified men. This would not necessarily be the man with the highest rating in each case. It should, however, be someone who has proved himself thoroughly competent on previous assignments and who is considered to have all necessary qualifications for the new job, and potentially for the job ahead if this is considered desirable.

DISPOSITION OF INADEQUATE PERSONNEL IN KEY POSITIONS

An effective system of control over appointments can go a long way toward minimizing the number of problem men in important staff, supervisory, and executive positions. Individuals who are considered to be fully qualified at the time of appointment, however, may coast, slip, or fail to keep up with changing needs and requirements. Where there has been no adequate control over the caliber of appointees, the number of key positions found to be inadequately filled is frequently high. Absence of a comprehensive rating plan prevents proper realization of the full extent and consequence of such inadequacies.

In the case of executive positions, failure to measure up fully to the requirements of the job often becomes a very serious matter, as the deficiencies of the responsible individual frequently impair the effectiveness of his entire organization. Thus an executive who is not "economy-minded" may easily spend 10 percent more in running his division than would a good "Scotsman." Likewise, an outstanding sales executive, who can really develop and get the most out of his organization, may easily influence the productivity of his territory by as much as 10 percent. This is in contrast to the popular misconception that the cost of such deficiency is confined to the salary of the individual concerned.

Most of the companies contacted recognize this as a major problem. Some, out of consideration for the individual or through reluctance to exercise a disagreeable responsibility, appear to "just grin and bear it," until the inadequately qualified executive finally retires. Others, equally mindful of their proper obligations to personnel, but also realizing the tremendous cost of inadequacy in key positions, insist that the proper functioning of the organization comes first, and that some equitable disposition be worked out for those who cannot meet the requirements. As someone expressed it, "You can afford to double the executive's salary and tell him to go fishing rather than tolerate incompetence in a key position."

Many companies face the issue and attempt to work out a mutually satisfactory arrangement with the individual, along some one of the following lines:

1. Premature retirement on pension or cash settlement.

2. Assignment to some special work, such as consultant, where advantage can be taken of the man's background and experience without impairing the organization's effectiveness. In such cases an impressive title, avoiding any inference of line responsibility, is frequently bestowed and full compensation is often continued, thereby tending to preserve morale. In one concern, the salary is the eventual pension, and payments to the pension fund are continued on the old basis, so that this rate will continue for life.

3. Elevation of certain major executives with long service to less strenuous "elder statesmen" jobs, making way for more active, younger men in key managerial positions.

4. Assignment of each such case to the vice-president in charge of industrial relations who is personally charged with responsibility

for and given wide latitude in working out an equitable solution. He may even take the individuals onto his own payroll if necessary.

STAFF AGENCY REQUIRED

It will be evident from the foregoing that there are many logical and essential steps in assuring that all responsible positions are capably filled. Full realization of this objective is not likely to result from casual individual efforts. It requires a carefully conceived, well co-ordinated and directed program for the company as a whole.

The active interest and support of general management is vital to such a program. Likewise, the wholehearted co-operation and participation of departmental executives is essential. But usually it requires a staff agency, with the necessary time, specialized experience and company-wide viewpoint, to develop, guide, and co-ordinate the whole program and thus assure its success. This is a logical assignment of the manager or director of personnel and his organization, including both central staff and divisional personnel men.

While working in closest co-operation with the interested executives, and in no way relieving them of their natural and appropriate responsibilities, the director of personnel must, if he is to be really effective, be given the fullest support and then be held responsible for achieving the desired results, instead of functioning merely in an advisory, "if asked," capacity. Logical functions of the director and his staff in this field include the following:

1. Direction and co-ordination of the program for inducting talent into the organization for training and ultimate development to positions of responsibility.
2. Direction and co-ordination of the training and development program.
3. Development and administration of the rating program in close collaboration with divisional executives and personnel men.
4. Review and certification as to adequacy of qualification of all nominees for appointive jobs, as a basis for final approval.
5. Active participation in the advantageous transfer and placement of personnel between departments in the interests of providing opportunities for further development of talent, of finding more suitable assignment, or of placing surplus employees.

6. Preparation of a comprehensive annual report to general management regarding the quality of personnel in all staff, supervisory, and executive positions, which summarizes and interprets the results of the annual ratings. This should indicate results by departments or divisions and by levels of responsibility, showing what proportion of the jobs are exceptionally well filled, satisfactorily filled, or poorly filled; stating what is being done toward correction of weaknesses, training, development; and recording the progress achieved.

Many companies feel that in making decisions directly affecting the destinies of individual employees, as in connection with rating, appointment, and compensation, it is well to have more than one judgment and responsibility. This protects the judges against undue personal influence and onus, and assures sound and impartial treatment. With this in mind, they prefer to look to a committee rather than any one individual in passing upon such matters.

This suggests creation of a personnel committee to rate and pass upon qualifications for appointment to all jobs above a certain level on the master salary schedule. As outlined more at length under "Committee Organization," page 70, such a committee might appropriately consist of the director of personnel, as the primary factor in personnel administration and development, the director of organization as the primary factor in establishing job requirements, and the divisional executive concerned in each case.

In the case of lower staff and supervisory jobs, reliance may appropriately be placed in divisional personnel men, or similar divisional committees, to perform the same functions.

Section 6

CONTROL OVER WAGES

An equitable wage structure, fairly administered, is a major objective in any well-managed company. While it is beyond the province of this report to present a detailed analysis of the various wage-control plans in use, certain features of control observed among the participating companies are of particular interest or significance. These will be discussed under the following headings:

Wage Policies
Job Evaluation Procedure
Control Procedure

WAGE POLICIES

Most of the companies maintain wage scales which compare very favorably with those prevailing in their own particular industry and in neighboring plants of other industries. This is done, not as a matter of philanthropy, but of sound business policy. The relatively small differential between low and high wage scales is usually far outweighed by the ability to attract and hold a superior class of personnel, by high employee morale and efficiency, and by comparative freedom from labor trouble.

Another major aim of most companies is that the wage structure be rational and consistent within itself. Thus men doing the same or equivalent work should receive approximately the same pay, at least within any one locality. Likewise differentials between jobs of different degree should reflect the difference in difficulty and responsibility between them, and hence provide adequate incentive for carrying the heavier load in each case.

In general, every effort is made to keep the whole wage plan and structure sound and simple so that it will be possible at all times to "lay all the facts on the table" and satisfy any fair-minded group of employees that all jobs are properly rated with respect to each other and that the schedule as a whole compares favorably with outside wage scales.

Relationship to Outside Rates

While, as stated above, most companies attempt to maintain wage scales which compare favorably with outside schedules, this policy needs further qualification. Some companies try to keep all their wage rates as high as or higher than rates prevailing on the outside. Some, indeed, use outside rates as their sole criterion in establishing their own schedules. Under such a policy, however, maintenance of a logical and consistent wage structure is practically impossible because prevailing rates, subject to many diverse influences, are seldom rational. Other concerns make sure that their rates for "key" or "bench-mark" jobs compare favorably with similar rates on the outside and then evaluate the balance of their jobs in proper relation thereto. Through this means they are able to orient their wage structures with respect to major outside influences, and yet preserve logical occupational differentials.

A variation of this method, finding effective application among companies in the same industry whose rates are largely influenced by each other, may be described as follows: (1) Rates for key jobs are maintained in favorable relation to their competitors. (2) Other jobs are properly ranked and rated with respect to these key jobs. (3) Finally, the adequacy of a company's schedule as a whole is checked, on the basis of relative generosity, with the other companies. This is done by comparing the average wage weighted according to the number of men at each rate with similar figures derived by applying the wage scale of each of the other companies to the same grouping of workers. With rates for key jobs, occupational differentials, and the schedule as a whole thus favorably established, a company should be in good position to satisfy its employees as to the soundness and adequacy of its wage structure.

Company-Wide versus Regional Rates

A few of the companies studied make job classification and wage determination a purely local affair, each branch or plant manager being responsible for establishing and maintaining wage scales which compare well with those prevailing in his locality. In view of the importance and complexity of the subject, however, and the increasing need for uniformity and consistency of policy and practice, a majority of the concerns have a common system of job classification, at least throughout any one department such as manufacturing or sales. This system, functionally directed and co-ordinated by a central staff agency, assures that the same or equivalent jobs will be placed in the same rate group or classification throughout major departments or even the entire organization.

In only a few of these companies having uniform job classifications are the wage rates also uniform. These particular companies have operations which are contiguous or closely related and the natural interchange between employees exerts a definite pressure toward uniformity. In one case, wage rates were found to be set and standardized for an entire industry through co-operative action. By far the greater number of companies, having widely scattered operations, price their wage scales in accordance with rates prevailing in each locality, even though they may have a uniform system of classification and job differentials. Thus truck drivers may be classified in the same wage group throughout the company, but the group rate may vary according to regional competitive influences.

Fixed Rates versus Ranges

About one-half of the companies surveyed follow a policy of paying fixed occupational wage rates regardless of variations in personal ability or length of service. The other half, seeking a means of giving tangible recognition to increasing experience and better-than-average performance, have adopted wage ranges in place of flat rates. These ranges vary from about three to five cents an hour for common labor up to as much as twenty-five cents an hour for skilled jobs. In some cases they overlap; that is, the top rate for a given job classification may be slightly more than the bottom rate for the next higher job classification. Often these ranges are divided into three or four definite gradations and designated by A, B, C, or D after the basic rate classification.

In nearly all cases advancement within the occupational wage range is based primarily upon merit as determined by periodic appraisal or rating. The service factor is given only incidental consideration. Promotions from lesser to higher grades are usually made upon recommendation of the supervisor concerned, with the concurrence of the personnel representative and approval of the local superintendent or manager. Demotions in grade are infrequent but do occur where reasons are sufficiently compelling.

One company with an interesting variation of this plan has starting rates for all jobs but no fixed maximums. As a result, its able and experienced men are exceptionally well paid and the others have hopes of similar attainment eventually. This practice, no doubt, is responsible in no small measure for the fact that although located in the center of a troublesome labor market, this company has never had any serious labor difficulty.

JOB EVALUATION PROCEDURE

The principal factors that need to be taken into consideration in establishing relative job values are:

Difficulty and complexity of the job as reflected in the apprenticeship, experience, skill, and general capability required.

Degree of responsibility, for such factors as quantity and quality of production, machinery and equipment, materials, direction and supervision of other employees, costs, and safety of others.

Occasionally, such factors as excessive hazard, hardship or expense imposed by working conditions need to be taken into account.

Volume or amount of effort required is frequently advanced as an important factor in job evaluation. This factor, however, should not be overemphasized, for two reasons: first, any company has a right to expect a full day's work from every employee; and, second, it is usually against company policy to assign regularly more than a reasonable day's work to anyone. While at some points operating requirements may impose a lighter load upon individuals in the same classification than at other points, it is necessary to maintain personnel capable of handling peak requirements when they do arise. "Stand-by capacity" is the justification for paying the same rate in such cases even though the normal work load may differ.

In some cases these broad elements of job value are broken down into subfactors to facilitate analysis and comparison.

Job Analysis

The first step in determining the value of any job is to secure an adequate description of that job, developed with particular reference to the factors upon which job value depends. Such an analysis is usually developed through the joint effort of a staff agency regularly engaged in the analysis of the various functions and operations from an organization or cost-control standpoint and the supervisors concerned. Sometimes the views of selected employees are solicited as to the adequacy of the job descriptions. Some of the participating companies ask each man to describe his own job and from this information develop a composite job analysis for each payroll classification. Other companies feel that this procedure is unnecessarily elaborate and that results are of questionable validity owing to a lack of sufficient discernment and analytical ability upon the part of rank-and-file personnel.

In general it is found that a satisfactory job analysis for rate evaluation purposes can best be obtained from someone who has a thorough firsthand knowledge of the job in question and a like knowledge of related jobs in the same and other departments. This is necessary in order that the relative importance of the various significant factors may be properly appraised and represented.

Job Classification

With a thorough knowledge of job demands thus available, the next step is to appraise and rank the jobs according to relative value, vertically by departments and horizontally across the company. Among the ten participating companies having comprehensive job-classification plans there are two general methods of evaluation in use—the over-all appraisal method and the point-rating method. Highlights in the application of these two plans as disclosed by brief examination in the course of the survey are outlined in the following paragraphs.

Four of the companies make effective use of the over-all appraisal method, with procedure substantially as follows:

1. A decision is made as to how close it is necessary and practicable to measure job values. This establishes the interval between wage grades and makes it possible to lay out a grading framework or "ladder," dividing the total wage range into ten or fifteen equal grades or "brackets." Many companies find it impracticable to measure job value closer than about five cents an hour or forty cents a day, and gradations are established on this basis.

2. A series of "key" or "bench-mark" jobs is carefully selected and tentatively spotted on the wage ladder at the respective levels shown to be appropriate by consideration of prevailing rates. These key jobs are usually well known and well standardized as to function; they have wide occurrence both inside and outside the company and generally apply to large numbers of workers. They thus afford a ready means of comparison and co-ordination between plants, departments, and companies.

3. The remaining jobs are then placed on the ladder in proper relation to these bench-mark jobs. This is usually a joint function of well-qualified analysts and supervisors having an authoritative knowledge of relative job requirements and values.

4. Appraisals are made only to the nearest wage grade because there is usually no purpose served by attempting to determine the exact ranking of jobs within each bracket, all of which carry the same rate. For this purpose a comprehensive firsthand knowledge of the different jobs, fortified by clean-cut job analyses, is usually sufficient to determine quite definitely which bracket a given job belongs in with respect to the others. In borderline cases it is sometimes necessary to compare individual job factors as an aid to final over-all appraisal and placement.

5. The final step is to co-ordinate and check the whole structure both vertically within each department and horizontally across the company, making sure that each job is (*a*) equivalent in value to all other jobs in the same bracket, (*b*) of less value than all jobs in the next higher bracket, and (*c*) of greater value than those in the next lower bracket. A very effective practical check on this grading process is to determine whether it would constitute a logical promotion from jobs in one bracket to related jobs in the next higher bracket. As a further check on job grading many concerns solicit the views of selected employees recognized as having long experience and sound, honest judgment.

This general method is simple, flexible, and effective. It is easily understood by supervisors and employees. It focuses major attention upon the main objective—determination of the relative value of each job as a whole—rather than upon the mechanics of the process, which is apt to be the case with the more complicated methods. It is usually accurate to the degree warranted, because even among jobs carrying the same designation and rate there is almost always considerable variation in actual function and responsibility.

Reliability of the method is directly dependent, however, upon the judgment of the evaluators as to over-all job value. As job analyses, at best, give only a general conception of over-all value, it is almost essential under this plan to rely upon men who have a wide firsthand knowledge of the many jobs and their relative requirements. The companies which use this method most successfully have such personnel available.

In this connection, one company has taken advantage of the impartial viewpoint, analytical approach, and firsthand knowledge of jobs and functions throughout the company which are available as a by-product of the constant study of organization and cost-control problems. Men engaged in this work collaborate with departmental supervisors in preparing job analyses and determining proper ranking, making special studies in the field where necessary. The departmental representatives usually have a more detailed knowledge of the jobs in their own departments and frequently have a good idea of their relative importance, and hence are most helpful in a consulting capacity. However, they seldom have sufficient knowledge of the functions in *other* departments to make sound comparisons. This equating process, therefore, falls largely to a central staff agency having a wide knowledge of functions throughout the company.

Six of the participating companies achieve the objective of wage evaluation through the use of the point-rating method of job evaluation. While there are various plans which differ as to detail, they may be generally epitomized as follows:

1. The various factors upon which job value is to be measured are determined and assigned arbitrary weightings in accordance with their estimated average importance. For example, one company uses the following factors and weightings:

Mentality	0–100 points
Skill	0–400 points
Responsibility	0–100 points
Mental application	0– 50 points
Physical application	0– 50 points
Working conditions	0–100 points

Another concern employs the following scale:

Knowledge and training required
Basic education required	0–100 points
Experience required	0–100 points
Aptitude required	0–125 points

Specific demands of job
Physical application	0– 40 points
Mental application	0– 40 points
Visual application	0– 40 points
Unusual features	0– 20 points

Responsibilities involved

For equipment	0–	25 points
For product	0–	25 points
For safety of others	0–	25 points

2. Instead of sizing up each job as a whole, the individual job factors are appraised and the several component values are then added to obtain the rating for the job.

3. In some cases a carefully selected list of key jobs is first rated and the relative ranking of other jobs is then established in proper relation thereto. This is done by rating and ranking the key jobs with respect to each job factor and then evaluating the same factors for the other jobs by direct comparison and interpolation. Thus, if the skill requirement of a job is determined to approximate that of one of the key jobs, it would be given the same numerical rating on that factor.

4. In this way all jobs are finally rated and ranked in order of value from lowest to highest.

Advocates of the point-rating system claim the following advantages as compared with the over-all appraisal method previously described:

1. Its effective use does not depend so definitely upon the availability of personnel having a wide and authoritative knowledge of all jobs and their relative importance throughout the company.

2. Once the rating of key jobs is established, the comparative ranking of other jobs in relation thereto tends to be more accurate and consistent, particularly between departments.

3. The basis for each job's rating is more easily demonstrable and is a matter of record. Dependence upon the evaluators' memories and continuity of assignment is therefore reduced.

4. By the same token, it is easier to delegate responsibility for establishing comparative ratings of other than key jobs to local personnel.

On the other hand, the following drawbacks and limitations of the point-rating system are generally recognized:

1. The whole system is predicated upon the selection and weighting of basic job factors and the rating of key jobs, which at best is a somewhat difficult and arbitrary process.

2. Because relationships shape up in the form of easily comparable numbers, there is a tendency to forget that these numbers

are founded upon rather broad assumptions. In the words of one company, "it is not a mathematical formula, and its over-apparency of mathematical accuracy must be appreciated."

3. There is a tendency for attention to be diverted to the mechanics of the plan, away from the primary object of establishing relative over-all job value.

All companies agree, however, that whatever the plan of job evaluation, it should be kept as simple and practical as possible.

Job Pricing

After these internal job relationships have been satisfactorily established, it is necessary to evaluate the whole wage structure with respect to outside wage scales. As previously indicated, this calls for a determination of policy as to just what relationship it is desired to maintain, that is, whether to orient the structure on the basis of all jobs, key jobs only, weighted averages, or smooth curves.

As a basis for such evaluation and current checking of relative position, many companies make periodic surveys of wage rates prevailing in the localities in which they operate. Where the policy is to meet competitive rates on key jobs and interpolate the others in proper relation thereto, the task of comparison is simplified. In some industries there is a growing tendency to make outside wage comparisons on a co-operative basis rather than to have each company make its own independent surveys. Under any circumstance, however, reliable comparisons can be made only on the basis of truly comparable functions, as similarity of job names is often misleading.

CONTROL PROCEDURE

Among the company plans for maintaining control over the administration of wages, the following features are of greatest interest:

Analysis of Wage Problems

Many companies have staff agencies which devote full time to wage problems, handling such analytical functions as the following:

1. Guiding, co-ordinating, and assisting in the preparation of job analyses.

2. Establishing relative job values in collaboration with the supervisors concerned.
3. Making comparisons and surveys of outside rates.
4. Maintaining records which currently show how the company's wage rates compare with outside scales and recommending changes considered necessary to maintain established wage policies.
5. Reviewing proposed changes in job classification or rate and recommending appropriate action, having in mind the effect of such changes upon the wage structure as a whole.
6. Advising management in connection with any wage negotiations.
7. In general, co-ordinating and furthering all steps necessary toward the creation and maintenance of a sound and equitable wage structure.

Where wage-earning personnel is largely confined to the factories, such an agency is often found on the staff of the top manufacturing executive. In other cases, where several departments are involved, it usually reports to general management. As a rule, however, instead of being organized on a separate basis, this activity falls within the province of either the organization, cost-control, or industrial-engineering departments, both central and divisional. This is a very logical arrangement, as the firsthand knowledge of job requirements gained in the study of organization and operating problems is of prime assistance in developing job analyses and establishing relative job values.

Approval of Wage Changes

There was found to be considerable variation among the participating companies as to the extent to which authority for changing wage rates is delegated. A number of concerns, particularly those which make no effort to co-ordinate classifications and rates between plants and departments, leave the determination of rates largely to the field executives concerned, only major or general changes being referred to the head office. It is even more common for such authority to rest at the divisional level of management—product-division managers or heads of major functional departments bearing final responsibility for maintaining suitable wage scales with respect to their own operations. As a rule, general management concerns itself only with the general control plan and structure and major changes therein, delegating to staff and operating executives responsibility for effecting proper co-ordination and making needed adjustments in individual classifications and rates.

Approval procedures followed by several of the participating companies which have fully co-ordinated programs are listed below.

1. In one concern, all changes in job classification or rate are reviewed and co-ordinated by a central staff wage and salary committee, passed upon by a co-ordinating committee of operating executives and finally approved by the managing board of directors.

2. Another company organized on a product-division basis maintains effective control through a plan involving a somewhat greater degree of decentralization. Classification of key jobs is co-ordinated and standardized through a central staff agency and approved by a company wage and salary committee consisting of the president and two vice-presidents. Authority for classifying their other jobs in proper relation to these bench marks is then delegated to division managements, subject to an annual review and co-ordination of all classifications. All changes in the rate schedules applying to basic classifications, even though adjusted to locally prevailing wage levels, are reviewed and co-ordinated by the central staff agency and approved by the wage and salary committee.

3. A third company not only looks to major plant and subsidiary managements to classify their own jobs in proper relation to established key jobs but also delegates to them authority for making necessary adjustments in individual wage rates in accordance with a general wage policy. Major changes in plan or structure are referred to general management. Effective functional co-ordination and supervision is provided by a high-caliber wage and salary administrator who works closely with the different divisions.

4. A somewhat different plan is followed in the case of several companies whose wage-earning personnel is largely confined to manufacturing operations. Here all ordinary changes in classification or rate clear through a wage-control agency attached to the central manufacturing staff and are finally approved by the vice-president or general manager in charge. This executive delegates to the staff agency responsibility for approving minor

changes and adjustments. Major or general increases are finally referred to general management.

From observation of these different plans, the following principles suggest themselves:

1. Establishment of wage policies and approval of the general wage structure (both as to basic classifications and rates, or method of pricing) would appear to be logical functions of general management.

2. Interpolation and adjustment of individual classifications and rates may appropriately be left to the approval of the operating executives concerned, with the concurrence of a capable central staff agency or committee functionally responsible for maintaining proper over-all co-ordination.

3. The degree of centralized co-ordination and control depends logically upon the extent to which changes in one plant or department may affect rates or classifications in other units of the organization.

Wage Application

Responsibility for proper wage administration does not stop with the approval of a sound and equitable wage structure; many inequalities can creep in from misapplication of the established schedules, carelessness, or lack of proper understanding of the intended uses. In order to preclude these possibilities, several of the participating companies conduct a periodic audit of the work actually being done by each employee to make sure it is in accordance with the specifications of the job for which he is being paid.

Another problem of wage administration has to do with overpayments. Many companies find that certain long-established rates are out of line with their approved wage schedules. While these instances can be corrected by cutting the rates to the proper levels, there is often a reluctance to adopt this expedient, particularly as it may apply to long-service employees. In such instances several companies continue the incumbent personnel at the high rates on a special basis but establish appropriate basic rates applicable to all *new* men, thereby paving the way for eventual realization of a fully logical rate structure. Ultimate correction of excessive rates can often be realized by holding them constant through successive increases in the general wage level until such time as they are in line with the desired wage schedule.

Section 7

CONTROL OVER SALARIES

Among many of the participating companies one of the most obvious and generally recognized needs is a better plan of control over salaries—one that is rational and equitable, and that relieves top management of the necessity of personally reviewing and approving each change.

Lacking such a plan and conscious of the abuses to which salary administration may be subjected, many chief executives or executive committees were found to be personally approving all salary changes for the entire organization. Not only does this practice appear to impose a considerable burden upon the top executives, but frequently they are hardly in a position to judge the merits of each case, lacking adequate information as to the worth of the jobs or the capabilities of the individuals concerned. About all that can be said for this plan is that, having to go to such a high level for approval, department heads are likely to be conservative in their recommendations.

Several of the participating companies, however, have developed effective control plans which permit delegation of authority for making salary changes and yet assure that adjustments are equitable and in line with good business judgment. These plans are predicated upon a master salary guide or schedule establishing relative values and appropriate ranges for salaried jobs throughout the company. Having approved such a schedule and having established the policies to guide its use, top management may confidently pass the major burden of salary administration down to departmental executives.

DEVELOPMENT OF A MASTER SALARY GUIDE

One-third of the co-operating companies were found to have master salary schedules. One concern carries the formal appraisal and classification of salaried positions to the very top. Three stop at the $20,000, $15,000 and $12,000 levels, respectively. Several others have not yet extended this treatment to positions above the

$5,000 level, although a number expect ultimately to embrace all salaried positions in the plan.

Job Analysis

As in the case of wage administration, the first step in salary evaluation is the preparation of job analyses defining those aspects of each position which have an important bearing upon its value. Where comprehensive job specifications, establishing the proper functions, responsibilities, objectives, relationships, and limits of authority for each position are available as a part of the organization manual, they provide an excellent basis for job evaluation. (See example, page 96.) Where such specifications are lacking, job analyses, covering factors upon which job value mainly depends, are specially prepared for this purpose.

In characterizing and appraising salaried positions, particular consideration is usually given to such factors and criteria as the following:

Nature and extent of job: General functions and scope; type and caliber of problems handled and decisions or recommendations made; approximate magnitude of production or sales, annual expenditure, and value of property, for which responsible.

Supervision received: Nature and frequency.

Supervision of others: Number and classification of employees supervised.

Contacts required: Most important contacts regularly made inside and outside the company.

Special job requirements: Particular knowledge, experience, and training required.

Source of candidates: Logical source, level, and type of positions (inside or outside the company) from which candidates should be selected for replacement.

Promotion: Logical advancement from this job.

Consequences of incompetence: Probable results of inadequate performance on the job.

Job Classification

As in the case of wage jobs, the next step is to disregard present salaries and appraise and rank the different positions according to relative worth, vertically by departments and horizontally across the company.

In this process most companies use substantially the same *over-all appraisal* method described for wage evaluation on page 134. The only difference is that for each bracket or level a salary range is established in place of a fixed rate. In some companies, brackets have wider ranges than in others, the spread between minimum and maximum salaries varying from 10 to 30 percent. There is some tendency to increase the percentage spreads at the higher levels.

Only one of the co-operating concerns uses the *point-rating* method for salary evaluation. In this connection one company, which has done a very comprehensive job of wage evaluation by the point-rating plan, contends that this method is impracticable as a basis for gradation of salaried jobs in view of the much wider diversity of functions and greater difficulty of measuring individual job factors.

Pricing Bracket Ranges

With all salaried jobs properly graded or bracketed, the final step is to establish an appropriate price range for each bracket. In this process, consideration is usually given to prevailing salary levels both inside and outside the company. Inside rates are taken into account through examination of the actual salaries paid for jobs listed within each bracket, discarding obvious under- and over-payments and deriving a representative range. Outside levels are established through comparison of salary ranges for common "key jobs" with other companies. Bracket limits are then established in proper relation to these two factors. In some cases the ranges are made to overlap.

Most companies aim to maintain salary scales which will enable them to attract and hold a high class of personnel. In this connection, it is often found, particularly in the case of specially qualified new men, that adequate initial compensation alone is not sufficient attraction. An even more important factor is the company's reputation for affording opportunities for the consistent growth and advancement of personnel according to their demonstrated capabilities.

As a rough check on the adequacy of factory salaries, one company in the equipment field has developed the following formula based on the relationship between supervisory salaries and the average wage rate of the employees supervised:

Assistant Foreman = 20 percent more than the average for his
   organization (approximately 40 men)
Foreman = 35–40 percent more than the average for his organization (7 or 8 assistant foremen and their men)
General Foreman = Double the average for his organization
Factory Division Superintendent = Five times the average for his
   organization

In most cases, a uniform salary schedule applies throughout
the company—at least throughout its domestic operations. One
concern, however, uses salary levels generally prevailing in each
operating locality as a basis for determining the schedules for
minor salaried jobs.

SALARY ADMINISTRATION POLICIES

There was found to be a considerable variation of policy and
practice in regard to the application and administration of their
salary plans among the participating companies. Some companies
limit the consideration of salary increases to one or two fixed times
per year except in the case of definite promotions. Other concerns,
seeking to spread the burden of anaylsis over the year and to
assure unhurried examination of each case, consider the propriety
of change in salary on each employee's service anniversary. Although not a matter of definite policy, there is a tendency to
restrict individual salary increases to around 10 percent and successive increases are seldom granted at intervals closer than six
months.

While fully appreciating the importance of establishing appropriate salary ranges representing the "market worth" of the
different jobs as a guide to judgment in considering individual
salaries, some companies recognize the danger of overstandardi-
zation in this field and insist that the individual and his just
deserts be given full consideration. Where some employee is
doing particularly outstanding work, beyond the normal expectancy of the job, these companies do not hesitate to increase his
salary above the normal maximum, upon presentation of sufficiently impressive evidence. A more common method of according special recognition without imposing permanent obligation is
through payment of some form of bonus to selected employees
who are considered to have contributed most to the enterprise or
for other reasons are felt to be specially deserving. Several of the

participating companies make effective use of such plans as a means of giving appropriate recognition to special achievement, particularly in the case of employees for whom an increase in regular compensation may not be warranted. A suggestion plan with generous cash awards for worthy suggestions is another device to the same end.

In regard to the payment of minimum salaries established for the various jobs, three general practices were found. As soon as an employee is appointed to a job, one company believes in paying him the established minimum salary for that job, no matter what the size of the increase involved, feeling that if he is worthy of the promotion, he will earn at least the minimum pay. Where such increase would be unduly large, other companies are inclined to make a partial adjustment, leaving greater range for subsequent encouragement. Still other concerns appear to substitute a title for compensation in making promotions, delaying any salary increase sometimes for quite prolonged periods until the appointee has made good on the job.

Some companies appear to take a short-range view of a long-range problem in granting salary increases. During prosperous times raises are granted in great profusion while in leaner years practically no increases are given. This practice seems to overlook the fact that salary adjustments constitute a permanent commitment and that there is no more justification for being excessively openhanded in making individual changes during good times than for deferring earned recognition during slack periods. In this connection, a number of the participating companies emphasize the importance of establishing an equitable salary schedule and then each year making the individual salary adjustments that seem fair and appropriate in the light of that schedule, regardless of fluctuations in the business cycle. In case of drastic stringency they prefer to adjust the entire salary schedule as necessary, rather than discriminate against individuals by withholding earned increases.

CONTROL PROCEDURE

The four principal control aspects of salary administration have to do with (*a*) the analytical agency required, (*b*) approval of changes in the salary structure or schedule, (*c*) approval of changes in individual salaries, and (*d*) periodic review of all salaries. The most effective plans found among the co-operating companies for handling these activities are outlined in the following paragraphs.

Analytical Agency Required

In many companies functional responsibility for development and maintenance of a sound and equitable salary structure is assigned to a central staff agency, such as an organization and cost control, industrial engineering, or personnel department. These agencies usually have a group of well-qualified specialists who devote full time to salary problems and related activities, handling such analytical functions as the following:

1. Developing a suitable salary-control plan.
2. Guiding, co-ordinating, and assisting in the preparation of job analyses.
3. Determining relative job values in collaboration with similar departmental specialists and executives.
4. Making outside salary comparisons.
5. Reviewing and making recommendations in regard to proposed changes in job classification.
6. Checking individual salary recommendations to make sure they conform to the established schedule and policies.
7. Making necessary analyses to determine how the pattern of actual salaries paid by departments throughout the company complies with established bracket limits, and whether there is a proper distribution within each bracket.
8. Pointing out undesirable trends and conditions in the entire salary administration program.

As indicated elsewhere, the knowledge of job functions gained in the analysis of organization problems throughout the company is of particular value as a basis for this work.

In order to co-ordinate departmental viewpoints and assure a broad and impartial consideration of salary matters, several companies have established wage and salary committees directly responsible to general management. These committees review the findings of the analytical agency and either take or recommend appropriate action in each case. As outlined on page 66, such a committee may appropriately consist of the director of organization, the director of personnel, and the divisional executive concerned with the salaries under consideration. Other executives are called into consultation as necessary.

Approval of Changes in Salary Structure

The master salary guide, establishing the appropriate limits for all salaried positions, is almost always approved by general management. It then serves as the vehicle by which general management delegates responsibility for routine salary administration to divisional executives. A normal course of development and approval of such a schedule is as follows:

1. The analytical or fact-finding agency develops the master guide in collaboration with departmental executives and specialists.
2. It is then passed upon by the wage and salary committee, which secures the endorsement of the different departments involved and submits the schedule for final approval of general management.
3. All subsequent changes in bracket limits normally follow the same course.
4. Changes in the classification of individual jobs which become necessary by virtue of changes of function or reappraisal of responsibilities are often decided by agreement of the wage and salary committee. Where the interested department cannot secure such committee agreement, and in all cases where such changes are likely to affect other classifications or large numbers of employees, the matter is referred to general management for final approval.

Approval of Individual Salary Changes

Among the participating companies there is a wide range of practice in regard to delegation of authority for approving individual salaries. In a number of concerns the president or executive council approves all changes. In other cases wide latitude is extended to divisional and even to field executives. It is rather usual for divisional executives to approve salary changes up to $400 or $500 per month provided these changes conform to the limits prescribed for each job by a master salary schedule and comply with the policies governing salary administration. In some cases divisional executives must secure the concurrence of the wage and salary committee as to whether the prescribed conditions have been met. In other companies, where the salary schedule and policies have become well established and executives are thoroughly trained in the principles of salary administration, this prior check is sometimes omitted and reliance is placed in an annual salary audit. In special cases where divisional executives feel that personal considerations warrant the granting of salary increases that exceed established limits and policies, they are at liberty to present the facts to general management for a decision. Major branch and plant managers are quite often authorized to approve salaries up to about $200 per month within the scope of established policies and schedules.

The several companies which have comprehensive budgetary control plans were found to make effective supplementary use of this device in connection with their salary-control programs. All salary increases which are considered to be justified are anticipated and included by name, amount, and date, in the departmental budget estimates for the year ahead. Likewise all anticipated retirements, transfers, and other payroll reductions are taken into account. This gives ample opportunity for the salary-control agency to make the necessary analyses, determine the effect upon departmental and company payrolls, and recommend appropriate action. Upon approval of their budgets, divisional executives are free to proceed with the indicated changes as planned or amended.

Even with a soundly developed master salary guide and a good budgetary-control plan, there is still need for some device to assure that advancement of individuals within the established salary ranges is handled in a rational manner. There is often a tendency for executives who are not thoroughly familiar with the principles of salary administration to want to raise too large a proportion of their people to the maximum for their respective jobs, giving insufficient recognition to differences in caliber of performance and often leaving little or no margin for subsequent encouragement of individuals who are likely to remain for a long time in their current jobs. In general it may be expected that within any one salary bracket, an average of the actual salaries paid should fall somewhere near midway between the bracket limits, as the promotion or retirement of higher-paid individuals would tend to bring in less experienced and consequently lower-paid individuals for replacement. Several companies keep watch of this index by departments and brackets as a check on this feature of administration.

Another more fundamental method of control finding application in several of the companies studied is to tie salary recognition into the merit rating plan. Under this arrangement, a man's progress from minimum to maximum for his job classification is dependent upon a thorough annual rating or appraisal of his capabilities and performance; only individuals with a high rating receive top pay. Sometimes this factor is taken into account in only a general way. In other cases, each classification is broken down into definite pay gradations or sub-ranges, designated A, B, C, etc., for each of which a certain merit rating is an essential qualification. This plan was found to have a very stimulating effect upon individual performance.

Periodic Review of All Salaries

Many salary-control plans lay principal emphasis upon preventing unwarranted salary increases. Initiation of increases is left to individual executives who vary as to judgment of their employees' capabilities; as to ability to convince their superiors of the need for increases; or as to willingness to present deserving cases despite previous discouragement. There is accordingly need for some plan to insure that *all* employees receive the consideration to which they are fairly entitled; that there are no "forgotten men."

Several companies make very effective provision for this need in their personnel-administration plans. They insist that at least once a year each employee be given very careful consideration as to:

1. His demonstrated capabilities, disclosed by a comprehensive annual rating.
2. His qualification for promotion or transfer to specific jobs—which may also be disclosed by his rating sheet.
3. Extent to which he has absorbed the full range of experience from his present job and needs a promotion or a switch of jobs at the same level to assure his continued growth and development.
4. His present salary, time since last increase, relation to established limits for his present job, and degree to which he is entitled to an increase in keeping with the established policies.

Such analyses are made by the employee's superiors, usually in conjunction with the personnel organization. In order to spread the burden of this important function over the year, several companies make such a review on or around the anniversary of each employee's service date, which gives it added personal significance. In other cases it follows as a natural resultant of the annual merit-rating process. In still other instances an annual review is made by the personnel organization, either independently or in collaboration with the executives concerned, to assure that each employee has been given the consideration as to promotion, transfer, and increase in compensation to which his progress and the opportunities available entitle him.

Section 8

CONTROL OVER COSTS

One of the important problems facing progressive management is the effective control of costs. Systems of accounting, statistics, and cost-finding have been devised, with the control of costs as one of their main objectives. Every participating company uses these methods, developed to varying degrees of scientific completeness, to guard against and to detect extravagance and waste, to point out unsatisfactory expense trends and items which are out of line, and to supply to the management other essential data upon which to base profitable operations.

THE HISTORICAL COST BASIS

The simplest basis for the analysis and comparison of cost records is the historical basis. The information may be taken from the regular accounting records with little additional expense, and is generally prepared in comparative form, the statements showing comparisons of costs with previous periods, with other units of the company, and so on. Many such comparisons show the current period in conjunction with former periods—by months, by years, by cumulative totals—for periods of from one to five years previous. Usually some common unit of measurement is adopted, such as the cost per unit of production, cost per hour of labor, and cost per machine-hour, so that the various factories will be on a comparable basis. Such statements are usually prepared by the accounting department, not infrequently at some appreciable time following the close of the period under review, so that the correction of some unsatisfactory situation is correspondingly postponed.

Special cost analysts are used in several of the companies to prepare the desired statements, point out any changes which appear to be significant, investigate unsatisfactory cost performances, and recommend corrective measures to the operating people. In some instances where this method of control is used, local managers are informed daily of unsatisfactory performance; in other cases such information is furnished only for weekly, monthly, or quarterly periods. It is not unusual for the manager of production, or a production committee, to review these cost comparisons and to question items which appear to be unsatisfactory.

From a control standpoint, however, such systems have many shortcomings. Not only is the information "post mortem" but the comparisons are, as a rule, on a historical basis rather than against the best-known possible performance. Furthermore, they generally provide no adequate basis for the delegation of responsibility and authority; frequently they do not give thorough coverage to all kinds of expense, but concentrate upon the productive operations. Other technical features, such as prorates, burden centers, and machine rates, make them too complex to be clearly understood by foremen and others directly responsible for expense items. Therefore, either innumerable approvals of miscellaneous expenses must be made by management higher up, or an approximation of the results of some previous period or year must be depended upon as a control or measure of the operations or activities of the current period.

A number of the participating companies, however, continue to obtain reasonably satisfactory results on this historical basis. In one company, analyses and cost comparisons are made monthly to cover a three- to four-year period, indicating any cost increases as related to sales volume. The comparisons, are accompanied by further analyses, showing which items might be reduced. In setting the next annual budget these items are taken into consideration. Weekly and monthly "logs" are also kept on production, and any unsatisfactory trends are corrected.

Another company makes an analysis and comparison of its cost records with previous periods, other plants, and similar factors. Each of approximately a dozen plants gets its own cost in comparison with the others, and is then expected to rectify any costs which are out of line. Because of the small number of products and the number of competing plants, the management believes such cost comparisons sufficient to provide adequate control. The production manager and the manufacturing committee review these costs, and make inquiry and examination wherever they consider necessary.

THE PREDETERMINED COST BASIS

For the past quarter-century it has been accepted cost-accounting practice to predetermine what the various costs will be, and thus have a more scientific basis for appraising current cost performance. Such procedure involves a comprehensive analysis of what needs to be done, as well as a close inspection and study of what is done at present. Wasteful practices or unnecessary operations are detected and eliminated. An endeavor is made to find the best procedure for accomplishing the remaining necessary functions, due consideration being given to such factors as safety, quality, time, and accuracy, as well as to cost.

The estimated or predetermined cost, which is chiefly applicable in those plants where production orders are based upon sales orders previously obtained, was found specifically used in only a few of the participating companies. However, in greater or lesser degree the plan was found to exist in connection with the budgetary-control systems of a number of the organizations. In one company, for example, which operates many plants and produces numerous items, and where the operations fluctuate rather rapidly, the estimated or predetermined cost is used. The cost-accounting department works constantly to anticipate economic and business conditions, and thus to keep the cost rates up to date. Efficiency studies are constantly being made by the manufacturing departments, and everything possible is being done to improve the performance and to reduce the costs. On the basis of past experience, and taking into account knowledge of current conditions, the predetermined cost has proved reasonably satisfactory in this company as a device of management control.

THE STANDARD COST BASIS

Modern management, however, has not been satisfied with knowing what its product *has* cost or what it *will* cost; it demands, instead, to know what it *should* cost. Accordingly, the *historical* cost and the *predetermined* (estimated future) cost have largely given way to the *standard* cost, which has been defined as a cost which should be obtained "under a given or assumed set of operating conditions and volume of output," but which is an attainable goal. This does not mean that it is an ideal cost, but a cost which could be reached if the plant were operated with the highest practical degree of efficiency. It means that a standard or goal is set for plant operations, for volume output, for raw material quality and cost, for labor efficiency and cost, and for each element of overhead expense. It thus becomes a yardstick for measuring efficiency.

Such a program calls for a basic analysis of every phase of operations, including manpower, wage and salary structure, the pattern of organization, materials procurement and control, expense control, and other similar aspects. Although more commonly used in connection with factory operations, the process is equally effective for sales, clerical, staff, and supervisory functions to determine what needs to be done, and how to do it most efficiently. Such analyses are made either by a special group selected by top management, by a department of organization which continuously makes such studies, by a cost-control group from within each department or plant, or by an outside consulting firm employed especially for the purpose.

Three Methods of Analysis

Any one of three methods of making this analysis may be used. One approach is by divisions of the organization. Each department is taken in turn and its activities are thoroughly examined; the usual practice is to ascertain what each and every person in the department does, and why. The possibility of eliminating functions is next considered; if the activity is essential, then an analysis is made of the methods used, and all improvements, short cuts, and other expense-saving possibilities are explored and incorporated in a recommended procedure. A new basic organization for the department is then established, showing the jobs required and the duties of each.

Another approach is by analysis of each practice or activity. In every company certain practices, for accounting, statistical, or legal reasons, must be carried out in the same way by every division of the enterprise. Many other practices, at least from a cost-control point of view, should be carried on according to a standard determined by scientific practice and tested results. Generally there cannot be several ways of handling an activity, all equally good. It is probable that there is only one best way. Accordingly, under this approach, a detailed analysis is made of each activity, showing step by step how it is now performed. Then all possible delays, unnecessary steps, and red tape are eliminated, and the most direct and economical procedure is established as the standard practice for that activity throughout a department or the company. As an example, the practice which covers the handling of procurement orders from the time of their issue until the delivery of the goods can be definitely analyzed and standardized by this process.

A third method of analysis is based upon an examination of the operating expenses. Such a procedure reveals not only the two major cost items of labor and materials but also such other costs as utilities, supplies, outside services, and the like. An analysis of these latter items by the commodity or service purchased indicates where proper reductions can be made and effective control instituted. Changes in quality, cheaper substitutes, and lower contract rates are then possibilities for savings which would be considered, along with means for decreasing consumption. For example, in one of the participating companies the manufacturing department spends approximately $80,000,000 a year. A segregation of these expenditures is first made into such general groups as labor, materials, power, fuel, water, and supplies. Each of these is then analyzed in detail to ascertain if any unnecessary expenditures have been made. To take one relatively small item, an analysis of the supplies group revealed that more than $10,000 of paper towels had been purchased during one year. A further investigation was made to determine whether the paper-towel consumption might reasonably be reduced. By applying this method of analysis to all groups and items the company is enabled to make real savings in its expenses and also to set up controls where needed to keep such expenses in line. Moreover, this is done without injury or handicap to any group within the organization.

All of these approaches have their place in establishing the basis for cost control, and it is probable that no one of them could of itself produce all of the facts required to determine what the costs should be. Further, because every operation of the company is covered, the analysts who make the investigations and recommend the standard procedures must include specialists on the various phases covered. Accountants, sales representatives, engineers, and production men are all essential for complete coverage.

Use of the Standard Cost

Approximately one-half of the thirty-one companies participating in this management study use the standard cost to some extent. Few of the companies have complete standard-cost systems, though the tendency is definitely in that direction. In some instances the standard cost at present applies only to certain plants, or to certain products, or only to the control of expenses. Only in two instances did the companies express definite opposition to the standard-cost concept of control—one of these was on the basis that if standards were set, and then realized, no further improvement would take place in the plants' performance even though there was still plenty to accomplish. This opposition is based, obviously, on a misconception of the standard cost, because as improvements of any type are made the standard is adjusted correspondingly. The primary purpose of the standard cost, as already stated, is to measure efficiency, rather than to produce an arithmetically exact cost.

Actually, many departmental activities remain fairly constant throughout the year. This is especially true of most of the staff departments, and except for seasonal influences, it is true also of most sales departments. Where this is true, an analysis which establishes the necessary functions, the number of people required, and the best methods of procedure, also establishes what the costs should be for the department. The total necessary monthly cost, detailed as to general types of expense, is thus established as a standard; variations therefrom can be readily checked each month, and the causes for the variations definitely ascertained. Corrections and adjustments can then be made as needed, either in the established standard or in the departmental personnel.

In other instances the costs are directly related to the volume of production. Where this is true, as in the manufacturing activities, recognition must be given to the volume factor in establishing yardsticks to determine good cost performance. Accordingly, the standards are prepared in written form covering a description of each operation, outlining the economies and improvements in procedure effected through the analysis, stating the number of people required, and detailing the expenses involved. The standard costs are established on the basis that everything will proceed as programmed. Usually a set of standards is set for varying rates of production, as for example, on the basis of full capacity, 90 percent capacity, 80 percent capacity, and so on. Thus, if the unit is working at 80 percent capacity, a standard is available to show the foremen what conditions should prevail as to the number of men, units of production, indirect labor cost, scrap loss, and other like elements.

To serve as a check upon the operations the production is calculated at the standard cost, and this is compared with the actual cost. Some of the companies furnish these comparative figures daily to their foremen; others furnish the figures monthly, but show their foremen how to gauge their own departmental efforts currently by means of daily checks on the production per man, the ratio of production to material used, and similar measures. Very often the statements given the foremen cover only the expense items over which they have control, and for which they are responsible. Such costs as depreciation, taxes, and general overhead, over which they have no control, are excluded; this tends to make the statements simple, understandable, and effective.

From a control standpoint, the standard-cost system aids in determining what the expenses should be, and also reveals at what points and in what items the expense performance is weak. It places the responsibility for costs on those who are best situated to control them, and it furnishes the information necessary for such control. It permits authority for expenditures to be delegated downward in the organization within the limits of the established cost standards. It is also useful as a basis for wage-incentive payments, and furnishes some of the information required for budgetary control.

The establishment and maintenance of these cost standards are usually the responsibility of a staff group in each major department or location. Where there is a number of such units, a central group audits the standards set by the local people in order to give a uniform measure of effectiveness. The cost standards are constantly under review, and anything which tends to reduce the costs is reflected in modified standards. Usually the consent of the manager is necessary either to establish new standards or to modify old ones. Because of the large sums of money often involved, some of the companies employ specialists on such items as forms and records, wage standards, maintenance and repairs, power, steam, water, stock loss, and scrap loss. In some cases the opportunities for saving are so great that the management assigns a group of these specialists to each factory or major location.

A TYPICAL CONTROL SYSTEM

Among the companies studied various methods of control are effectively used in the handling of expenditures. While a complete analysis and description of a system of control is not feasible in this study, it is believed desirable to point out briefly some of the more important characteristics generally involved in such a plan. Accordingly, the plan of factory cost control evolved by one of the participating companies is briefly presented.

Paralleling the five production divisions of the plant are five divisions of the works comptroller's organization. Each of these has attached to it a group of three or four high-caliber "cost engineers" (fifteen to twenty for the entire plant), usually engineering graduates, some with advanced business training, carefully trained and picked not only for general ability, but also for personality, tact, and diplomacy. One of these cost engineers is assigned to each of the departments, or to a group of smaller departments, which comprise a production division. Their job is to work closely with the foremen and superintendent in studying all operations and determining the most efficient methods for such things as the handling of direct and indirect labor, maintenance, materials and supplies, and waste. With the concurrence of the superintendent they establish standard performance and costs representing the best that can be done with all conditions favorable.

These same cost engineers also work with the budgetary-control division in establishing the monthly over-all control and the yearly forecasts. They assure themselves that the various cost and expense statements properly represent the facts and then review and interpret the control statements to the supervisors concerned, advising them as to the correction of deficiencies.

In this work they make simple time studies or ask the assistance of the wage-standards division in making more extensive time studies. They also request the engineering division to make studies toward the solution of technical and processing problems, removal of bottlenecks, improvements of facilities, layout, and similar matters.

It has been found advantageous to have the cost engineers, who are to make the physical analyses and who are thoroughly familiar with all operations, also familiar with the handling and accounting of the cost figures in order to follow them through to the presentation and interpretation of results. In this way each foreman and general superintendent can look to his cost engineer for the full picture of his operations. It should be added that these cost engineers are looked upon as comparable in rank to the departmental foremen and are considered prime candidates for higher operating or comptroller's department jobs. They are regarded by the management as the "business managers" of the departments they serve.

A very careful study is made of indirect costs such as maintenance. Foremen are trained to be specific in their maintenance requisitions, looking upon the maintenance organization just as a home owner would the plumber. If the cost engineers are not convinced that some practice is the most economical possible, they get all the facts together and attempt to convince the foreman or superintendent as to what looks best. If they do not succeed, they may allow for the questionable practice in a tentative standard (separately reported) until after a period of trial, perhaps a year. They never allow retrogression in the standard costs or the "whitewashing" of doubtful procedures through their inclusion in the permanent standards or budgets until after at least a year's trial, and then only after being definitely convinced that the procedure being followed is the best that can be developed. Each supervisor's showing against his standards and budget is reported to him monthly, with interim statements daily or weekly on such items as direct labor and similar costs of major importance. The cost engineers review the statements with the various supervisors or foremen concerned, obtain their explanation of deviations, and meet with the general superintendent once a month to discuss progress and results.

The standard costs and budgets are attainable, but lean toward the ideal side. They cover all elements of out-of-pocket cost, whether or not such cost can be controlled by the particular foreman. Deficiencies in other departments show up as excess cost and responsibility for its correction is placed where it belongs by that general superintendent at the monthly meeting of his group. These monthly cost-control meetings are attended by the assistant works comptroller, the cost engineers, and the foremen concerned. In these meetings, as at all other times, every attempt is made to adapt the nature and language of the control system to the foreman's needs and to educate him on its value, rather than try to impose technical cost-accounting terminology upon the operating department.

Performance against the standards in well-established operations runs within 5 percent; if it gets much above this, the cost engineers investigate for causes. One thing which the standard costs have brought to light for correction is the excessive cost of short runs and frequent changes. Changes in planning to enable longer runs resulted in a saving of $40,000 a year in one department alone.

In setting standards or budgets on items of indirect labor an attempt is made to recognize minimum requirements for different production rates, sometimes by economic steps, and sometimes as a direct ratio of production or of direct labor. This forces the supervisors to analyze and determine the possibility of cutting down on their clerical and other indirect help as production declines, or to get enough production scheduled by the planning division to occupy their full force at any stabilizing level.

Although much has already been accomplished during the time that this plan has been in effect, the company hopes that, after further experience with standard costs as a means of control, it will be able to estimate deviations with sufficient accuracy to permit using them in its general cost accounting (instead of using actual figures of cost in the general cost accounts), and thus make a substantial saving in clerical work.

Section 9

CONTROL OVER METHODS AND MANPOWER

Experience indicates that there is a constant tendency to expand the functions and personnel of any department in response to the many demands placed upon it. This expansion is ordinarily a slow and gradual process. It is seldom of such proportions at any one time as to excite question. All the people may be obviously busy and it is therefore often assumed that the department is functioning efficiently. In many cases legitimate increases in the volume of business mask the fact that activities of questionable justification have been undertaken by a department. There is also a tendency for forms, reports, functions, and methods to be continued after they have outlived their usefulness. As a result many companies find that from time to time it is necessary to inspect and analyze the work actually being done in order to effect proper control over functions, methods, and manpower. There are two processes by which this is ordinarily done—(a) by complete analysis of each department's activities, and (b) by analysis of individual practices. A few companies make such analyses on a continuing basis, through a central staff agency, and by means of specialists attached to the larger departments, as described in pages 49–53.

ANALYSIS OF EACH DEPARTMENT'S ACTIVITIES

All the functions being performed by a department can be examined by surveying in detail the activities or duties performed by each of its individual employees. This is usually done by having a member of the reviewing agency spend a day or more with each man to study his activities, both as to their character and the time they require. This is supplemented by a statistical review of the work performed over a representative period. When all the jobs have been surveyed in this manner, the resulting inventory of activities is carefully analyzed. The many functions, reports, and other work are considered in relation to the requirements of the business as a whole, and those which are not essential are eliminated. The remaining essential activities are next simplified as far as possible, and the most efficient methods and procedures for performing them are established. These eliminations and changes in method make some entire jobs unnecessary and result in many fractional jobs. Related activities are then arranged into logical full-time assignments by combining these fractions, which permits a further reduction to be made in the number of positions. Finally, each necessary job or group of like jobs is covered by a specification which shows not only the activities to be performed, but also what constitutes satisfactory performance and how it is to be measured.

From this one basic analytical process comes the information for determining:

1. The essential departmental activities.
2. The best methods for performing these activities.
3. The number and type of people required.
4. The pattern of organization.
5. Relative job values and classifications.
6. Standard costs.

In addition, the basis for a system of merit rating in terms of performance on the job, as well as much of the data required for a comprehensive system of budgetary control, is available from this analysis.

Current Control

Having established the necessary functions and the personnel required to perform them, some control must be set up to assure that the organization is kept currently in line; otherwise it tends to revert to its old faults during the changes and additions which naturally follow the fluctuations in business.

In those companies which have budgetary-control systems, each department estimates its manpower requirements by months or quarters, usually for a year in advance. These estimates are predicated upon anticipated activity and are revised as necessary, particularly with respect to the immediate period in advance. Control then involves checking the reasonableness of the departmental budgets submitted and comparing actual performance against approved budget estimates. In addition to control on a departmental performance basis, the top executives are concerned with company-wide control of manpower. Accordingly the manpower budgets of all the departments are tabulated and summarized into total company figures. Some of the companies include also figures on overtime, contract work, and payroll dollars. Such a statement shows which departments will be needing men and which ones will have excess personnel. The advance notice provided through the budget permits suitable provision to be made. Overs and shorts can be matched up where possible; the use of overtime or contract work can be discouraged in times of slack employment; and many other means can be adopted to stabilize employment and control manpower on a company-wide basis, provided the need is brought to light by advance planning.

In the absence of a budgetary-control system, various means are employed by the participating companies to control changes in the authorized manpower. The effectiveness of such methods appears to depend very largely upon the care taken to investigate and determine the necessity for the proposed changes. Some of these plans are:

1. The divisional executive responsible for the department must personally approve additions to the department's payroll.

2. Various committees review personnel requirements and approve new additions. In the home office, this may be an office administration committee; in the manufacturing department, a manufacturing committee, etc.

3. A central agency (or its departmental affiliates) reviews all requests for increased manpower and, when any doubt exists as to necessity, investigates on the ground the need for the increase. If possible, adjustment in method or curtailment of activity is arranged to obviate the necessity for the proposed addition.

In other companies the departments are permitted to make additions, but must justify them later. For example:

1. Each manager must explain quarterly any increases in the personnel of his department to the executive committee. Statements are prepared quarterly by the comptroller showing the manpower in each department and the increases in each.

2. Ratios are established between productive and nonproductive labor and between supervisors and workers, and any manager who violates these ratios must explain the reason to the home office.

ANALYSIS OF INDIVIDUAL PRACTICES

Another widely followed method for inspecting and analyzing the work being performed is to study each activity individually from start to finish. Every step in the sequence is analyzed with a view toward determining the most practicable methods and equipment, the proper qualification of personnel, and the best order in which to perform the various steps or component operations. Such an analysis is not limited by departmental boundaries, the activity being traced through all its aspects, wherever they occur. Furthermore it may be applied to any activity, whether sales, clerical, production, or specialized staff functions. This method of analysis finds application where it is desired to examine and improve particular practices either as to cost, time-saving, quality, or accuracy; or where it is advantageous to establish a uniform method throughout the company.

Standard Practices

Having established, by means of careful analysis, the one best way for handling a given activity, it is often desirable to standardize that practice throughout a department or the company. In many concerns the same manufacturing, selling, accounting, purchasing, credit, traffic, and other activities are carried out at a number of plants or branch offices. In certain of these activities there are legal, statistical, and accounting considerations which require establishment of uniform practices. Beyond this there are other reasons why the standardization of practices is worthy of consideration by top management:

1. **Determination of manpower needed.**—A given volume of work, whether it be office or shop work, if performed in a standard manner under like conditions and at a uniform rate, should require a certain number of man-hours regardless of where the work is done. A basis is thus afforded whereby actual performance can be checked against desired performance.

2. **Determination of cost.**—In addition to the natural expectancy of lowered cost, it is desirable from a control standpoint to know what the cost of doing a specific piece of work *should be*. This would include not only payroll cost but material, supplies, and other items as well. Standard-practice determination furnishes such measures.

3. **Determination of time.**—The factor of time is important not alone from the standpoint of cost but for such other reasons as improving service to customers, meeting delivery promises, handling orders, preparing reports, and submitting estimates. The

time element, derived in reliable manner through standard-practice development, provides the basis for planning, scheduling, and assigning work to individuals, departments, plants, or offices.

4. **Assurance of quality or accuracy.**—In the determination of standard practice the quality of work expected is established quite as definitely as the quantity. Hence, for factory operations quality of performance is prescribed and for office operations, accuracy of performance.

5. **Facilitation of supervision.**—With methods or procedures standardized, situations which are variations from normal are minimized. This enables executives to concentrate attention on those matters which are exceptional, resulting in a consequent improvement in supervision.

6. **Interchange of personnel.**—If throughout an entire company an activity is carried out in identical manner, those engaged in the activity can be shifted from one unit to another with no reduction in proficiency and with no loss of time for learning.

7. **Training new employees.** — The standardization of practices customarily implies standard instructions or procedure manuals, either of which provides a new employee with full information as to his specific duties with respect to any activity. Moreover, it takes no longer for a new employee to learn a well-defined standard method than to learn by word of mouth a procedure which may change from day to day. Then, too, the learning process can proceed with a minimum amount of coaching and explanation upon the part of the new employee's supervisor or associates.

8. **Reliance on procedure.**—The frailties of human nature are such that it is much safer for management to fix definite methods of carrying out repetitive activities than to depend upon the uncertainties of memory and variable judgment of those involved in the activities. Only by prescribing fixed practices can consistency and permanency be given to the conduct of such activities.

9. **Capture of basic information.**—One of the most important objectives of establishing standard practices is to corral certain of the basic operating data which otherwise repose solely in the minds of long-service employees. Such information is the rightful property of the company, as it has been gathered on time paid for by the company. However, unless, through the analyti-

cal procedure of standardizing practices, it is gathered piecemeal from those possessing it, certain portions of it are lost every time there is any turnover of personnel. To be sure, a synthesis of such captured data may not produce the best way of performing a given activity, but the foundation for developing the proper standard practice does lie fundamentally in this information.

10. **Incorporation of policies.**—The preparation of standard-practice, instruction, or procedure manuals provides the opportunity for incorporating positive statements of policy. For example, if company policy decrees that the purchase of an item involving an expenditure in excess of a certain sum shall be on the basis of bids from three vendors, such a provision can be written into the standard purchasing procedure. Numerous company policies can be given positive definition, and therefore uniform interpretation, through the medium of standard-practice statements. Moreover, a means is provided whereby checks can be instituted as to compliance with policies, a method of control not easily realized otherwise.

Even the most painstaking analyses obviously cannot anticipate all of the improvements and methods which are developed from time to time, but at least for an appreciable period the best practice can be established. There is nothing in the process of practice standardization which precludes adoption of better methods whenever discovered. In fact, by the very process of detailed and careful analysis, the foundation is laid for the constant search for and adoption of improved methods. It is only when the full facts about a given method are known that an intelligent appraisal or comparison with another method can be made.

It is not intended, however, to imply that all practices should be standardized. Large numbers of practices are of relatively minor importance and should be left to the discretion and judgment of local managements. Other restrictions are often imposed by variations in equipment, layout, and other local conditions. Usually only the most important practices warrant standardization throughout a department or a company, and even those are customarily submitted to field or division managements for review and adaptation to local requirements before going into effect.

The degree to which compliance with standardized practices is mandatory varies among the companies and even within a given company regarding different types of practices. In several instances, local plant managements are under no restrictions as to how they handle the factory operations under their respective jurisdictions. Preferred practices have been developed by competent staff agencies, but there is no compulsion as to their adoption. What methods are followed and what means are used to meet cost, quality, and quantity requirements are matters left to the management of each plant. Control by top management is a matter of end results reflected by budget or profit-and-loss performance. Other companies modify this plan to the extent of encouraging an interchange of ideas among the various plant managements. Occasionally members of the management group in a given plant visit other plants of the company to study methods and exchange ideas. Several companies hold periodic meetings of plant managers and staff specialists where for several days common problems are discussed. In one instance specialists work in various plants, reporting new ideas, methods, and practices to headquarters. Particularly good discoveries are written up and distributed in bulletin form to all plants. Local managements, thus apprised, use their own judgment as to whether or not these ideas are to be introduced into their own plant operations.

Another plan followed by a few companies is to delegate the authority and responsibility for determining manufacturing practices to regional executives. All plants coming under a given regional management adopt the methods of processing, maintenance, and so on, that the regional specialists decide are the best. Among these regional specialists an interchange of ideas is brought about through corresponding staff executives at headquarters who, however, do not arbitrarily impose standard practices on all plants.

In several companies central agencies carry on exhaustive studies of processing methods, equipment performance, method-study technique, waste elimination, procedures of production control, and similar operating problems. Representatives of these headquarters staff departments constantly visit the plants of the company, consulting and advising with local managements. Well-prepared reports of these studies are written up for distribution to all plants. The central office staff group works in an advisory capacity rather than dictating methods and practices.

Several companies centralize control over manufacturing, sales, and office practices through specialists and staff agencies at headquarters. Standard methods are worked out by these home-office specialists in conjunction with experts in various plants or branch offices of the company under typical operating conditions. Standard practices thus derived have been practicably demonstrated and their use becomes mandatory. In one company complete authority and responsibility resides in a home-office staff department for designing and constructing all buildings, providing all necessary plant facilities, selecting and ordering all equipment, laying out and arranging all equipment, prescribing all methods of manufacture, and, finally, operating new plants and processes at the start until all production problems are worked out. In some companies the head-office sales staff develops and standardizes the practices for ordering of merchandise, warehousing, loading, delivering, displaying, and all other physical operations involved in store or branch-house sales activities.

More than half of the companies use office procedure manuals which govern the practice to be followed for the regular routine office methods throughout their respective organizations. In many of these same companies there are staff agencies at the home office frequently under the comptroller's department, whose function is to study and analyze office methods, establish performance standards, and investigate new equipment. Out of such studies are developed the standard practices which comprise the office manuals. It is the further responsibility of these central agencies to keep all manuals up to date. In most companies standard practices are changed only when careful study and factual analysis confirm the need for modification. This prevents aimless tinkering with office procedures but does not discourage continuous and critical examination of prescribed methods.

Section 10

CONTROL OVER CAPITAL EXPENDITURES

In contrast to the lack of effective control over many major management problems, practically every company participating in this study has established some form of control over capital expenditures.

CURRENT APPROVAL OF INDIVIDUAL PROJECTS

In many of the companies this control is embodied in a series of approvals. Under this plan all projects involving more than a designated minimum amount are presented in formal shape, with pertinent information and substantiating reasons. Unless an engineering analysis accompanies the request, the engineering department or some other suitable agency may be asked to survey the proposal with a view to determining cheaper alternatives and checking estimated costs and savings. The requests are then individually reviewed, successively endorsed, and finally approved by the authorized agencies or individuals.

Authority for this final approval is delegated in varying degrees according to levels of management. Furthermore, a wide variation exists among the companies studied as to the limits assigned to these levels. This variation is indicated in the following tabulation:

Level of Management	High Limit	Low Limit	Representative
Board of Directors.......	Only those requiring a bond issue	All over $500	All over $25,000
General Management.....	$300,000	All over $25	All between $1,000–$25,000
Divisional Management...	$150,000	0	All between $500–$1,000
Field Management........	$2,000	0	All up to $500

Thus, under representative practice a project over $100,000 originating in the field would require the successive approvals of the field manager, divisional manager, general management, and finally the board of directors.

When well conducted, this system furnishes an effective control over individual projects, but it also has several shortcomings. Since the projects are considered individually, it is practically impossible to forecast the company's cash position or to preplan its financial operations. Further, while authority for the individual approvals may be limited to $100 or $500, there is usually no limit on the number of such authorizations which can be made. To get around this, some companies require a list of such authorizations to be submitted monthly or quarterly, but this covers funds already spent for which plausible reasons can usually be advanced. The highest executives of the company are required to analyze and pass upon the merits of numerous rather small expenditures, and this becomes a burden. Finally, and most serious of all, the lack of thorough preconsideration makes it impossible to select the most worthy and essential projects and program them first with due consideration for the company's financial position.

CAPITAL BUDGET

To obviate these objections many companies make use of a capital budget. Under such a system all divisional managers prepare annual estimates of all capital additions and major maintenance expenditures required in their departments during the year. These estimates indicate for each individual project a brief statement of purpose, the amount of money required, the anticipated savings, the improvement in quality or the avoidance of loss, and the time the work should start and be completed. These departmental estimates are then assembled and considered by a central analytical agency, such as the engineering department or appropriations committee, which classifies the projects according to urgency and merit. Usually there are three general groups: first, those which are absolutely essential; second, those which are desirable because of good payout; and, third, those which are desirable but not immediately necessary.

After analysis and classification, the project lists are submitted to general management, together with notations on those which are considered unworthy. This group further reviews the projects with respect to over-all company considerations, the general financial condition of the company, and the equitable allocation of funds among departments, and finally recommends to the board of directors those projects it is willing to endorse.

The board of directors considers the proposed capital budget from the point of view of economic conditions and the company's financial position, with particular emphasis on the total amount of money to be reinvested. Some companies endeavor to reinvest annually the amount of their total depreciation, thus maintaining the assets at a certain level. The board may consider the major projects individually, but its main concern is the total amount to be approved. This approval, however, represents only an allotment of the aggregate amount in relation to other demands as well as the company's financial and capital position. It does not give anyone the authority to go ahead on any project.

Even though it has been included in the capital budget, each individual project of any consequence must be worked out in detail and submitted to the home office for review and approval. The central analytical agency makes a thorough investigation of each project to determine its soundness and necessity. The basis for delegating additional authority to divisional managers is thus established, since total departmental limits are authorized by the budget, and an independent appraisal is made as to the desirability of each individual project included therein. Under this arrangement divisional executives may have final approval up to a higher limit (say $25,000), provided the project has been included in the budget and is endorsed by the analytical agency. This relieves the general executives of the burden of reviewing and passing upon any but major requests or those which are not covered in the budget.

In case of adverse economic changes or financial disturbances, the individual projects can be curtailed as necessary upon notification from general management. Likewise any unforeseen but necessary projects can be submitted for consideration on a special basis. Sometimes unforeseen projects may be substituted for some other less urgent or worthy one at the discretion of general management. Many companies revise their capital budgets quarterly.

The sample control specification on page 173 and the discussion of an appropriations committee, page 67, outline in more detail this method of controlling capital expenditures.

CONTROL WITHIN AUTHORIZED AMOUNT

Most companies prepare a cost and time schedule for each authorized project. Generally the accounting department registers

CONTROL OVER CAPITAL EXPENDITURES

ANNUAL BUDGET

1. All capital expenditures will be covered by an annual capital budget.
2. By November first each year, each Divisional Executive will develop within his division and submit to the Appropriations Committee an itemized estimate of all such expenditures for which justifiable need is definitely anticipated during the following year, giving substantiating earnings, payout, or other reasons in each case. Individual projects should be divided into three classifications:

    Class A. Essential to satisfactory operation
    Class B. Desirable on an earning basis (payout within ——— years)
    Class C. Desirable from the standpoint of logical expansion and development but not urgent.
3. The Appropriations Committee, consulting as necessary with the divisional executive concerned, will critically review these divisional estimates as to necessity, justification, urgency, cheaper alternatives, and other considerations and will then consolidate and submit the estimates to the Executive Council with its recommendations.
4. The Executive Council will review the consolidated estimate from an over-all viewpoint, satisfying itself as to the necessity, justification, and urgency of each project, considering the propriety of deferring Class C and less promising Class B projects to be used as "fill-in" jobs during slack periods to help stabilize employment and so lessen the shock of depression, taking into account proper co-ordination between divisions, eliminating all items considered questionable or unworthy, and submitting a final budget estimate with recommendations to the Board of Directors by December first.
5. The Board of Directors will consider the estimated totals from the standpoint of investment policy, taking into account the availability and judicious allocation of funds, general business, economic, and financial conditions, and prospects ahead, and will finally pass upon the budget (in principle)

APPROVAL OF INDIVIDUAL PROJECTS

6. Within the scope of this blanket authorization, individual projects and expenditures will be subject to further analysis and approval before they are actually undertaken, as follows:
7. Budgeted projects under $1,000 will be approved by the Divisional Executives concerned, within their respective total budget allowances, either individually or on the basis of requirements anticipated (and submitted in the form of an itemized list) for each month in advance.
8. All projects over $1,000 must be reviewed and passed upon by the Appropriations Committee, as a basis for approval, (a) as to whether they are economically warranted (considering assured earnings, payout or other advantages, cheaper alternatives, justification of separable parts, risks, etc.), and (b) to make sure they are generally consistent with, and within the limits of, the approved budget.
9. Divisional Executives may authorize budgeted projects between $1,000 and $25,000 (within their total budget allowances) provided the proposals have the endorsement of the Appropriations Committee.
10. All projects not endorsed by the Appropriations Committee and, in any event, all projects over $25,000 must be referred to the Executive Council for final approval within the total capital budget.
11. Any project over $1,000 not provided for in the approved budget must be referred to the Executive Council for approval.
12. Whenever adverse changes in business and economic conditions or prospects (unforeseen in establishing the budget) indicate the desirability of deferring projected expenditures, the Executive Council will, at its discretion, restrict, suspend, or cancel capital budget balances and projects, reporting such action at the next meeting of the Board of Directors.

CONTROL OF EXPENDITURES WITHIN THE AUTHORIZATION

13. The Accounting Department is responsible for furnishing appropriate reports to those concerned, showing the current status of actual expenditures and commitments with respect to budget and project authorizations.
14. Before any project expenditure exceeds the authorized amount by more than five per cent it must be referred to the original authority for a supplementary grant.
15. Before any divisional budget is exceeded, a supplementary allowance must be authorized by the Executive Council.
16. Before exceeding the total capital budget, a supplementary grant must be obtained from the Board of Directors.

REALIZATION OF ANTICIPATED BENEFITS

17. Divisional Executives will be responsible for seeing that the anticipated benefits relied upon in the justification and approval of capital expenditures are fully realized.
18. Once a year, the Appropriations Committee will submit to the Executive Council a report summarizing the extent to which projects which it has passed upon during the previous two years have proved out satisfactorily (classified as to "definitely satisfactory," "questionable," and "unsatisfactory").

Approved (date)
  Executive Council
  Director of Organization
  Comptroller

FIGURE 7.—Capital Expenditures Control Specification

each project and assembles the cost and progress data upon it. Monthly reports are usually prepared for all such projects, showing what happened during the current month and cumulative to date. Expenditures are closely watched. If the project overruns the appropriation a supplementary grant is usually required, although some companies permit a tolerance up to 5 percent. Such supplementary grants are made on the same basis as the original authorization. Any department which anticipates overrunning its total budgeted allowance must notify the general management well in advance and seek further funds. Similarly, if the total capital expenditure budgeted appears to be insufficient, the general management must seek an additional grant from the board.

FINAL CHECK OF RESULTS

Many companies have a regular follow-up procedure for determining whether the advantages anticipated from capital expenditures are realized. Where improved quality of product and advantages of that nature are involved, some agency is usually called upon to check the results and report the degree to which this objective has been realized. In the case of a project based upon an estimate of savings, the actual amount realized in operation is compared with those anticipated. This comparison may be followed until the estimated rate of saving is attained, until results are determined for a year or two, or until the project has paid out in full. The purpose of such final checks is not only to confirm the judgment of those responsible for the project as a guide for the future, but also to show up technical or engineering faults which might be remedied at a little extra cost and thus to realize fully the intended objectives.

Section II

CONTROL OVER SERVICE DEPARTMENT
EFFORT

Staff or service departments, such as engineering, research, and statistical, find themselves in a difficult situation in many companies. Expected to undertake any service requested and always liable to criticism as to speed and adequacy of performance, such agencies frequently feel constrained to maintain an unjustifiably large organization and to render an unnecessarily elaborate service in order to minimize such criticism. Their willingness to undertake work invites more, which in turn requires increased personnel. On the other hand, they are criticized for their tendency to expand and for the greater cost of their departmental operations.

Under these circumstances it is not unusual to find the sales department regularly using men from the engineering department on strictly sales problems; or perhaps the research department spending a considerable portion of its time on routine control work for the manufacturing department. One case was found where an executive needed some information regarding the influence of temperature upon product behavior. He wanted an approximate answer from the research department which, with some reference work, might have cost $100. Some months later he was surprised to receive a very elaborate report on the subject which cost $10,000.

Such situations point to a need for control within this field. What is required is some way to determine what work should be undertaken, and what requests should be refused. Furthermore, it is necessary to decide how far to go on those projects which are approved, and about how much money to spend on each. No department should hesitate to call upon another, if it feels that it requires the assistance of the other in solving its problems. In practically every one of the companies reviewed each department is free to call upon any other for assistance. In most of the companies, however, the request must be made by a responsible executive of one department upon someone in a comparable position in another. Some companies provide limits of authority on amounts department heads may request. For example, a commodity staff manager might request a research study costing up to $500; his superior up to $1,000.

In about half of the participating companies studied, each of the staff departments has its own budget, which covers the usual run of ordinary requests from other departments. When some unusual request is made, it requires an addition to the budget, and in obtaining the extra funds both the asking department and the one doing the work are likely to be conservative. In some companies the staff agencies budget only the work of a general nature which cannot be allocated or charged to any specific department. The various departments include in their respective budgets the amount they want to spend on research, engineering, or similar service, defend the amount, and get it approved in their budgets. The staff departments then charge the requesting departments for the work done for them.

In many of those companies which have no budgetary system, each staff department management has authority to question the necessity for work requested. This may take the form of asking the requesting department to clear with the president or vice-president, because of the fact that additional help may be needed to handle the work. Sometimes the staff department is permitted to send work to outside firms rather than add employees or purchase special equipment.

CONTROL OVER LINE OF PRODUCTS

A company's line of products has a most important bearing upon its success. The problem of determining and controlling this line is therefore of vital concern to management. This problem has two closely related aspects:

1. Keeping the line designed to meet ever changing market demands—offering strongest competitive appeal as to nature, variety, quality, and price.
2. Preventing overdiversification and eliminating unprofitable items.

The first of these considerations involves the development of entirely new lines of products, the introduction of additional sizes and varieties into existing lines, or the improvement of items already in the line. The second involves the constant and critical examination of all products in order to weed out the slow-moving, obsolete, duplicate, or only slightly different items, altering related products as necessary to maintain a logical, unbroken line.

Despite its importance many concerns seem to lack a fully comprehensive plan of control over this field. It is true that many have impressive product research and development agencies which are continually creating new and improved products. There does not appear, however, to be a correspondingly effective effort directed toward simplifying and rationalizing the line and eliminating unprofitable items. Thus, the list of products tends to become more and more extensive, with many relatively obsolete and semi-duplicated items.

Policies or aims in regard to the extent of their product lines differ among the participating companies. Some concerns strive for complete coverage and offer a line of products to meet every demand of their natural markets. A constant effort is made to fill out any gaps in market coverage and to match any and all competitive innovations. Other companies aim at selected or limited coverage, confining their lines to those items which will reach the most profitable portion of the market. In general, they concentrate upon high volume and consequent low cost. Still other concerns adhere to a policy of manufacturing a limited range of products for which they are best fitted, purchasing supplementary items to fill out the line and so enable the sales department to meet customers' full requirements.

Any comprehensive plan of control over the line of products logically divides itself into three major parts:

Product planning, or the analytical function of determining what products will constitute the most profitable line.

Product development, embracing the technical functions of product research and design.

Product authorization, involving the final determination and approval of the product line and any changes therein.

PRODUCT PLANNING

Product planning is the process of determining just what the line of products should be to secure maximum net realization from the intended market. Its aim is to insure that the line is confined to logical, well-designed, and individually justified items which will place the company in the strongest competitive position. This is largely an analytical problem, involving the following important aspects:

Market Analysis

An obvious need in designing or checking the line of products is to determine, as accurately as practicable, what the market wants, giving consideration to such factors as

Needs, preferences, and service requirements

Potential volumes and prices

Competitive offerings—nature, variety, quality, price, and share of the market

Probable reaction to changes in the line and effect upon demand for other products

Shifts, trends, and new developments

Such analyses afford the basis for the formulation of a logical or ideal product line, best suited to market demands, toward which to work in strengthening and simplifying the actual line as it becomes expedient to make the necessary changes.

Analysis of Line of Products

After determining, as far as practicable, what the market wants, the next logical step is to examine the company's line of products to see how closely it conforms to these wants and to determine the possibilities of simplification, elimination of unwarranted items, the advantageous redesign of others, and the development of entirely new items. As a basis for this analysis, which should be repeated at appropriate intervals, it is desirable to develop and summarize for each product such pertinent information as the following:

Identity and character
Sales for past several years
Prices
Costs
Profit or loss on both a unit and a total annual basis

Simplification

With this basic information available, the first objective is to weed out all unjustifiable items and varieties through combination, simplification, or elimination of unprofitable products and those approaching obsolescence.

Despite the fact that the economic importance of keeping the product line trimmed down to profitable limits has been preached for years, it is amazing to discover how little positive control is exercised over this problem by many companies. One company dismisses the question with the statement that it is up to the manufacturing department to complain of low-volume items. Another reports that it has no continuous plan but that once in a while a concerted effort is made "to get rid of the weak sisters." As a rough guide toward keeping their product lines free of unnecessary, questionable, or excessive varieties, a few companies have adopted such expedients as the following:

1. A conscious endeavor is made to drop an existing product for each new one added.
2. A minimum profitable volume or economic lot size is established for each item, and any product whose annual sales fall below this quantity is dropped from the line.

In some lines, the matter of product standardization and simplification is largely an industry problem and can best be approached through co-operative study, often with the guidance and service of the Division of Simplified Practice of the United States Bureau of Standards.

Rationalization

Hand in hand with the elimination of unjustifiable varieties goes the problem of redesigning the remaining products or creating new items to cover the desired market range with a minimum number of properly graded items. Often the best features of many products may be combined in a few which will offer the strongest appeal to the trade and through decreased variety and increased volume result in reduced costs and improved profit ratios. Likewise nonduplicated products may often be redesigned to advantage and entirely new items developed to round out and strengthen the line. This process should finally result in a logical list of products approaching as closely as practicable the ideal specifications developed through analysis of market requirements.

As indicated in the foregoing discussion, product planning is primarily an analytical function, involving the factual determination of what products will most profitably meet market needs. In the case of any extended product line, this analytical function is a continuous, full-time assignment for high-caliber staff specialists. Market demands are constantly changing and require corresponding modification of the product line. There is need for frequent review to eliminate unprofitable items. In connection with each proposed change in the line, there is need for careful analysis and development of all pertinent facts as a basis for approval. And finally, such an agency may appropriately serve as a clearinghouse for all product suggestions from customers, inventors, field force, and technical staff.

A few of the participating companies have organized effectively for handling this important function. Among these, the following plans are of particular interest. Several companies have set up staff merchandise departments primarily to handle the various aspects of product planning. This arrangement is described more at length on page 54. Other concerns have a staff group performing essentially the same functions, attached to the product research and engineering department or to a products committee. Still others scatter the component activities such as market analysis and product simplification and rationalization among different major departments.

Several product research and engineering departments maintain a staff of technical men in the field, investigating complaints, observing service requirements, talking with users as to their needs and preferences, and appraising the performance of competitive products. Their findings, sent in currently to the home office, constitute a valuable guide in planning and designing the line of products to fit market requirements.

PRODUCT DEVELOPMENT

While closely related to the field of product planning previously described, product development is logically a separable function. It embraces the technical functions of product research and design which are logical assignments of a product-engineering department. It is concerned with the creation of new products and the improvement of existing products arising either out of its own activity or in response to requests from other agencies. The product-planning function, on the other hand, is concerned with appraisal of market, cost, and profit potentialities as a basis for deciding, first, what product developments are worth undertaking, and, second, whether completed developments or other changes should be incorporated in the line. For more expanded treatment of control over product development and research, see Section 13.

PRODUCT AUTHORIZATION

Product planning and product development, important as they are, merely crystallize facts and formulate proposals for final consideration and decision. The determining voice in what products the company is to make and sell invariably rests with management. Because of their primary interests, all consequential changes in the line of products—involving additions, withdrawals, or major changes in specification—are invariably approved by the top executives in charge of sales, manufacturing, and product development, respectively. Sometimes these approvals are secured individually. More often these three executives serve as a products committee to review and approve such changes and to guide the work of the product planning and development agencies. For further detail on products committees, see page 69. In some companies, the president or general council or even the board of directors may give final approval to the more important changes on the strength of the products committee's recommendations. In the case of companies organized on a product-division basis, on the other hand, a large measure of autonomy is usually accorded the different divisions in determining their own product lines. Thus, each division may have substantially the same plan of control as described above for an entire company. In some instances there is an overriding control to assure proper co-ordination of the various divisional product lines in the interest of the enterprise as a whole.

As a basis for decision at any level, each change in the product line should be covered by a formal proposal, supported by such pertinent information as the following:

Probable and potential sales volume and price
Probable effect upon sale of other products
Cost to equip for manufacture and distribution
Production and distribution costs
Probable net realization

Such information would normally be developed and presented by the product-planning agency.

TYPICAL CONTROL PLAN

Two of the participating companies have particularly interesting plans for control of their product lines. One of these companies, organized on a product-division basis, has established a nice balance between decentralization and over-all co-ordination of its product-determination activities, as follows:

Each product division, of which there are nearly a score, has its own product-engineering staff and carries proprietary responsibility for the determination of its own product line. Under the spur of accountability for conducting a profitable business, each division is continually active in reviewing its line, dropping unprofitable items, and developing profitable new or improved products. However, inasmuch as each division is held strictly accountable on a profit-and-loss basis, there is a tendency to "fight shy" of long-range developments which may be mostly outgo for the first few years. Then, too, certain product problems cut across divisional boundaries. The company has therefore set up two strong central staff departments to insure that these wider interests are properly served.

The technical aspects are handled by a central engineering and research staff with adequate laboratory facilities. This agency devotes itself to the more fundamental research problems, the development of new products not falling logically within the province of any one division, the co-ordination of projects involving several divisions, and the interdivisional standardization of practices, parts, and materials.

A new-products department examines major new-product proposals from a broad economic and market standpoint in order to determine whether they are in the company's interest and how to handle the manufacture and sale. It also undertakes the actual promotional work on any development which does not clearly fall within the province of a certain division or which some division is reluctant to undertake until it is a proved success. To this end, the staff department may secure a development appropriation, hire one of the product divisions to undertake the trial manufacture and sale of the new product or line on a service basis until it is proved out, and finally recommend its permanent assignment to one of the product divisions or to a new division created for the purpose.

In another company, whose organization structure follows a functional pattern, the procedure of product control is epitomized as follows:

All proposals relating to new products, regardless of source, are first submitted to the research and engineering division. This division considers the practicability of any such proposal and, if promising, its staff patent engineers explore the patentability of the proposed product. The division then consults with the sales department relative to such factors as market possibilities, volume, and price. Similarly, it consults with the manufacturing department as to feasibility from a production and cost point of view. Predicated on this collective opinion, the division then outlines the research, engineering, and development program. This program is next submitted by the director of engineering and research to the vice-presidents in charge of sales and manufacturing for their concurrence, and if of sufficient magnitude, to the president for final approval.

Each project is classified according to its degree of urgency. It is then planned, scheduled, and budgeted. Constant surveillance is exercised over each project program, both as to time and cost. Monthly progress is reported to those concerned on a standard form. After a project is once agreed upon and placed on the docket, the director of engineering and research has full responsibility and authority as to how far the project is to be carried.

When a project is completed, including its design, models, specifications, etc., the division prepares a complete report, setting forth the estimated cost, sales, price, and profit. If the new product is then approved by the heads of development, manufacturing, and sales (also by the president if necessary capital expenditure exceeds a maximum figure), it is released for production.

This company is one of the few having a positive and continuous plan of control over unwarranted diversification of its product line.

Its engineering and research division is charged with responsibility for systematically studying the simplification possibilities in its line, numbering thousands of products. The division regularly assembles and analyzes the following data on duplicative products:

Product numbers illustrated by catalogue cuts or photographs
Sales for past three years
Average sales
Rank of products in order of sales volume
Prices
Factory costs
Profit or loss per year by units and products

These data, along with recommendations for eliminating or redesigning products, are sent to the sales department, which assumes responsibility for the continuation of questionable items.

CONTROL OVER REPAIR AND REPLACEMENT PARTS

Somewhat related to the question of product simplification is the problem of producing repair and replacement parts for items no longer included in the regular line. This is a situation, obviously, which faces only certain industries such as those producing assembled products, silverware, chinaware, and similar goods.

Without question, a manufacturer of a machine or other piece of assembled equipment is obligated to provide repair and replacement parts for a period of time after the discontinuance or obsolescence of the particular product. But for how long a period is this an obligatory and profitable service? Within the limited scope of this study the actual practice ranges from practically no time to a period as long as any customer is able to keep the machine hanging together.

It would seem that this problem warrants more careful consideration than appears to have been given to it in many cases. Some companies have made a start by discontinuing the regular stocking of any repair or replacement part when the annual volume falls below one economic run per year. Thereafter any calls for the part are met by special manufacture. To handle such work they have established a machine shop separate from their regular manufacturing operations. In this shop they make use of their older mechanics who require light-duty assignments and whose knowledge of the old models is of particular value.

CONTROL OVER RESEARCH AND DEVELOPMENT

The exercise of proper control over the nature and extent of research effort and expenditure is often a perplexing problem. Some companies apparently make little effort at control. In effect, they acquire a competent technical organization, turn it loose, and hope for results that will be of justifying commercial advantage to the company. Other concerns strive for more positive control either through an annual budget or current approval of individual projects or both.

CONTROL THROUGH THE BUDGET

Among the participating companies which rely upon budgetary control over their research activities, the following features are of particular interest:

1. A budget estimate is prepared by the research director to cover all departmental expenditures for the ensuing year. This is usually broken down into specific major projects, routine service, and other activities.

2. Where practicable, allowance for service in behalf of specific departments is worked out with the heads of those departments upon whom falls the burden of justifying the required expenditures.

3. Budget estimates are subjected to critical review through the usual budgetary channels and finally approved. In this process, consideration is usually given to the justification of individual major projects, and to the comparison of total amounts with previous years, or as a ratio to expected sales.

4. One company, subject to severe cyclical swings, attempts to avoid disruption of its trained staff and long-term development program during slack times by an overriding research budget based on 2 percent of sales averaged over the past five years. During exceptionally good years a reserve is accumulated from which to draw when sales are below normal.

5. The research director is normally given some latitude in the diversion of funds from one undertaking to another as needs and prospects materialize during the course of the year, so long as he stays within his total appropriation. Projects not anticipated in the original budget are covered in supplementary authorizations through the same channels. In this connection, limitations imposed by his budget give the research director an excellent defense against unwarranted demands for technical service.

CONTROL BY INDIVIDUAL PROJECTS

Other companies place primary reliance upon the current review and approval of individual research projects, sometimes in connection with an annual research budget. The most effective practice along these lines embraces the following features:

1. Before any development project of appreciable extent is undertaken, an analysis is made to determine and, as far as practicable, to evaluate the objectives to be accomplished in terms of savings, sales and profit potentialities, probable effect upon demand for other products, and equally pertinent considerations.

2. A formal proposal, incorporating the results of this analysis and indicating the contemplated research program, schedule, and cost, is then drawn up. Emphasis is laid upon the importance of specifying whether the appropriation sought is expected to complete and conclude the project or is merely a "first payment."

3. In the case of product-research projects, approval often rests with a products committee, consisting of the top executives in charge of product development, sales, and manufacturing, respectively. In other cases, projects may follow the same course of approval as for capital expenditures, according to the amount involved.

4. In connection with more fundamental research, where results and costs cannot be so definitely anticipated, approval generally rests with general management based upon representations as to need, prospects, and value submitted by the research director.

5. Once approved, each project is closely followed as to performance and cost, and periodic reports are rendered to those interested.

6. Whenever, in the research director's judgment, developments indicate that further work is of questionable value, the project is suspended pending reappraisal by those concerned. Pe-

riodically the entire list of projects may be reviewed as to progress and prospects by the products committee or other authorizing agency as a basis for decision to continue, curtail, or suspend the work.

TYPICAL CONTROL PLANS

One company, having several hundred technicians on its research staff and with upwards of a thousand concurrent projects under way, has demonstrated that the techniques of management control can be applied with full effectiveness to research activities. The elements of this company's control are:

1. Proper organization of the entire staff with adequate administrative personnel and logical departmentalization of work and workers.
2. Manuals prescribing the functions, responsibilities, and procedure of each unit of the department and defining its relationship with other units.
3. An annual research budget.
4. Thorough analysis of each individual project before any work is undertaken, consideration being given to objectives and their commercial value, required work, time, and cost.
5. Final review of each project of appreciable size with approval by the research director, the heads of sales and manufacturing, and, if of sufficient importance, by the president.
6. Classification of each approved project by degree of importance: AAA projects are urgent and take precedence; AA and A projects rate as active and are given current status; those with B rating are moved into the A classification as circumstances warrant; the C group are "rainy-day" projects.
7. Assignment of a project number to each item that goes on the docket; all records and correspondence relating to any project bear the assigned number.
8. A planning of each project from the standpoint of what units of the department will be involved, what individuals in those units will be assigned, and for what period of time.
9. Time schedule covering every stage of the project, including those phases dependent upon other departments, such as procurement of needed materials through the purchasing department.
10. A posting of current progress and expenditures on a control

board which records all active projects and shows the status of each.

11. Weekly check as to progress and cost of each project by the research director in conjunction with the section head responsible.
12. Monthly report of all active projects to the president and the heads of manufacturing and sales departments.
13. Semiannual review of the entire docket by the heads of research, manufacturing, and sales, at which time projects that lack promise are dropped.
14. File of project folders containing for each project complete information as to the source of the project, reason for starting it, when it was authorized, and all other related information, thus providing a complete case history of each project for future reference.

A control such as the foregoing prevents any research activity from going very far astray. It likewise permits measurement of costs against results, precludes duplication of effort, and in this particular company relates to fundamental as well as applied research.

The company whose procedure is outlined above operates under the functional plan of organization. A somewhat different procedure of control is needed by companies which are organized on a product-division basis, and where research is carried on by each division in addition to that conducted by the central research department. All development effort must be co-ordinated in these instances; otherwise, some activities will be duplicated and others will be overlooked entirely.

Ordinarily the central unit concerns itself with problems common to several or all of the divisions. It conducts most of the fundamental or underlying research. Projects are undertaken for individual divisions if they so request. The divisional units confine their research activities to translating the more fundamental developments into practical application in their respective fields of operation. The divisional research departments report to their division chiefs but maintain close functional relationship with the central research department. In one company the personnel for the division groups is drawn from the central department. This enables the central staff to develop sources of good research talent and to train technicians in the most effective manner. The basis for a continuing and understanding relationship between central and divisional personnel is established.

In this same company all work is programmed on a project basis. For those originating in a division an appropriation request is submitted upon approval by the division manager. These requests go to the central research department and, if endorsed, are passed up to the agency which authorizes all appropriations. Over and above this project control is the annual budget. Each division through its manager submits its annual research budget. These go to the central research department where they are consolidated with that of the department to make one over-all research budget for the year. The total amount of the budget is not a fixed percentage of sales, although sales, profits, long-range programs, and similar factors are considered in granting the total annual appropriation.

CONTROL OVER EXTERNAL RELATIONS

All the preceding sections of this report have been concerned with internal relationships in the management of the various companies studied. This section touches briefly upon certain phases of company external relationships—those involving the general public, the industry, and government. Events of recent years have greatly accentuated the need for more than incidental attention of corporate management to these relationships.

PUBLIC RELATIONS

It is unfortunate that business in general delayed so long the public presentation of its case, collectively and individually. For years the public has heard only the misrepresentations, garbled half-truths, and big-business baiting of unscrupulous politicians, labor agitators, and those of similar stripe. Corporate management for the most part has been inarticulate. It has seemingly been reluctant, even unwilling, to tell anything to those outside the innermost circles. It has been unmindful of the natural curiosity of ordinary people about our great industrial enterprises. This interest, with rare exceptions, is healthy and is not prompted by ulterior motives. If sufficiently well informed, most people are inclined to think the best rather than the worst of business and its leaders. On the whole, the public is genuinely interested in the personalities that direct our large, successful corporations; it is impressed by the developments of industrial research; being American, it is success-minded.

One company, conscious of the soundness of telling its story, has had an established public-relations program for many years. Its attitude toward this activity is summarized in the following quotation:

Our public relations policy is simply the provision of means for the Company to make itself understood and the transmission of the opinion which the public holds, back to the management.

In its organization the Public Relations Department has provided the necessary machinery for such a contact with representatives of the press, who are afforded easy access to a responsible source of authentic information about the business. In this way the time of the Company officials, which would otherwise be taken up with matters of this sort, is conserved.

This Company believes that it is not sufficient for it to do an efficient job in designing, manufacturing, and distributing its products, and in other ways properly operating a business. It is equally important that the public be acquainted with the nature of the job we are doing. The character of a business is what that business actually is; its reputation is what people believe it to be. It is our aim to make these two as nearly as possible synonymous.

The Public Relations Department aims to give the facts about the business to anyone who has a right to know them. It recognizes that there is no short and easy route to the attainment of good will toward a business, i.e., to sound public relations. It knows there is no magic about it. In that spirit the Company has been telling its story since 1920 through all the legitimate channels which are available; and, if the reputation which the Company now enjoys is to be retained and is to be still further increased, we believe it probable that a like course of action will be followed in the future.

Sound public relations for any business begin, of course, with honest and efficient operating policies. If the internal situation is unsound, no amount of publicity can cover up that fact.

The key to sound public relations is an informed and satisfied personnel from president to sweeper—every employee a booster for the company. As with any such activity, however, there is need of some centralized responsibility and control if full advantage is to be taken of the opportunities in this field. Of the thirty-one companies studied, about half now have public-relations departments. In some of these all the top executives are expected to work closely with the public-relations agency. Company policies and activities are always considered from the point of view of public reaction before a final decision is taken. Company announcements, speeches of officers, refusals to make contributions, company representation at various functions, and even the personal outside activities of top executives are previewed by the public-relations department. In most instances the head of that department reports to a top-management level, either the president, a major vice-president, or a committee of top executives. In a few cases there is a public-relations staff organized as a division of the advertising department. In a few other instances, public relations is affiliated with industrial relations, both activities being headed up by the same individual.

INDUSTRY RELATIONS

While some difference in corporate practice naturally exists, the predominant policy of the companies studied is to participate actively in the affairs of industry, particularly their own industry. Through the medium of trade association memberships, most of the companies give positive endorsement to the collective study of common problems. Company representation through its top executives provides authoritative stimulus to association action.

Most companies, furthermore, encourage their executive and staff personnel to join professional societies or associations and to take a prominent part in the activities of such groups. A large proportion of these companies generously permit members of their organizations to present before meetings of professional societies the activities, practices, and procedures developed in their respective companies.

GOVERNMENT RELATIONS

Corporate relations with government may be classified as defensive, offensive, and co-operative. As such, they involve many individuals and departments of a company, and, except for general policy determination, are not amenable to centralization in any respect. Defensive activities might relate to tax refund cases and action on existing legislation. Among offensive activities may be mentioned sales to government departments and action regarding proposed legislation. Co-operative activities suggest such undertakings as government-sponsored standardization projects and preparedness programs. These few illustrative activities would involve various top executives, the legal department, the accounting department, and various technical departments.

Government relationships are so diverse that, beyond establishing a broad position, no individual or agency can practicably assume responsibility for them all, and in no company studied has any attempt yet been made to create a department of government relations.

CONTROL OVER FOREIGN OPERATIONS

While it is important in domestic operations to establish controls which permit delegation of authority to those directly responsible, this is of even greater significance in foreign operations.

Some companies which rely largely on personal approvals to control domestic matters have tried to extend the same treatment to foreign operations, with unfortunate results. The approval method has some chance to work domestically where the conditions and methods of operating are relatively uniform, where the factors of time and distance are short, and where the top executives are familiar with all the conditions involved. In foreign countries, however, there are all sorts of variations as to conditions, traditions, laws, methods of doing business, language, customs, currency, and, in fact, every type of circumstance. Not only do these variations exist between countries, but there are often marked local differences within a country. As a result the judgment of a responsible person on the ground is usually better than that of some head-office executive whose decisions are necessarily influenced by the procedure followed at home.

One participating company reports that during its early foreign ventures, executives together with the necessary staff assistants were sent out to establish the foreign operations. The practices followed were patterned after those at home, and had the unqualified approval of the head-office executives. Sizable losses continued, however, until a thorough investigation was made which showed not only that the small foreign operations were organized on the same elaborate scale as the huge domestic ones, but that the American methods used were not suitable in those countries. The American staffs were sent home and nationals engaged in their place. Methods used by competitors in those countries were adopted. The ventures have been most successful under these new conditions.

Another company engaged for many years in extensive foreign operations, states the case as follows:

We early became convinced that operations in numerous foreign countries could not be satisfactorily run from the United States. Local organizations are essential. To conduct the business in even one foreign country would require daily voluminous reports from someone in that country able to give adequate details of all changing conditions. This would require so much time as to make it most uneconomical.

As a consequence, the home office does not attempt to dictate the local operation of the foreign companies. Instead, qualified executives are picked and are given full responsibility. These executives are, of course, informed of any policy changes and adjust their own operations accordingly.

Foreign executives are expected to handle their own affairs in the light of local conditions. If these executives are unable to make sound decisions on their own, they are replaced by others who can and will do so.

ORGANIZATION ASPECTS

The foreign organization plan is largely influenced by the nature and extent of the foreign activities. In some companies this involves merely the sale of domestic-manufactured products through foreign agents or distributors. The organization in this case usually consists of an export department with a manager and staff of specialists and correspondents in the head office. In addition there is ordinarily a group of field representatives devoting most of their time to contacting local distributors in their respective foreign areas.

Where the volume of business is large or where direct company sales representation is used, sales organizations are established in the various foreign countries. A frequent plan of organization is to set up a subsidiary domestic corporation within which to centralize all foreign operations. Under this main subsidiary, local companies are organized in the different foreign countries where business is conducted and where laws and other reasons make such incorporation necessary.

Several of the participating companies carry on manufacturing as well as sales operations in foreign countries. Under these conditions the importance of organization is accentuated. Again the domestic subsidiary company is usually organized together with the necessary foreign subsidiaries. The more extensive operations have ordinarily been in Europe, and a common practice has been to set up a European subsidiary in full charge of all activities on that continent. Such subsidiaries have their own manufacturing, sales, finance, accounting, and other departments. Close functional relationships are maintained with the corresponding departments of the parent company, officers and department heads of the foreign subsidiary keeping abreast of latest developments by frequent trips to the United States. While the heads of these foreign subsidiaries operate with a large measure of independence, it is not uncommon to find the comptroller-treasurer of the subsidiary reporting directly to the parent company.

Primary responsibility for foreign operations almost always rests with a high official at company headquarters. This individual is commonly a vice-president of the parent company and is also the general manager of the domestic subsidiary through which the foreign operations are conducted. His immediate assistants are specialists on particular parts of the world in which the company operates. These assistants spend most of their time traveling and contacting the foreign organizations, taking to them new ideas, policies, methods, information, and bringing them generally up to date on what is new. They also check progress, conditions, and personnel and report back to the vice-president. Most of the companies engaged in foreign work find these personal contacts essential to good results.

Also at headquarters, reporting to the vice-president in charge, are various staff assistants. These include merchandising experts, foreign-advertising specialists, and the people handling documentation, price lists, codes and cables, statistics, paper routine, and similar functions.

Only in the case of extremely large operations are the treasurer, comptroller, and factory manager positions duplicated at the home-office of the foreign organization. The parent company's factory manager, treasurer, and comptroller, as well as the heads of other staff departments, have functional responsibility for their respective aspects of foreign operations. The vice-president, however, is fully responsible for the successful and satisfactory over-all operation of the foreign subsidiaries. The managing directors of the various foreign companies are directly responsible to him. Direct instructions, policy information, and other major matters are transmitted from the vice-president to the managing directors. Except for the comptroller-treasurer the other headquarters departments usually act in an advisory capacity, providing such help and information on their functions as is new or requested by the foreign companies. The maintenance of a separate corporation to handle foreign operations appears to help in preserving independence and freedom from too much domestic influence by these departments. Where foreign operations are carried on through an export department rather than through a separate corporation, it is not unusual to find communications from all headquarters departments to the foreign companies clearing through the export department.

PERSONNEL ASPECTS

The conduct of foreign operations, particularly if on a sizable scale, is characterized by the high caliber of personnel in charge both at home and abroad. The reasons are not hard to find. As mentioned previously, the very remoteness of operations necessitates the delegation of much authority and responsibility. Local conditions are peculiar and are changing frequently, thus making it difficult for a head-office executive to keep closely informed. Personal contacts with major executives are infrequent. No elaborate staff is available to give assistance. This means that the individual in foreign service is on his own and must make most of his own decisions. In the selection of the personnel for their foreign operations most companies are exceedingly cautious. A man's wife is subject to as careful scrutiny as the man himself. Training for foreign service is thorough and rigorous. Promotion to management positions is almost always up through the organization; foreign managers are seldom hired on the outside. In most of the participating companies, Americans are used only in the key positions, although nationals are often trained and take over the highest posts in time. Some of the companies require one top manager to be an American capable of taking over the entire company in case of war or other emergency which might involve nationals.

CONTROL ASPECTS

The mechanisms used to control foreign operations are practically the same as those used by many companies in the domestic field. Most emphasis is placed on results as reflected by profit-and-loss statements. Where there are separate subsidiaries with their individual accounting statements, this method is particularly effective. Those companies operating through agents record all sales and expenses by country. In addition, they check their own sales against total imports into the various countries. From the profit shown and from comparison with the total trend, any weak spots are detected. Traveling auditors and manufacturing and sales specialists check and report on conditions within their respective fields.

A few of the companies make use of budgetary control. Expenditures are estimated for a year in advance, and quarterly revisions of a more accurate nature are made. Such items as salary increases, donations, advertising, entertainment expenses, and the like, together with the other usual expense items, are anticipated and included in the budget. A close estimate of sales by class and size of product is an important factor in many companies because the goods must be manufactured in the United States well in advance of the date required in the foreign market. Some companies follow the policy of fabricating abroad all parts which can be produced economically and supplying the remainder from domestic plants. Good estimates are required to co-ordinate production of the complete product. The sales estimates are based on economic analyses of conditions within the various foreign countries. Full information and statistics upon which they are based are usually checked at headquarters to confirm the interpretations of the management of the foreign companies.

The extent of authority granted foreign managers is somewhat wider than that enjoyed by a corresponding individual at home. The intent seems to be to establish these limits on a normal operating basis for the prevailing conditions. Accordingly there are different limits assigned to the managers in different countries according to the size of their operations. Any large or unusual item is usually cleared in advance, except in case of emergency, when it is reported afterward. Changes in basic policy, any large capital expenditure, or any major change in organization or operations require head-office approval. Appointments or promotions to key positions likewise require the prior concurrence of the vice-president in charge of foreign operations. All other personnel matters are usually handled locally. One company reports that it allows its foreign managers full authority on salary increases up to $3,500 a year; in another the limit is $1,300. Establishment of selling prices is usually left to the local foreign management, although some companies with world-wide distribution control the prices from the head office.

CONTROL OVER DEMANDS UPON
EXECUTIVE TIME

How to relieve major executives of the many unwarranted demands upon their time and attention, leaving them free to concentrate upon the more important matters which they alone can appropriately handle, is a problem of real consequence to management. As indicated elsewhere, the most effective means to this end are (*a*) a sound plan of organization with the functions, objectives, relationships, and limits of authority clearly established for each agency and each key job, and (*b*) well-designed systems of control over the various activities that need it, permitting the effective delegation and decentralization of responsibility and authority.

Many executives, however, and particularly those who have risen through successive steps in the same division, find it difficult to divorce themselves from the problems and detail of their former positions; or their subordinates have not been developed or encouraged to assume their full responsibilities and to bring to their principal's attention only major matters, presented in well-considered and crystallized form; or through lack of more appropriate means of control, reliance is still placed upon personal approval of every move before it is made. Again, it is often found that field executives, functionally responsible to a number of staff or product-division managers in the home office, are so deluged with inquiries and requests through these functional channels as to interfere seriously with the proper discharge of their primary functions.

All of these conditions tend to burden executives with matters that never need concern them and hence prevent full concentration of time and effort on the major problems and objectives of the business. While a clean-cut plan of organization will go a long way toward minimizing such tendencies—particularly if it is developed in close collaboration with the executives concerned and has their full understanding and support—there is always need of a periodic check to see how well the plan as prescribed in the organization manual is working out in practice.

ANALYSIS OF EXECUTIVE ACTIVITIES

In this latter connection, one of the best practical tests of organization effectiveness is through analysis of the demands upon executive time and attention—in effect a time study of each executive's working day. While this means of control is used by only a few of the participating companies, it would seem to warrant more extensive application because of its simplicity and effectiveness. It would normally fall within the province of an organization agency to make the necessary analyses, and because of the personal aspects of the assignment, the whole approach should be one of *assisting* each executive, preferably at his invitation, to free himself from unnecessary burden and detail, rather than publicizing or reflecting in any way upon his personal methods of management.

A program for the periodic (perhaps annual) review of organization practice and effectiveness along these lines might properly involve the following steps:

Board of Directors

1. Through review of minutes, agenda, reports and proposals, and possibly attendance at a meeting or two, make an inventory of all matters considered by the board over a representative period, noting action taken in each case.

2. Analyze and classify each item as to whether its consideration by the board appears to have been necessary or appropriate within the scope of the trusteeship function as defined and delimited by the board, or whether it could appropriately have been taken care of at a lower level, under policies established and powers delegated by the board.

3. Make a report to the board chairman, presenting the results of this analysis, and suggesting the need of any further delegation, policy clarification, or other change to facilitate or increase the effectiveness of board functioning from an organization standpoint.

General Management

1. Make a similar review, inventory, and analysis of all matters considered by general management over a representative pe-

riod (possibly a week)—both by the general council, if any, and by the general executives individually—taking into account personal contacts, telephone calls, reports, and correspondence, and considering the adequacy of presentation and the action taken in each case.

2. Make a report to the council chairman in regard to the council, and to each general executive in regard to his own activities. Such reports should point out matters which could appropriately be handled by divisional management under existing or needed policies and authorities, specifying the suggested disposition in each case. They should also call attention to the need for better preanalysis and clarification in presenting matters for decision, and should recommend any other changes needed to facilitate the functioning of general management.

Divisional Management

Make similar analyses of the demands upon the time and attention of divisional and field executives.

Committees

Through attendance at meetings and a study of the matters considered, perform the same service for each major committee, giving thought in each case to its necessity, setup, and effectiveness from an organization standpoint.

SUPPLEMENTARY DEVICES FOR CONSERVING TIME

Other devices found in some of the participating companies for lightening the burden upon major executives, include the following:

1. The use of high-caliber personal assistants to the major executives who handle much of the detail that would otherwise burden their principal's attention. These assistants, who are usually not in direct line of authority, digest proposals to facilitate final consideration and action, interview callers, coordinate matters between subdepartments, and otherwise conserve the time of their principals. In one large company each of the five general executives has such an assistant, whose caliber might be indicated from the fact that the positions are rated on a parity with such jobs as works manager, traffic manager, credit manager, and chief engineer. Such an arrangement does not interfere with the direct contact between

major executives and their line subordinates when matters of justifying importance are involved.

2. The effective use of a capable staff organization to analyze, digest, and make recommendations to facilitate executive action on proposals submitted.

3. Limitation of the number of subordinates reporting directly to any one executive.

4. Physical separation of the offices of major executives and their subordinates, usually on different floors. At the same time, it is generally insisted that, as far as possible, the latter confine their contacts to a minimum number (say not over one a day) and then take up only worthy matters in well-crystallized form, instead of "running into the chief's office with every problem or thought as it occurs."

5. Insistence that all but emergency matters be submitted to principals in written form; "the urgency of many situations and the importance of many ideas fade in the process of putting them down in black and white."

6. The endeavor of one company to govern the allotment of executive responsibility so that each executive will have at least one-third of his time available for personal supervision in the field, another third for constructive thinking, planning, and betterment, and not over one-third required for administrative routine.

7. Reduction of the time and attention of field managers consumed by the deluge of literature, correspondence, requests for information, surveys, and similar demands emanating from home-office departments. Some companies clear all such material and requests through a central agency whose function is to question its value and necessity, suggest easier ways to develop needed information, and finally pass upon each case, bringing any controversial items to higher authority for decision.

Obviously too many limitations or interpositions between an executive and his immediate subordinates will destroy those personal relationships for which there is no substitute in successful business management. A working arrangement can be developed which will preserve the natural contacts without wasting the time of either executive or subordinate. The president of one company classifies into three categories the decisions or actions involving a subordinate in his relationship to his superior:

a) Those which are clearly within the province of company policy, where the subordinate knows exactly the viewpoint of his superior—such decisions are made without reference to or consultation with his superior.

b) Those having the characteristics of the first but which involve considerable importance—these decisions are made but the superior is fully advised so that he will be familiar with the action taken if any reference is made to it subsequently.

c) Those which involve considerations outside present interpretation of policy or are of major importance—these decisions rest upon advance consultation with the superior.

CONTROL OF OVER-ALL PERFORMANCE

One of the principal purposes in freeing executives of detail is to permit them to concentrate major attention on performance of the company as a whole. This function involves the co-ordination of all parts of the organization, and direction of their activities toward attainment of the over-all results desired. As in the case of the individual control procedures, the first step must be the determination of the task to be done—the planning of objectives.

First, there is the broad general objective for the company as a whole. It is in terms of this objective that the general effectiveness of the organization is measured. It is usually established by the board of directors, through approval of the objective proposed either by general management or originated by the board itself. Such an objective is ordinarily expressed in terms of profit for the year, based on a certain volume at an estimated cost and selling price. It is usually stated by months or quarters, in order to provide a basis for progressive following of results. There may also be other auxiliary objectives, such as a decrease in the accident rate, or improvement in the cash position. Actual accomplishment compared with these objectives is the measure of over-all performance.

The establishment of the objective is an important consideration. Since the organization is to be held for its accomplishment, it must be reasonably attainable. All conditions having a bearing on the outcome, such as the sales outlook, forecast of general business conditions, cost trends, labor conditions, and industry developments must be taken into consideration. The test of the objective is to determine what the accomplishment has been in the past; what the present rate is; what accomplishment is desired; and then to judge whether the desired improvement is reasonable to expect.

In some companies a single, dominant individual sets the objectives and looks to general management to meet them. He stands by, criticizing, suggesting, investigating, approving, and driving to obtain the results desired. In other companies the objectives for the year are worked out within the organization, reviewed by general management, and passed to the board as a commitment for the organization. The board examines the general objective, determines whether it is satisfactory, calls for any adjustments thought necessary, and finally accepts it as the goal for the organization.

It is not enough to establish the general objective. As a matter of fact, that concerns mostly the first and second zones of management. To be really successful the co-operation of every person in the organization is needed. The general objective must therefore be translated into terms of each and every department. For example, the sales department's objective may be to sell a given volume at a price, and with a certain expense; that of the manufacturing department may be to produce the quantity and quality desired, at a given time and cost. These departmental objectives may in turn be broken down to divisions, locations, and individuals. The final test is to have every single person with his own particular objective, all being co-ordinated to produce successive cumulative results leading to the general objective for the company as a whole.

As a practical matter, the preplanning of objectives must necessarily include the changes, the costs, and all other factors involved in attaining them. The result must be matched and weighed against the costs of attainment in order to judge its merit. A complete and comprehensive plan is therefore the very essence of establishing objectives. Such a plan likewise provides the gauge against which to measure performance.

This process is not one of accounting analysis whereby probable expenses are matched against those of last year. It is a well-rounded plan. It is the responsibility of the executives in charge to consider all improvements to be made during the year and preplan the action which will bring them about. Aside from affording a preview of annual results from a dollar-and-cents standpoint, it permits shaping action in advance to meet impending situations instead of meeting them unprepared on short notice.

BUDGETARY CONTROL

One of the methods for preplanning and co-ordinating the activities of the organization is through a system of budgetary control. This system provides a way for preplanning all operations for various periods in advance and for committing the various departments and divisions of the business to a well-considered performance estimate. It also supplies the means for checking results, uncovering weaknesses, and making corrections before it is too late.

Further than that, it provides an effective means by which top management, particularly the board of directors and general management, may delegate authority to divisional and departmental executives without sacrificing over-all control. After having considered and satisfied themselves as to the preplanned objectives and requisite conditions and expenditures upon which they are based, such as payroll, salary increases, repairs, new facilities, advertising, and similar factors, the two top levels of management need be concerned only with watching performance against objectives, delegating to divisional and departmental management the final review and approval of individual items and expenditures within the blanket authorization. However, it is usually necessary to obtain specific approval, as a budget addition, of any item of consequence not provided for in planning the budget.

Each unit and section of the company has its own budget, and in some companies certain individuals, such as salesmen, have a budget. The person responsible for each budget figures his own objectives, costs, and other criteria of performance, follows up to see where and why he failed of accomplishment, and takes steps to correct the weakness. The person who approves each budget also makes a careful check of actual results against the budget estimates and requests explanation of any unsatisfactory item.

Of the thirty-one companies studied, sixteen use budgetary control in some form. Some have comprehensive systems covering all operations and all units of the company. Others limit this form of control to one or more departments, and have no over-all system for the company as a whole. Some of the companies not now using the system have tried it in some departments and discarded it, either because they felt it was not accomplishing its purpose, or because it lacked sufficient flexibility to permit changes in the plan commensurate with business activity. In the latter case the system was based on an estimated sales volume, and when anything happened to the sales estimate the whole plan had to be recalculated. This being such a task, the plan was discontinued and some other form of over-all control adopted. Otherwise it appears that the dissatisfaction was due to faulty application rather than to any shortcoming of the system itself.

Among the budgetary-control plans observed, those which work best and which are truly effective devices of management have several outstanding characteristics.

First, they receive the wholehearted support of the top executives, who insist that the budgets be well prepared and as accurate as possible, constituting a soundly planned, well-considered program, to which those who prepare them are committed and held accountable.

Second, a central staff agency, such as a budget department or bureau having well-qualified personnel, devotes its time to following the budgets for the top executives. This agency analyzes costs, expenses, and results, compares them with other periods and other divisions, and establishes the reasonableness of the budgets submitted. It also co-ordinates the departmental budgets into company-wide figures with summaries for such items as research, donations, salary increases, manpower, and payroll, and points out the salient features to general management. It likewise checks to see that the results of more economical methods and processes are reflected in the budgets. This check offsets the tendency of those preparing the budgets to leave themselves plenty of latitude in order to be sure of meeting the estimate. The budgets are improved in accuracy and effectiveness to the extent that costs are based upon thorough analyses of all activities and that adequate standards are established to cover necessary functions.

Third, it is considered important to secure the maximum possible participation of the organization in both the preparation of the budgets and in following progress. For example, the department managers in some companies prepare the budgets and commit their departments to certain performance. A more effective plan appears to be that followed in other concerns where, for example, each individual salesman makes a budget of his year's expected results as to units, dollar volume, and expense. These budgets, which are reviewed with the branch manager in detail, indicate specifically what accounts are to be added, which ones might be lost, and to what accomplishment the salesman will actually commit himself. From these reports the branch managers prepare and submit their budgets to the district manager, who in turn analyzes, criticizes, and finally approves them as commitments of the branch managers. The district manager in turn prepares a district budget, and so on up the line. By this process each person commits himself to a definite accomplishment, against which he is checked and can check himself. The results are usually impressive.

Fourth, the system must be flexible to accommodate unavoidable fluctuations in business volume. One of the common objections to the budgetary-control plan is that it is predicated on a sales estimate, and if anything happens to alter the estimate (and something usually does) it is a long, difficult task to recalculate the budget on the revised basis. To get around this, the flexible budget has been introduced. Under this plan there is a sliding scale at intervals of, say, 10 percent. In other words, there is a series of budgets covering expenses and results at varying rates of activity. Under this plan the budget comparison is not made until the period's activity has been determined. When this is known, the budget for that rate is compared with the actual results to determine the effectiveness of management. The flexible idea applies particularly to departments, such as manufacturing, where there is a direct relationship between production rate and cost. In many departments much of the operating cost does not change materially, regardless of the change in rate of operation. As a result some companies have a separate budget which covers such departments, while the regular operating budget covers only those departments where a flexible budget is practicable.

There are many variations in the mechanics by which the different companies accomplish their budgetary-control plans. The important thing about them all, however, is that clear thinking, analysis of operations, and planning for the future are stimulated throughout the organization; every part of the company is committed to a particular accomplishment, which adds definiteness and purpose to the efforts of management.

FIVE-YEAR PLAN

One of the companies has what it terms a "five-year plan" to supplement its budgetary-control plan. Each supervisor and manager is expected to lay out a five-year program of development and improvement for the operations under his jurisdiction. These plans are definite for a year ahead, and necessarily somewhat less definite for the longer outlook. The programs and objectives are carefully thought out and reduced to writing. They cover all contemplated betterments or changes in the balance sheet and income statement; the outlook for such matters as sales volume, price situation, cost reduction; improvement in facilities, processes, and methods; improvement in product and quality; development of new products; improvement in personnel and training. These long-range programs are carefully reviewed in departmental meetings, and finally each manager presents and explains his program and objectives for five years ahead in a meeting attended by general management and all department and division managers.

This affords an excellent opportunity to acquaint top management with developments under way and in prospect, adds perspective to the definite one-year program, stimulates and coordinates constructive long-term planning, and discloses which managers are really contributing to the enterprise. Control over the current year's operation is effected through the annual budget. The long-term objectives serve only as a general guide. Once a year each executive reappraises his projected program in the light of existing conditions and submits a revised plan for the next five years. Any departures from the previous objectives are explained and justified.

This method of planning applies also to such things as the cash position, retirement of bond issues and other financing, handling of reserves, plant expansion, modernization, and the like.

PROFIT-AND-LOSS CONTROL

Under this system of general control, each operating department, plant, or unit is held rigidly accountable on a profit-and-loss basis. The common objective for the company as a whole is to operate at a profit. What then could be a sounder objective or a better measure for departmental effectiveness than the profit-and-loss showing of each?

Some fifteen of the thirty-one companies reviewed have systems of this kind. One of these, as a typical example, holds each operating department for results on a monthly profit-and-loss basis. Approximately two weeks after the close of the month, statements showing income by sources and detailed cost and expense items, total costs, gross profit, and net profit are available to the managers concerned. Often these statements are prepared by the manager's own local accounting department, in which event the manager sends in an analysis to the head office along with the statements, explaining each unsatisfactory item and indicating what has been done in correction.

Usually under this system the manager is endowed with a proprietary responsibility to run his unit in a way to make it profitable. He also has considerable authority in the ordinary matters of operation within the limits of the company's general policies, which he must know and understand. For instance, he can add all the people he wants to his payroll, but he knows they must earn their way and that he must be able to justify their addition in terms of profit and loss.

As a rule the purely staff and service departments do not have a profit-and-loss statement. They are usually provided with monthly statements of expense, which are carefully checked against the budgets covering such expense items, but their cost is included as overhead or administrative expense.

In some of the companies both budgetary control and profit-and-loss control are used. These systems actually complement each other and, taken together, make a very effective plan of control. The budgetary control then becomes the forecast or objective, and the profit-and-loss statements are compared with the estimates to determine actual accomplishments. The profit-and-loss control appears to be particularly effective in measuring the performance of entire companies or fully integrated portions thereof, such as product divisions, regional divisions, or subsidiaries, each responsible for its own production and marketing operations.

A number of the companies with purely functional organizations are also using this system. In such cases it meets with some difficulties in determining the "income" or "sales" between departments. For example, the manufacturing department turns the product over to the sales department. At what price should the transfer be made? If the cost price is used, the manufacturing department always breaks even and has no profit. This problem is usually handled by having some executive establish the transfer prices, usually based on what an equivalent product is quoted in the market. It appears that there is considerable discussion between departments concerning such transfer prices, and this is one of the most unsatisfactory features of the plan when applied to the functional type of organization.

There is a further complication in that this system creates interdepartmental profits all along the line. If the profit for each of the departments were added, it would far exceed the total company profit. Accordingly reserves are used to cover the internal profits and eliminate them from the total.

One company organized on a product basis, breaks down its profit-and-loss statements to type of product, so that the company can tell which of the products are making or losing money. Another company, organized on a regional basis, makes an annual profit-and-loss analysis for each plant by products in order to determine any weaknesses in the product line or the costs. In still other companies, profit-and-loss statements are prepared only at six-month intervals as a check on the effectiveness of the departments from an over-all standpoint.

It is usual to expect an operating department to cover its direct expenses and a portion of the general overhead and to show a profit in addition. Where there are many prorates, such as research or administrative expense, managers are inclined to eliminate them in calculating their own performance. In other words, they want to be charged only with those costs and expenses for which they are directly responsible, and which they themseslves can reasonably control.

PART D

BOARD OF DIRECTORS

FUNCTIONS OF THE BOARD

COMPOSITION OF THE BOARD

ORGANIZATION OF THE BOARD

PROCEDURE OF THE BOARD

REPORTS TO THE BOARD

PART D

BOARD OF DIRECTORS

The place of the board of directors in the functioning of top management is broadly discussed in Part B, Section 1. Much additional and pertinent information on boards of directors was gathered during the course of this project and, because of the interest manifested by many executives, is herewith presented under the following outline:

1. Functions of the Board
      Twenty-two major responsibilities
      Job specifications used by one company
2. Composition of the Board
      Considerations of size
      Management representation
            Executive or officer boards
            Officers on board
      Outside representation
            Professional directors
            Public and employee representation
      Election of directors
      Term directors
3. Organization of the Board
      Officers
      Duties of top officers
      Board committees
      Executives responsible to board
4. Procedure of the Board
      Meetings
      Agenda
      Conduct
      Executives appearing before board
      Fees and expenses
5. Reports to the Board
      General practice
      Outlines of two examples

1. FUNCTIONS OF THE BOARD

The powers and duties of boards of directors are set forth in rather broad and inclusive fashion in the by-laws of most companies. Stipulations as carried by by-laws run from a simple fifteen- or twenty-word statement to a substantially more extensive delineation of the board's functions.

Functions ordinarily exercised by the board (whether or not covered in the by-laws) include action regarding:

Basic Policies and Objectives.—Without exception the board of directors determines the basic policies and general objectives of the enterprise. Formulation and recommendation of policies frequently originate with management, but final determination and approval rest in the board of directors. Typical illustrations of such policy determination are:

Major changes in line of products
Major changes in method of distribution
Major changes in basic price structure
Establishment of employee benefit plans

Company Performance.—A prime function of all boards is the over-all appraisal of progress made and results secured by management, preferably through comparison with established yardsticks and objectives. (See also Item 5, Reports to the Board, page 235.)

Organization Structure of Company.—Determination of the basic organization structure and major changes thereof predominantly reside in the board of directors, although in one-fifth of the companies this function is exercised by management. In one instance the management on its own authority has recently changed the basic organization structure from a functional to a product basis.

Selection of Corporate Officers.—The selection and removal of corporate officers in every instance is the function of the board of directors. The board also exercises the authority in most companies to define the duties of all corporate officers, including assistant secretaries and assistant treasurers. Frequently the by-laws set forth in varying degrees of specificity the duties of such officers as chairman, vice-chairman, president, vice-president, treasurer and assistant treasurer, secretary and assistant secretary, and comptroller or auditor. All other executives are usually appointed by management, although in a few instances the board exercises the right of approval of major executive selection. In one company the board approves such appointments down to a salary level of $7,500 per year, which includes department managers and assistant managers.

Professional Services.—Practice varies considerably with respect to the engaging of professional services, although a rather general pattern of action is evident. For instance, in two-thirds of the companies independent auditors are appointed by the board, not an unusual practice being to delegate this duty to a nonofficer committee of the board. In six cases selection of independent auditors is a prerogative of the stockholders, and in less than 10 percent of the companies covered is the choice of independent auditors officially delegated to the general management. In two-thirds of the companies the management exercises the authority for engaging outside engineering, legal, and advertising services. However, certain exceptions to this general practice are found even among these companies, e.g., if an extensive management survey were to be conducted, or if the expense of the professional service were to exceed $50,000, then board approval is obtained. This is largely because of the size of the expenditure, as well as the nature of the service.

External Relationships.—There is virtually an equally divided viewpoint regarding the handling of relationships with government, the industry, and the general public. In half of the companies the determination of company position relating to this field is regarded as a board function, while in the other half the management has full authority to act, with no restriction beyond reporting to the board what action has been taken. In one instance responsibility for policies guiding external relationships is divided: those with governmental agencies requiring board approval, whereas those dealing with the industry and the public rest with the management.

Financial Structure of Company.—It is the invariable practice of all companies that any change in the financial structure of the enterprise be authorized by the board and approved by the stockholders.

Corporate Income.—The management of the corporate income, as regards surplus and dividend action, is distinctly a board function in every company.

Expansion and Rehabilitation.—Authorization, financially and otherwise, for any major plant expansion or rehabilitation is another function exclusively residing with the board in all companies. To relieve the board of detail, generally speaking, only appropriations of $25,000 or more require board action. However, two companies follow the practice of requiring board approval to all expenditures over $500 where the equity of the stockholders is involved.

Working Capital.—The determination of the amount and sources of working capital is a board function in approximately one-half of the companies and a management function in the remainder. There are by-law provisions in several cases which stipulate this action as a board function. In one instance a by-law provision even specifies the actual amount of money to be reserved as working capital.

Subsidiaries and Affiliates.—In only one-fourth of the companies are financial relationships with subsidiary or affiliated companies a matter for board consideration. Where the management has authority for this function, a few companies state that the board sets limits for loans or credits within which management has complete freedom of action. The designation of the officer or officers who shall vote the stock of subsidiaries or affiliates owned by the parent company is customarily a board function. Similarly, the board of the parent company selects the officers who are to hold directorships in partially or wholly owned subsidiaries as representatives of the parent company.

Depositaries.—The board, in most instances, selects the banks, trust companies, or other depositaries of the company's funds. This frequently is provided for in the by-laws.

Employee Benefit Plans.—Introduction or modification of such benefit plans as pensions, which ordinarily involve substantial financial commitments, require board action in all instances. In one-third of the companies stockholder approval is also required.

Salaries.—The board, whether through by-law provision or by its own action, fixes the compensation of corporate officers. Similarly, extra or incentive compensation for officers and other executives generally is a board determination.

Salaries for executives other than officers are customarily left to general management. However, in several companies the board, usually acting through a committee, approves all salaries above a certain amount, varying from $3,600 to $20,000 per year. In one company the board must pass on all salaries over $5,000 and, in addition, must approve any change in the basic salary scale by which all positions rated less than $5,000 per year are evaluated and classified.

Size of the Board.—The by-laws of a majority of companies fix the number of directors. But in an appreciable number of cases the by-law provision is flexible, stipulating an upper and lower limit to the size of the board. Where a flexible provision exists, the directors usually submit to a vote of the stockholders any change in the size of the board within the limits specified.

Vacancies in the Board.—The uniform practice followed is for the directors to fill all vacancies in board membership caused by resignation, disqualification, or other cause. A director thus chosen serves only until the next annual meeting of the stockholders, at which time he must stand for election along with all other directors.

The practice of filling a vacancy varies in those companies having term directors. In certain instances the board fills the vacancy only until the next annual stockholders' meeting—whereas, in other cases the board fills the vacancy for the entire unexpired term of the particular directorship.

Organization of the Board.—Unless otherwise provided in the by-laws, the board chooses its own presiding officer and any other officers, such as vice-chairman and secretary. In addition to such committees as may be stipulated in the by-laws, the board at its discretion establishes other committees and chooses the personnel thereof. (See also Item 3, Organization of the Board, page 227.)

Amendment of By-Laws.—Additions to or amendments of the by-laws are generally initiated by the board of directors, though in most instances such amendments must be approved by the stockholders. Occasionally a provision appears in by-laws authorizing the directors to amend the by-laws without reference to the stockholders.

Stock Certificates.—The board approves the form of the stock certificates. The board also must be satisfied and grant approval for the replacement or reissue of certificates lost, destroyed, or mutilated.

Stock Transfer and Registration.—The board is charged

with the responsibility of establishing rules and regulations for the issue, transfer, and registration of stock certificates.

Appointment of transfer agents and registrars of transfer is also a regular function of the board. In like manner, the closing of transfer books and the period of closing is a board responsibility frequently provided for in the by-laws.

Annual Report to Stockholders.—A further duty or responsibility of the board, one occasionally mentioned in the by-laws, is the rendering of an annual report to the stockholders showing the condition of the company's property, business, and finances for the fiscal year. This report is generally first presented at the annual meeting of the stockholders.

Clarification of Board Functions.—It would appear eminently desirable in any company to define clearly and specifically the functions, responsibilities, and limits of authority which are to be reserved to the board and those that are to be delegated to general management, in order that directors and executives may have a clear conception of their respective parts in the whole scheme of management. This clarification can appropriately be provided for in the organization manual if it is considered impracticable to expand the by-laws sufficiently for such purpose. One company has thus defined its board functions in its organization manual as follows:

MATTERS REQUIRING ACTION BY THE BOARD OF DIRECTORS

All matters involving major transactions or policies require action by the Board of Directors. This instruction specifies those matters, on which action of the Board of Directors is required, which occur most frequently in the regular course of business. Executive and administrative officers shall refer such additional items to the Board, as in their judgment require its action.

General

Definite commitments in respect to matters on which action of the Board is required shall not be made prior to such action except on the approval of the President or his delegate.

Items to be included in the agenda of a meeting of the Board shall be submitted to the Secretary not later than the fourth working day prior to the meeting.

The Secretary shall give appropriate notification of action taken by the Board to those interested or involved.

The Comptroller shall show reference to action taken by the Board on all financial and accounting transactions in connection with which action of the Board is required.

Specific Items Requiring Board Action

Specific action is required in respect to the matters listed below, unless otherwise specified in footnotes as having been covered by blanket action or by delegation to officers.

a) Employees

    Employment at rates in excess of $——— per annum.

    Specific cases of recommended changes in rates of pay when present or proposed rates are in excess of $——— per annum.

    All extra compensations.

    Retention in service of employees who are 65 years of age or over, submitted annually.

    Changes in employees' pensions and other benefit plans.

b) Organization

    Election of officers of the Company.

    Appointment of members of the Executive Committee and other committees.

c) Operations

    Qualification or withdrawal of the Company as a foreign corporation in any state, territory, or country.

    Plant acquirements and disposals (routines therefor shall be specified in general accounting directions).

    Annual budget of the Company's operations.

    Development expenditures (routines therefor shall be specified in general accounting directions).

d) Purchase or Sales

    Purchase or sale of a going business.

    Purchase or sale of patents when amount involved exceeds $———.*

    Purchase or sale of securities and subscriptions thereto.*

    Purchase or sale of Company's own stock or bonds.*

e) Borrowing and Loans

    Issue of bonds.

    Issue, discount, and renewals of notes . . . .

    Loan of Company funds.*

* The General Accounting Direction covering "Approvals Required on Payments . . . ." indicates the items on which the Board of Directors has taken blanket action or has delegated approval or authority to officers of the Company in respect to payments involved under these matters.

Advances to other companies.

Mortgages of lands, buildings, or other assets of the Company.

f) Payments

All dividends.

All payments to the Trustee of Company's Pension Fund.*

All contributions.

g) Contracts and Leases

Contracts, other than routine contracts entered into in the ordinary course of business.

Contracts or agreements involving the acquisition or grant by the Company of a license under patents where the amount of royalties or other money payments under such license exceeds $——— over the term of the license.

Leases of premises where the rental for the full term of the lease exceeds $——— or the rental for a period of one year or less exceeds $———.

h) Legal

Change of location of principal place of business in any state when Board action is deemed necessary by the Legal Department.

Designation of agents to accept service of process.

Execution of surety bonds and guaranties, other than those required in the ordinary business of the Company.

i) Profits and Reserves

Accounting transactions involving Undivided Profits or Surplus except routine closing of Profit and Loss and Undivided Profits Accounts.

j) Reports to Stockholders

Reports to stockholders.

k) Depositories

Designation of depositories for Company's funds and securities.

2. COMPOSITION OF THE BOARD

The membership of the board of directors is governed by two considerations—essential representation and workable size. There are three points of view which generally are represented; those of management, ownership, and qualified outside business experience. The extent to which these viewpoints are found desirable establishes the minimum size of the board. The upper limit on size is determined by practicable consideration of workability. The board is a committee and as such its effectiveness has some relationship to size. The general consensus favors small boards. In large boards protection against ponderous or perfunctory action frequently is provided by means of an executive committee.

Among the participating companies the board size ranges from seven to thirty-six; the most common size is fifteen and the average size is thirteen. The latter figure checks closely with another study made recently by the authors covering the size and composition of the boards of several hundred of the largest industrial, utility, and distribution enterprises in the United States.

The by-laws of approximately two-thirds of the companies specify or fix the size of the board. In the remaining companies the by-laws have a provision stipulating that the board may have any number of members between a minimum and maximum figure, in which case the stockholders generally determine annually the number of directors for the ensuing year. This flexible provision has the advantage of facilitating changes in the size of the board whenever such action seems desirable.

From the standpoint of representation, practice varies widely among the thirty-one companies included in this study. An analysis of their boards, however, reveals the following proportionate representation:

Active officers .... 42 percent
Former officers .... 7 percent
Ownership (substantial) .... 19 percent
Outsiders .... 32 percent

Management, former and present, constitutes about one-half of the membership of this average board. Perhaps it can be generalized that those who are at present or recently have been engaged in the active management of an enterprise carry predominant representation on the board of directors.

Management Representation

Executive or Officer Boards.—The extent of management representation in the thirty-one companies studied ranges from a single active executive on the board to 100 percent of board membership, i.e., to a board composed solely of salaried officers devoting full time to a company and its subsidiaries. Only a few of the participating companies had executives or officer boards. **The** advantages and disadvantages inherent in this type of board are:

Advantages

1. Generally all key executives are on the board, and hence **all** important functions are represented when basic policies and problems need solution.

2. Matters requiring board consideration receive quick action (for mixed or representative boards the executive committee is the agency which fulfills this requirement).

3. Special or emergency board meetings can be held with greater facility.

4. More frequent board meetings are practicable, with the result that board consideration and deliberation is being given constantly to company affairs.

5. The managing board is a recognition of the undesirability of occasional rubber stamp or *pro forma* action of board members representing an outside point of view.

Disadvantages

1. It is difficult to maintain a sufficiently clear distinction between the needs and essential viewpoints of the three fundamental elements of top management—trusteeship of stockholders' interests, general management of the business, and divisional management.

2. The interests of ownership, theoretically at least, are not given adequate protection.

3. The board, in effect, merely endorses the action of the board members themselves in their capacity as executives.

4. Members of the board occupy a somewhat anomalous position in that, as vice-presidents and other officers, they are subordinate to the president, but as directors they are, as a group, his superior; in one position they report to him, whereas, in another, theoretically, he reports to them.

5. One of two results might obtain: either top management may operate, virtually, by committee action, or the president may dominate and run a one-man show.

6. If the company rigidly enforces its retirement policy, it cannot retain valuable former or retired officers in an advisory or consultative capacity by inviting them to serve as directors.

7. The board lacks an outside point of view in the consideration of its problems.

8. The board may be composed of a group of highly specialized or functionalized executives with little background in general business administration, i.e., the board may consist of good specialists, but not of individuals possessing all-round business experience and judgment.

Executives of companies operating under the mixed or representative type of board were asked their opinion concerning the managing type of board. Their viewpoints, as the following examples indicate, range from emphatic endorsement to equally emphatic disapproval.

Favorable

1. Feasible and entirely practicable
2. Emphatically desirable; would like to change to the management type

Unfavorable

1. Neither desirable nor feasible
2. Lacks balance in every direction
3. Lacks proper perspective
4. Lacks objectivity of viewpoint
5. Provides no check on management
6. Gives large shareholders no voice
7. Company has full-time service and thoughts of officers anyway
8. Outside point of view and counsel necessary
9. Our company changed in order to bring in an outside viewpoint

Officers on Board.—Just what officer or executive representation should have board membership is generally a matter of qualification of the individual, relative importance of his position, length of service, or tradition in the company. While an exclusive executive board is not generally regarded as desirable, genuine doubt is also expressed as to whether a single officer can adequately represent the various functional or divisional viewpoints pertinent to the problems coming before the board. Hence most companies favor substantial representation of active management on their boards.

Following is a tabulation showing the representation of management positions on the boards of the thirty-one participating companies:

Chairman (not always an active, full-time officer)......All cases
President ....All cases
Executive Vice-President (position occurs in only one-
      third of the companies) ....All cases
Major Product or Regional Executive...............Most cases
Manufacturing Executive ....14 companies
Marketing Executive ....10 Companies
Raw Materials Operations Executive (oil and steel com-
      panies) .... 6 companies
Finance Executive
    Through Vice-President .... 5 companies
    Through Treasurer .... 5 companies
    Through Secretary-Treasurer .... 5 companies
Accounting Executive
    Through Vice-President–Comptroller .... 3 companies
    Through Comptroller .... 2 companies
Purchasing Executive (handling procurement of major
      raw materials) .... 3 companies
Research and Development Executive .... 2 companies
Legal Executive .... 2 companies
Secretary .... 3 companies
Foreign Operations Executive .... 2 companies

Ex-Officers on the Board.—In about a quarter of the companies certain former officers have continued on in a consulting and advisory capacity as members of the board after their retirement from active, full-time service.

Outside Representation

Most boards include other types of representation in addition to management. One of these is ownership, which, if substantial, is always entitled to some voice in determining the general course of the business. One executive advanced the opinion that "to look for a successful company is to find one, part of whose directorate has a considerable financial stake in the enterprise." Mere stock ownership alone, at least from a management standpoint, is not sufficient justification for board membership. However, if those who, in addition to being large shareholders, have the other qualifications of directors, their counsel is of unquestioned value because they are likely to think in terms of long-range company welfare.

Another type of outside representation is that selected on the basis of wide business experience and demonstrated ability. Individuals chosen on this basis should bring to board deliberations an outside and independent viewpoint that is invaluable. Some familiarity with the company and its industry and a sufficient interest to attend meetings and give thoughtful consideration to company problems are further essentials for this type of representation. For the most part such directors are active executives in other enterprises—industrial, commercial, financial, or legal. Some concern as to the difficulty of attracting competent directors of this type was expressed by several companies. This situation appears to be of sufficient permanency that some alternative source of such outside directors will be sought.

Professional Directors. — One promising possibility seems likely to be the professional director. Such a director may be described as one who has no present full-time or active executive position in any enterprise; whose previous experience, whether broad or specialized, equips him to contribute constructive ideas and counsel on corporate policy and problems; who confines his services to a few noncompeting companies; who devotes a proportionate share of his time between board meetings to the affairs of these companies; who receives a substantial annual compensation from each company served; and who does not represent the government, the public, the management, or any financial institution, but rather the shareholders, small as well as large.

On the basis of this definition, the attitude of various top executives to the idea of professional directors is surprisingly favorable. In a few companies certain existing board members are in effect professional directors, and the following considerations indicate that a definite trend in this direction may develop:

1. It is becoming increasingly difficult to secure competent men who are busy running their own companies.

2. Recent legislation has imposed additional liabilities on directors.

3. As compared with services expected, fees paid are nominal; particularly is this true where no large stock ownership provides adequate financial or other incentive.

4. Adverse, personal, selfish, or dual interests may influence

service; i.e., directors may serve for what they can get out of a company rather than what they can contribute.

5. Hazards of "strike suits," i.e., stockholders' suits, designed solely as a nuisance and thus coming under the classification of legal racketeering, are a deterrent. (A recent development in this connection is the action taken by several companies "to indemnify directors and officers for expenses reasonably incurred in defending suits where they shall not be found liable.")

6. Men of the caliber qualified to be professional directors are becoming increasingly available as a result of the early and rigidly enforced retirement age; among such men are many who have not a few years of vigorous life ahead and who have no disposition voluntarily to assume business inactivity; moreover, to permit such talent and experience to go unused is an economic waste of high order.

7. The current practice of quite a few companies is to retain the services of their own "elder statesmen," i.e., former key executives who are relieved of the brunt of day-to-day battling with business problems, but are continued on in an advisory or consulting capacity, active enough to keep abreast of current conditions and developments, but free enough to do the contemplative and reflective thinking necessary to long-range planning and policy-making. While such men would not necessarily qualify as professional directors, their retention does indicate a tendency to look to men beyond normal retirement age for advice and counsel.

8. The two most frequently expressed doubts as to the feasibility of professional directors are related to: (a) the availability of qualified men; and (b) the danger that such individuals would invade the province of executive management, a situation difficult to prevent because of the intense interest which professional directors should have.

Public and Employee Representation.—There is little interest or enthusiasm among the participating companies for the idea of having representation on the board of either rank-and-file employees or the public at large. One company among the group does have a director who would essentially qualify as a representative of the public. Another company at one time had an employee representative on the board, but discontinued the practice after a few years. In general the opinion regarding this idea may be summarized as follows: election to a board of directors should be chiefly, if not solely, on the basis of what the individual can contribute to the consideration and solution of the company's problems.

Election of Directors

Nominations for directors generally arise within the board itself and election is by vote of stockholders. The voting is frequently carried out on the cumulative voting plan. Vacancies are filled by the board until the next annual stockholders' meeting, or in the case of several companies having term directors, for the entire unexpired term of the director whose place has become vacant.

Term Directors.—As contrasted with the practice of electing the full complement of directors annually, one-third of the companies follow the term or classification plan; i.e., only a certain group of directors come up for election each year, and election is for a term of years. The prevailing term was found to be three years, although in some companies directors are elected for a four- or five-year term.

Those companies which have term directors find certain definite advantages in the practice, as indicated by the following quotations:

"Term directors are likely to serve out their full term; hence their services are available to the company for at least that period."

"The plan of having term directors prevents sudden and complete changes in board personnel and policy, an event which might theoretically occur when the term of the entire board expires at the same time."

"Stability and continuity in the directorate is insured; cumulative voting might interfere with this."

"Because of the present form and content of proxy statements, it is more convenient to solicit proxies for only a portion of the directors and less confusing to stockholders."

3. ORGANIZATION OF THE BOARD

Regardless of size, boards of directors have found it practicable to have certain organization within the board itself. To some extent responsibilities or functions are delegated in accordance with this organization. The following paragraphs treat of a few phases of this feature.

Officers of the Board

In three-fourths of the companies studied the office of board chairman exists. In eight companies the chairman is a full-time officer, and in six other instances he is a part-time official. The positions of chairman and president are combined in one individual in eight companies. Among the remaining companies the by-laws either make no mention of a chairman or it is optional whether a chairman shall or shall not be elected from the directorate. The term of office for the chairman is, as with all corporate officers, one year.

In seven companies there is also a full-time office of vice-chairman, a position stipulated in the by-laws of several companies.

Duties of Top Officers

The four top officers are: chairman, vice-chairman, president, and executive vice-president. None of the companies studied has all four positions, a few have three, most have two, and several have only one.

In those companies where two or more of the top officers are full time and active, the assignment of duties and responsibilities between them is not entirely clear. Such delineation of duties as may be set forth in the by-laws is usually so general as to convey very little actual information.

A few companies broadly divide the duties between the chairman and president (or between the president and executive vice-president) by having the chairman direct his attention primarily to external affairs of the company, e.g., government relations, industry relations, public relations, association activities, whereas the president, as chief executive officer, confines his attention to internal company affairs.

In one company the chairman assumes responsibility for foreign affairs of the company, while the president handles all domestic matters. In another instance the chairman acts as chief financial officer. In still another case the chairman devotes his efforts largely to financial and legal matters. In a further case the vice-chairman is in charge of production and the executive vice-president is also general counsel. The vice-chairman of another company is also the chief engineering executive.

In every instance, the chairman, whether a full-time or part-time officer, presides at the annual meeting of the stockholders and at all directors' meetings when he is present.

Board Committees

An interesting and important feature of board organization is the nature and extent to which there are subcommittees of the board. The practice of the companies studied is quite varied; some have no committees, while others follow the committee plan rather extensively.

The Executive Committee.—This committee is the most frequently reported, two-thirds of the companies having an executive committee—a requirement stipulated in most cases in the by-laws. Ordinarily this committee is small in membership. The size ranges from three to nine members, the most frequent number being five and the average six.

The composition of the executive committee is variable. In eight instances the executive committee is composed solely of officers; in three other companies all but one member are officers; and in an additional three companies 60 percent of the members are officers. In eight cases outside directors outnumber the officer directors.

The officers having membership on the executive committee include the chairman in ten instances, the vice-chairman in three, the president in all cases, the executive vice-president in nine, the vice-president of manufacturing in seven, the vice-president of sales in three, the secretary and/or treasurer in six, and the vice-presidents of engineering or research, of finance, and of legal activities in one case each.

The executive committee, generally speaking, is vested with full authority to act for the board of directors between meetings of the board itself. It is a powerful administrative agency. Such committees are obviously established to facilitate action of an emergency or interim character requiring board consideration. Membership, even when partially comprised of outside directors, almost invariably is local to the headquarters of the corporation. In most instances the active officers constitute a quorum of the executive committee.

In addition to the broad powers of the executive committee, a few companies mention certain specific responsibilities of the committee, such as setting the salaries of all officers; authorizing appropriations over $25,000 for capital expenditures, maintenance, and rehabilitation; approving all salaries over $10,000; authorizing the investment of company funds; working out major problems for presentation to the entire board; and authorizing the writing off of doubtful accounts.

Meetings of the executive committee are held at no regular intervals in one-fourth of the companies having such committees. In the remaining instances regular meetings are scheduled, a few being held weekly, others monthly, and the remainder at longer intervals. In every instance it is reported that meetings are conducted under customary parliamentary procedure, minutes being kept and votes being recorded when so requested. In most of the companies the secretary of the board of directors serves also as secretary of the executive committee.

Finance Committee.—Less than one-fourth of the companies have finance committees. When such a committee does exist, it is slightly larger, on the average, than the executive committee. On the other hand, the proportion of officers on the finance committee is somewhat lower and meetings are held less frequently. Typical responsibilities and powers of the finance committee were found to include:

1. Having the annual budget prepared and submitting it to the board.
2. Considering and making recommendations to the board in regard to all proposed purchases of properties or securities over $100,000.
3. Passing upon the salaries of all officers and employees in excess of $20,000 per annum.
4. Exercising such further powers as may be conferred from time to time by the board.

Auditing Committee.—The membership of this committee in the companies where it exists is comprised of nonofficer members of the board, usually three in number. For the most part, the duty of this committee is to employ the independent auditors and review the auditors' report. As condensed from the by-laws of one company, the committee on audits was authorized:

1. To select and employ a firm of certified public accountants to audit the books and accounts of the company and report to the committee.

2. To report to the board of directors the progress and scope of such auditing work.
3. To transmit to the board of directors the consolidated balance sheet and related statements with the certificate of the auditor at the end of each fiscal year.

Investment Committee.—The membership of this type of committee is mixed, being comprised of both officer and outside directors. The duties of the committee are essentially the approving of securities and other corporate investments.

Salary Committee.—This committee is found in quite a few companies and for the most part is comprised of outside members of the board. Its duties are variously reported as being to submit recommendations to the board on all salaries over $4,000 a year, to fix salaries of the three top officers, and to approve all salaries over $3,600 a year.

Incentive Compensation Committee.—The incentive compensation committee found in a number of companies is generally comprised of nonofficer directors, or at least of nonparticipating members of the board. The principal duty of this committee is to determine executive bonuses and extra compensations.

Pension Committee.—In the several companies having this type of committee, the membership is comprised of outside directors, and the duty of the committee is the determination of executive pension plans and provisions.

Special Committees.—Occasionally boards of directors find it desirable to appoint committees to study and report on matters of a nonrecurring character. Such assignments of special committees as the following illustrate this practice:

Setting up of a research department and program
Nomination of officers
Consideration of the personal situation of an ex-officer
Determination of plan of stock ownership for officers
Location of foreign plant
Purchase of an allied company
Dissolution of a partially owned company
Revaluation of capital assets

Executives Responsible to the Board

The president, in most respects, is the only officer regarded as directly responsible to the board. However, in 15 percent of the companies either the treasurer, or comptroller, or both, as well as the president, is responsible to the board. In one company a provision of the by-laws stipulates that "the general counsel, treasurer, auditor, and secretary, and their respective offices shall be under the supervision of the finance committee," which in turn is a committee of the board.

4. PROCEDURE OF THE BOARD

The conduct and frequency of board meetings represent quite varied practice among the companies studied. Certain aspects or phases of board procedure will be taken up in some detail in the following paragraphs.

Meetings

Two out of three boards meet monthly. In a few cases, one or two of the summer meetings are omitted. The next most common frequency is quarterly, a practice found in 20 percent of the companies. One board of the mixed or representative type meets twice a month, and the company reports an attendance record of better than 75 percent. The executive or managing type of board generally meets more frequently, weekly in certain instances and daily in others.

Special meetings of the board, particularly of the mixed type, are reported as being held occasionally by about half of the companies. Such meetings are a frequent practice in a few instances, whereas in other companies such meetings are rarely, and sometimes never, called.

The length of board meetings averages about one hour, although here again the practice is varied. The normal length of a board meeting, as reported by the various companies studied, runs from twenty or twenty-five minutes to as much as four or five hours. Some questions might naturally arise as to the actual interest and contribution which could be derived from a board of directors which, during the course of a year, might meet four times, or even twelve times, with an average meeting of less than half an hour.

Recognition, however, needs to be given to the fact that the time directors spend in regular board meetings does not always tell the full story. As one executive put it, "Board meetings often serve merely to ratify hours of informal discussion, numerous telephone calls, and exhaustive memoranda which cover all phases of problems with which directors must deal. Through such processes far-reaching decisions are crystallized which may take less than a dozen lines in the minutes of a meeting."

Agenda for Board Meetings

Agenda are prepared to program and facilitate the conduct of meetings for most boards, although in several companies this procedure is not followed. In these latter instances, no indication was given as to the method followed in providing some direction to the deliberations and consideration of the board.

Furnishing board members with advance copies of the agenda is not a practice followed in any uniform way by the various companies. It would seem that time would be conserved and that more considered action could be taken at board meetings if directors knew in advance what matters were to come before them; yet only a few companies followed the practice of providing board members with copies of agenda in advance of meetings. In one case the agenda are mailed to the directors ten days before board meetings, and in the other cases they are distributed some two to four days before meetings. Several companies give notice to directors concerning matters of unusual importance coming before the next board meeting, even though the customary practice is not to send out advance agenda. About half of the companies place the agenda before directors at the meetings. However, a few companies do not furnish agenda to the board members even at the meetings. Such reasons as the following were given for not providing directors with agenda in advance of board meetings:

1. Matters of unusual importance, and hence ones requiring much thought and deliberation upon the part of directors, are customarily discussed and considered over several meetings.
2. Directors are busy individuals and would probably give little attention to matters listed on an agenda before meetings, even if they were regularly advised in advance.
3. Considerations of secrecy make it inadvisable to permit any inadvertent divulgence of important matters before the actual board meeting.

Conduct of Board Meetings

A rather meticulous adherence to parliamentary procedure seems to characterize the conduct of board meetings despite an occasional suggestion of informality. Action of the board is, without exception, determined by vote of the members. Recording of individual votes generally is made only in those instances when a member votes "no," or wishes to register as "not voting," or requests specifically that his vote be recorded.

Minutes of meetings are kept, but in only a few instances are board members furnished copies. A general practice is to read the minutes of the preceding meeting for approval at the current meeting. To save the time involved in this procedure, several companies send copies of the minutes to the board members for approval or correction, after which they are returned to the secretary.

Executives Appearing Before Board

Do executives who are not directors appear before meetings of the board? A surprising number of companies, more than two-thirds, follow this practice. The frequency of such occasions ranges from "rarely" to "constantly and regularly." Even those companies where the practice has not been followed manifested genuine interest in the idea.

One company states that at the start of every board meeting each vice-president makes a brief report (five or six minutes) concerning matters of consequence under his jurisdiction. This has the desirable effect of keeping not only board members, but the other vice-presidents, currently advised of important problems and developments in the major departments of the enterprise. These oral reports in the aggregate consume twenty-five to thirty minutes, after which the vice-presidents retire and the board meeting proceeds.

In another company the president makes it a point to have each of the key executives appear before a board meeting at least twice a year. Other companies recommend the practice of inviting non-director executives to appear before board meetings for the following reasons:

1. Outside directors are given advice on and an insight into some of the more technical phases of the business.
2. These same directors are afforded an opportunity to meet, see, and learn something at firsthand of the key men of the organization.

3. Those directors not in constant touch with the business are enabled more intelligently to pass upon recommendations for appropriations, promotions, salary increases, bonus earnings, and organization changes.
4. The executives themselves are given a feeling of recognition and encouragement.

Fees and Expenses

Compensation of directors varies. All companies participating in this study reimburse directors for traveling expenses incurred in connection with attendance at board meetings. Most companies, in addition, pay fees for attendance, the amounts being about equally divided between $20, $50, and $100 per meeting. Several companies compensate directors for attendance at committee meetings on the same basis as for attendance at directors' meetings. About one-half of the companies that pay fees for attendance at meetings exclude those directors who are full-time executives and who are on the salary roll of the company. Two companies pay annual stipends to outside directors regardless of the number of meetings attended. Five companies report that no fees are paid to any director.

5. REPORTS TO THE BOARD

No phase of the board of directors picture appears more varied than the extent and nature of the current factual data about the company which are supplied to outside board members. Full-time officer members of the boards are obviously in possession of or have ready access to all operating data. In certain of the participating companies, outside members of the board are kept informed of company operations only by means of the most meager factual information reported orally at board meetings by the president or other officers. On the other hand, many companies compile quite comprehensive reports and furnish these to each director in advance of, or at, every meeting.

It can be argued that outside directors, most of whom are actively engaged in running their own enterprises, will not take the time to analyze and interpret any extensive assembly of figures. Obviously, there is a limit to what, and how much, data are genuinely significant to these directors in the exercise of their functions. There should, however, be very little difficulty on the part of management in determining what are the essential criteria for appraising company performance, and nothing less than a full yardstick would seem adequate or desirable. Under any circumstance, if all significant data are regularly reported to the outside directors, these individuals can act more intelligently and thereby render greater service to the business which they are helping to direct. It would appear obvious, therefore, that management, if it is to err at all, should err in the direction of more, not less, elaborate reports to the nonofficer directors.

Men who by position, ability, and achievement qualify as corporation directors have, or should have, the facility to analyze and interpret quickly a substantial body of operating data. The sense of trusteeship which they should feel as representatives of the shareholders would suggest a desire for more data than it appears that many of them now receive.

The practice of making interim reports to board members, i.e., keeping directors apprised of company affairs between board meetings, is also quite varied in the participating companies. Some managements, in addition to providing comprehensive reports to directors at regular board meetings, report on important developments, such as a labor situation, by letter or other means to outside directors between board meetings. They also seek their advice on important matters which may arise between regular meetings of the board. Other managements, even in instances where the board meets only quarterly, make no interim reports to nonofficer directors.

An interesting practice is followed by the management of one company in presenting operating and financial data to its board at monthly meetings. A set of large wall charts is prepared each month. These charts present financial, production, and sales data. Even the balance sheet is drawn up in magnified form. The purpose of these charts is to focus the attention of board members on each item being discussed by the president. Prior to adopting this practice, the directors were provided with reports, and during the president's discussion they were often observed thumbing through the reports and giving their attention to pages or portions not being discussed. Now, after the full presentation by the president, the directors are handed the reports as heretofore.

The extent to which the managements of two companies present salient operating information to their directors at their regular board meetings is illustrated in the following report outlines:

Company A presents:

a) Income statement
b) Balance sheet
c) Operating Report No. 1
  Orders by product division this year and last
  Unfilled orders by product division this year and last
  Inventories by product division this year and last
  Payroll by product division this year and last
   Amount and persons
   Average hours worked
  Tax accruals
  Number of stockholders (by quarters)
  Adjusted compensation
   Amount and percentage
  Payments to pension fund
  Number of employees
   Hourly and salary
   By functions
d) Operating Report No. 2
  Gross earnings, monthly and year ago
  Manufacturing cost, monthly and year ago
  Manufacturing profit, monthly and year ago
  General expenses, monthly and year ago
  Operating profit, monthly and year ago
  Adjusted operating profit, monthly and year ago
  Added income, monthly and year ago
  Gross income, monthly and year ago
  Deductions from income, monthly and year ago
  Net income, monthly and year ago
e) Operating Report No. 3
  Sales billed
  Cost
   Manager controlled
   General controlled
  Operating profit
   Operating cost
   Selling cost
   Administrative cost

Company B presents:

Sales, in dollars by products and by months
Income, in dollars by products and by months
Production, in dollars by products and by months

Manufacturing cost, in dollars by products and by months
Purchases, in dollars by products and by months
Selling price, in dollars by products and by months
Balance sheet items, by months and year to date
Full income statement, by months and year to date
Accumulated earnings, by months and year to date
Statistics per share, earnings and dividends
Securities to be sold
Changes in security portfolio
Weekly report on production and shipments by units
Weekly report on net sales in dollars
Weekly report on accounts receivable
Cash report
Appropriations to be acted upon
    Description and amount
Unexpended appropriations
Consolidated disposition of profits

PART E

DATA SHEET USED FOR FIELD INTERVIEWS

GENERAL PLAN OF ORGANIZATION

BOARD OF DIRECTORS

STAFF DEPARTMENTS

COMMITTEE ORGANIZATION

MEANS AND METHODS OF CONTROL

DATA SHEET USED FOR FIELD INTERVIEWS

All of the material from which this volume has been prepared was obtained by means of discussions with key executives in the participating companies. To give direction to such interviews, to insure comparability of data gathered, and to expedite the entire program of field work, it was essential to have a data sheet or list of questions.

Much time and effort were devoted to the preparation of this data sheet and it is reproduced below with the thought that it may be of interest to some readers of this report.

I. GENERAL PLAN OF ORGANIZATION
  A. Company Organization Chart
      1. Number and titles of management positions in each division or department
      2. Organization manual
      3. Date prepared and by whom
  B. Explanation of unusual features of organization structure
  C. Basic changes in organization structure in recent years
  D. Contemplated changes and reasons therefor

II. BOARD OF DIRECTORS
  A. Composition
      1. How many directors?
      2. Is size flexible or fixed?
      3. What executive officers are members of board?
      4. What interests do other board members represent?
      5. What is method of selecting board members?
      6. What has been the trend in size of board?
      7. What has been the trend in proportion of officers on board?
      8. Would a board comprised solely of active officers and executives be feasible?
      9. What place would professional directors have in your company?

10. Should professional directors be chosen essentially on a functional or specialized basis?
11. How is chairman of board selected and what is the term of this office?
12. Does the chairman devote full time to the company?

B. Organization
1. What are the regular and continuing committees of the board?
2. What is the membership of each?
3. What responsibilities and authority are assigned to each?
4. What are typical special committees of the board?
5. What have been their assignments?
6. What is the frequency of committee meetings, conduct of meetings, procedure of action, follow-up, etc.?

C. Functions
1. To what, if any, extent does the board delegate:
   a) Determination of the major policies and general objectives of the enterprise?
   b) Establishment of basic organizational structure and major changes thereof?
   c) Determination of external relationships, such as with government, industry, general public, etc.?
   d) Management of the corporate income, e.g., surplus and dividend decisions?
   e) Methods (bonds, stocks, bank loans) to be employed in financing expansion and rehabilitation?
   f) Changes in the financial structure?
   g) Determination of amount and sources of working capital?
   h) Determination of financial relationships with subsidiaries or affiliates?
   i) Selection of outside auditing and other professional services?
   j) Establishment of pension, insurance, and other employee-benefit plans?

2. What responsibility does the board have for selection of corporate officers?

3. What executive selections must be approved by the board?

4. What type of executive decision must have board approval?

5. What executives report directly to the board?

6. What other functions, responsibilities, and authority does the board reserve exclusively to itself?

7. What control devices does the board use to appraise executive performance, such as special reports, professional surveys, etc?

8. Broadly, what is the division of duties and responsibilities among board chairman, president, and executive vice-president?

9. What is the relationship between the treasurer and the comptroller? What are their respective duties? Is either elected by the stockholders?

D. Procedure

1. How often does the board meet?

2. Are special meetings occasionally called?

3. Is there an agenda for each meeting?

4. Who prepares it?

5. How long in advance of meeting are board members advised of the agenda?

6. Is board action determined by vote and is record made of members' vote?

7. How is action of the board made known?

8. Are reports, resolutions, etc., issued by the board?

9. What follow-up procedure on board action is instituted?

10. Are minutes of board meetings kept and are members furnished copies?

11. Do executives, not members of the board, have an opportunity of appearing personally before the board on matters with which the particular executive is involved?

12. How is attendance of members at board meetings assured?

13. How are board members kept advised of company conditions between meetings? Are interim reports sent to directors?

III. STAFF DEPARTMENTS

A. Which of the following are regarded as staff functions, to whom does each report, and what central and divisional organization is to handle each?

1. Accounting
2. Advertising
3. Auditing
4. Budget
5. Credit
6. Economics and Statistical
7. Employee Relations
8. Engineering—Facilities
9. Engineering—Product
10. Expense Analysis and Cost Control
11. Industrial Engineering
12. Insurance
13. Legal
14. Merchandising
15. Office Management and Service
16. Order and Distribution
17. Organization
18. Patent
19. Public Relations
20. Purchasing
21. Real Estate
22. Research—Product
23. Research—Market
24. Research—Methods
25. Tax
26. Traffic
27. Other

B. What responsibility does each staff department have?

1. Complete control of function—relieving other departments
2. Consulting advice and service only

3. Policy recommendations and interpretation
4. Policy administration and enforcement
5. Procedure determination and enforcement
6. Staff personnel in other departments, branches, **or** subsidiaries, as to:
    a) Selection or approval
    b) Training
    c) Dismissal or transfer
7. Issuing orders, standard instructions, etc., to **the** functional representatives in other departments, branches, or subsidiaries

C. What is nature of staff relationship to:
    1. Board of directors and officers?
    2. Other departments?
    3. Subsidiary companies?
    4. Branches?

IV. COMMITTEE ORGANIZATION

A. What company or interdepartmental committees have continuing status?
B. For each such committee:
    1. What is its composition?
    2. How are members chosen?
    3. How is chairman selected?
    4. What are its purposes and functions?
        a) Formulate policies
        b) Establish procedure for carrying out **policies**
        c) Make decisions and issue orders
        d) Serve in advisory capacity to executives
        e) Provide co-ordination among departments
        f) Act as fact-finding agency
        g) Develop and train junior executives
    5. What is the nature of subjects considered **and by** whom submitted?
    6. What is the extent of its **authority?**
    7. How often does it meet?
    8. Is an agenda prepared for each meeting, who prepares it, and how far in advance of meeting do members have the agenda?

9. Is committee action determined by vote and is the vote recorded?
10. What is the means of follow-up and who is responsible?
11. How is action made known and effective?

C. What means or expedients are used to insure committee effectiveness?
1. Limitation on number of committees
2. Limitation on size
3. Full-time secretary or other fact-finding agency to develop material
4. Limitation on length and frequency of meetings
5. Insurance of attendance
6. Termination of committees that have outlived their usefulness
7. Limitation on number of committee memberships held by individuals

V. MEANS AND METHODS OF CONTROL
A. Organization
1. How is basic structure determined?
2. With regard to organization planning?
   a) Has a future plan been worked out?
   b) Who is responsible?
   c) What is the procedure?
3. Is organization plan subject to periodic review?
   a) By whom?
   b) At what intervals?
   c) Under what procedure?
4. To achieve organizational effectiveness, how have you met these problems?
   a) Limiting number of individuals reporting to a single executive
   b) Precluding the danger of too-finely divided functions
   c) Developing company rather than departmental allegiance
   d) Preventing an accumulation of miscellaneous and unrelated activities under a single executive

e) Adjusting duties and responsibilities of an executive position to the individual

f) Maintaining proper balance between inbreeding and inducting outsiders into organization

B. Policies

1. What is the procedure of policy determination?
2. How are policies made known to executive and subordinate personnel?
3. What check is provided as to compliance with, and interpretation of, company policies?
4. Are department or division heads expected to recommend changes in policies?

C. Appropriations and Expenditures

1. Capital Expenditures
   a) What review and check are exercised?
   b) To what extent is authority delegated to the different levels or zones of management?
   c) If departments have an annual budgeted appropriation, what control is provided over the manner in which this amount is expended?

2. Maintenance Expenditures
   a) What review and check are exercised?
   b) To what extent is authority delegated to the different levels or zones of management?
   c) If departments have an annual budgeted appropriation, what control is provided over the manner in which this amount is expended?

3. Operating Expenditures
   a) What review and check are exercised over expenditures for:
   Materials and supplies
   Traveling expenses
   Dues and memberships
   Donations and subscriptions
   Payroll
   b) To what extent is authority delegated to the different levels or zones of management?

    c) If departments have an annual budgeted appropriation, what control is provided over the manner in which this amount is expended?

4. Professional Services

    a) What review and check are exercised over expenditures for such professional services as accounting, engineering, legal, and medical?

    b) To what extent is authority delegated to the different levels or zones of management?

    c) If departments have an annual budgeted appropriation, what control is provided over the manner in which this amount is expended?

5. Outside Contracts

    a) What review and check are exercised over expenditures involved in negotiating outside contracts?

    b) To what extent is authority delegated to the different levels or zones of management?

    c) If departments have an annual budgeted appropriation, what control is provided over the manner in which this amount is expended?

D. Employee Relations

1. How is the quality of hourly employees maintained?

a) Selection	*d*) Transfer
b) Training	*e*) Promotion
c) Rating	*f*) Dismissal

2. How is the quality of staff and executive personnel maintained?

a) Selection	*d*) Transfer
b) Training	*e*) Promotion
c) Rating	*f*) Dismissal

3. What policies and practices are followed with respect to executives and others in key positions who, because of personalities, superannuation, and other causes, raise serious personnel or organizational problems?

4. With regard to wages and salaries:
   a) How is general wage level of productive and clerical workers determined; of supervisory and staff employees?
   b) What procedure is followed in establishing occupational differentials?
   c) At the several levels or zones of management, what authority is delegated for individual wage or salary advances?
   d) Are salaries above a certain level, e.g., $4,000 per year, based on any job-evaluation plan?
5. With regard to collective bargaining:
   a) What is the degree of centralized responsibility and authority?
   b) What is the status of the personnel or industrial-relations department?
6. With regard to grievance handling:
   a) What is the procedure?
   b) What is the status of the personnel or industrial-relations department?
7. At what level or zone of management does the authority exist for administering pension, insurance, and other employee-benefit plans?

E. Operations
   1. Manpower
      a) How is basic force determined?
      b) How is force kept in adjustment to changing rate of operation?
      c) At what executive levels does authority exist for expanding and decreasing the force?
      d) Is there any periodic review to eliminate nonessential work and to maintain the force at an economic minimum?
   2. Products
      a) How is the line of products determined and changed?
      b) Is the line subject to periodic review?
      c) Are norms or standards used to indicate the possible need for eliminating items?

d) How is the standard of quality determined?

e) Who is responsible for such other merchandising considerations as guaranties, servicing, styling, and packaging?

3. Facilities

a) Who is responsible for keeping facilities adequately up to date, and competitive?

b) Who is responsible for the abandonment, dismantling, and disposal of facilities?

c) Who is responsible for the specification and selection of equipment and facilities?

4. Prices and discounts

a) At what executive level does the authority for price policies and practices exist?

b) What procedure is followed in changing prices and discounts?

5. Market Areas and Channels

a) Who has authority for entering new market areas or withdrawing from existing areas?

b) Who decides the location and extent of warehouses, and other market service facilities?

c) Who determines the channels and methods of distribution?

6. Planning and Co-ordination

a) How is the rate of operation determined?

b) How far in advance is the rate of operation determined, i.e., is long-range planning practiced, and what period is covered?

c) In this connection are finance, procurement, production, personnel, and sales programs integrated both as to rate and time period?

d) How are operating schedules and delivery dates determined?

e) How are size and distribution of inventories determined?

7. Foreign operations

a) Through what type of agency are foreign operations conducted: home-office department, subsidiary company, or holding company?

      b) What is the extent of responsibility and authority delegated to the several zones or levels of management?

      c) What are the principal means of control?

F. External Relationships

    1. To what executives are the following relationships assigned?

      a) Public

      b) Governmental

      c) Industry

G. Departmental Service

    1. What steps are taken to control demands for the services of such departments as research, engineering, statistical, and legal?

H. Demands upon Executive Time

    1. What methods are used to relieve executives of unnecessary and time-consuming administrative detail?

    2. How are home-office demands upon field force controlled?

I. General Effectiveness

    1. To what extent is performance measured and control exercised by the following groups?

      a) Budget

      b) Profit-and-loss control

      c) Cost control

      d) Manuals

      e) Reports and charts

      f) Standards

INDEX

INDEX

255